The Management
of Corporate
Business Units

Recent Titles from Quorum Books

The Management of Corporate Business Units

PORTFOLIO STRATEGIES FOR TURBULENT TIMES

Louis E. V. Nevaer and Steven A. Deck

Q

QUORUM BOOKS
NEW YORK • WESTPORT, CONNECTICUT • LONDON

Library of Congress Cataloging-in-Publication Data

Nevaer, Louis E. V.
    The management of corporate business units : portfolio strategies
for turbulent times / Louis E. V. Nevaer and Steven A. Deck.
    p.   cm.
    Includes index.
ISBN 0–89930–284–X (lib. bdg. : alk. paper)
    1. Portfolio management—United States.   2. Strategic management—
United States.   I. Deck, Steven A.   II. Title.
HG4529.5.N485   1988
332.6'0973—dc19   87–32586

British Library Cataloguing in Publication Data is available.

Library of Congress Catalog Card Number: 87–32586
ISBN: 0–89930–284–X

First published in 1988 by Quorum Books

Greenwood Press, Inc.
88 Post Road West, Westport, Connecticut 06881

Printed in the United States of America

The paper used in this book complies with the
Permanent Paper Standard issued by the National
Information Standards Organization (Z39.48–1984).

10   9   8   7   6   5   4   3   2   1

Benedict IX
1033–1044, 1045, 1047–1048

CONTENTS

FIGURES

INTRODUCTION

The business world of 1990 is radically different from the business world of 1950. The business environment today is more intensely competitive than ever before. Structural changes in the U.S. economy such as the emergence of structural deficits, technological advances, the nature of maturing economies, trade imbalances, industrial globalization and a redistribution of purchasing power from the United States to our major trading partners have left no industry unaffected. During the past four decades the pace of these basic structural changes and the resulting economic dislocation has been so rapid that a new management discipline has emerged to assist the corporate executive in dealing with the newly competitive marketplace: strategic planning and portfolio management. The use of strategic and portfolio planning as a management tool, however, has proved lacking of context to be a viable and relevant form of management discipline alone.

This book addresses the crucial inadequacy strategic planners have encountered: managing corporate business units. The inability to determine the implications of the prevailing economic conditions on the firm's business units poses a major obstacle in the implementation of portfolio strategies. Unless the corporate officer can assess the conditions of the economic context in which the firm operates, he cannot establish an optimal business unit portfolio matrix that can harness the benefits of the interrelationships that exist among business units. The ability to incorporate the prevailing economic context into strategies is necessary if objective benchmarks by which to judge a business unit or an entire portfolio's performance is to yield valuable information to the firm trying to meet the challenges of foreign competition. The task of implementing effective portfolio strategies capable of succeeding in a highly competitive environment is a difficult matter. The want of an objective process for evaluating portfolio performance has long interfered with the implementation of a responsive portfolio management strategy capable of delivering a sustainable competitive advantage. The discussion in this book is designed to address this need.

This book stresses the importance of context—the economic and political environment in which the firm operates—in the management of corporate business units and the implementation of portfolio strategies. The manner in which strategic goals are established and how business unit interrelationships are developed enables the firm the insight necessary to secure a defendable market position. Managing corporate business units requires a thorough set of strategies that reflect the economic context in which the firm operates. The reasoning behind the notion of strategic thinking is to offer a management tool capable of delivering a reliable, responsive and accurate system for assessing the performance of any individual unit within a portfolio which is a requisite to the proper management of corporate business units. Most firms, whether medium-sized concerns with exclusively domestic markets or large industrial multinationals with extensive overseas operations, are very diverse in their organizational structure. The inherent gap in communication and real-world expertise between the corporate level and the business level necessitates a system by which a more precise reading of the portfolio's performance is achieved. Managing corporate business units through strategic thinking addresses this concern. In so doing the ability of the firm to establish strategies, execute development plans and secure sustainable market leadership positions is enhanced.

This is no longer a luxury, but a necessity born out of the loss of market shares American firms have suffered at the hands of foreign companies. The economic dislocation which has plagued American balance sheets must be reversed if the significant inroads are to be made in reducing the trade deficits and loss of leadership position of recent years. In this sense, then, this book builds on the work of others, such as Peter Drucker and Michael Porter, in an effort to present viable proposals the corporate executive can use to enhance performance and reverse the decline of American industry. The executive must be able to build on strengths, incorporate horizontal organizational structures among business units within the business portfolio, anticipate changes brought about by the central role technologies now play in determining competitive edges among firms, shift from short- to long-term thinking, encourage calculated risk taking among line managers and incorporate sound strategies which reflect the prevailing economic context.

The arguments made in this discussion revolve around the identification of problems, the offering of solutions, and case studies which demonstrate the effectiveness of the recommendations presented. The first part discusses the problems afflicting corporate America. During the past four decades there has been a major shift in the balance of economic power away from the United States to other nations in the West, most notably West Germany and Japan. The structural changes in the economy resulted in the demise of the Bretton Woods system which governed the international monetary order from the postwar era through 1971. The contention that the problems of today are rooted in the history of this time is analyzed in detail.

The ensuing period of economic turbulence created an environment with markedly different terms of trade. Thus a period of decline began as other nations took dominant positions on the world economic stage. The recovery period for the war-ravaged nations of Western Europe and Japan was characterized by export-driven economies and long-term management. American firms, in contrast, rested on their laurels while foreign firms secured competitive advantages through cost, differentiation, or focus strategies. The introduction of strategic planning and portfolio management has done little to reverse the decline of corporate America.

With this background in mind the track record of traditional strategic planning and portfolio management is reviewed. During the course of the discussion several fundamental flaws emerge which play an instrumental role in explaining why American firms have not been able to manage corporate business units. Corporate America has not been able to build on its strength and defend its market shares. Throughout the past decade few firms have implemented portfolio strategies that generate new business, given relevance to the economic context in which the firm operates, and emphasized the long term over the immediate quarter. During the past two decades few firms have been able to establish competitive advantages. Managing corporate business units has become more difficult because the implementation of portfolio strategies is an unclear process. The history of Pacific Telesis International, the international arm of Pacific Telesis Group, embodies the failures encountered throughout corporate America that have resulted in the economic dislocation. Its beleagured history is discussed as are the foreboding implications of this firm's failure.

The second part offers solutions on how the stumbling blocks to the management of business units can be overcome. Introducing the use of context to establish an objective reference point addresses the need to, as Michael Porter phrases it, "relate the company to its environment."[1] The problems of recent years are caused when managers neglect to consider the current economic environment when developing strategic plans. The solution offered is the use of the constant-dollar Dow to

provide an inflation-adjusted representation of stock market performance. Its role as the broadest based economic indicator enables the
market to signal the direction of the economy as well as reflect all possible
interpretations on the meaning and impact of news developments. The
result is an instrument which offers context to corporate strategies and
allows for the precise evaluation of the performance of a single business
unit or an entire portfolio.

The stage is then set to introduce a systematic approach to addressing
the structural problems of traditional portfolio planning. Proposals are
offered on how business can be generated, how horizontal interrelationships can be established, how to increase commitment by long-term
planning and how to incorporate the economic environment into business plans. These techniques allow a firm to exploit not only lines of
business, but also more focused "lines of expertise." In the same manner, economies of scale become economies of scope through the harnessing of potential benefits possible through the harnessing of SBU
interrelationships. The result is a firm more sensitive to developments
in the marketplace and with an internal organization in a position to
capitalize on opportunities and anticipate threats. The second part ends
with a case study of a firm who has demonstrated a keen ability to
develop sound strategies in a turbulent industry and which has emerged
as a formidable force in the market. Digital Equipment Corporation,
moreover, has positioned itself in strategic market niches in the computer industry. The ability to anticipate market shifts and react to new
developments have made it a permanent and profitable firm in markets
in which even such huge giants such as IBM have encountered declining
sales and a drop in profits. The secrets of DEC's success—the secret to
avoiding the pitfalls of traditional portfolio planning—are explored especially in light of the irony of the juxtaposition of Pacific Telesis International and DEC case studies. One firm entering a rapidly growing
industry has been unable to establish a significant presence while the
other facing great turbulence in a consolidating industry has strengthened its position.

The third part of this discussion builds on the first two and brings
together the solutions into a management system for the implementation
of portfolio strategies in these turbulent times. The bringing of context
into strategic planning becomes more important as the world becomes
a global village. Indeed, the emergence of nations such as Taiwan and
Korea as important export-driven economies foreshadows a more intensely competitive world in the near future. Thus a program designed
to address the internal and external problems encountered by American
firms is welcome. The arguments made in favor of adopting the solutions
offered in this discussion in a strategic thinking approach are comprehensive. The notion of "lines of expertise" allows for the internal or-

ganization of the firm, its business units, and the portfolio matrix in a manner which reflects the need for long-term planning and the horizontal organizational structure which results in competitive strategies. The notion of "market area planning" incorporates the need for considering the current economic context affecting the firm—local, regional, and global. These contextual insights affect the market analysis so as to identify which competitive strategy—cost, differentiation, or focus—is the most effective in given market segments or niches. Thus, reference points and objectivity are brought into the process of evaluating business unit performance and the role each business unit plays in the portfolio as a whole.

The discussion centers on how firms can establish an internal organizational structure that results in optimal use of corporate resources and gives the firm the tools necessary for thriving in the new competitive environment. The role of technology as a weapon, and the use of joint ventures and alliances to increase competitiveness through enhanced economies of scale are analyzed. The need for leadership with a vision of the corporate place in the marketplace is stressed, as is the need for bolder risk taking that can be used to capitalize on opportunities as they first develop. The firm which can develop its lines of expertise and implement market area planning is one with a clear vision of the future that can direct its energies into activities which will facilitate the realization of goals.

The result is a focused competitive strategy capable of delivering on several fronts: the need to overcome the structural limitations of portfolio planning, the incorporation of context into strategies, the identification of basic economic trends which affect business, and the need to anticipate opportunities and threats. The numerous case studies offered in this section suggest that the several American firms such as Primerica, Walt Disney, Heinz, and American Airlines have met with success implementing strategies than can deliver a sustainable competitive advantage. The challenge, then, lies in the widespread implementation of portfolio strategies throughout corporate America. This is necessary in order to reverse the economic dislocation of past decades. The continuing lackluster performance of corporate America in the face of foreign competition must be reversed. The discussion offered in this section constitutes a blueprint designed to play an important role in the task of restoring the vitality and competitiveness of the American firm in today's intensely competitive environment. In times of turbulence and volatility, nothing less will do.

NOTE

1. Michael E. Porter, *Competitive Strategy: Techniques for Analyzing Industries and Competitors* (New York: Free Press, 1980), p. 3.

PART I

The Problem: The Failure of Strategic Planning and Portfolio Management

THE FAILURE OF STRATEGIC PLANNING AND PORTFOLIO MANAGEMENT

The world has experienced a major shift in the balance of economic power during the past two decades from the United States to our major trading partners. This fact has caught many American firms by surprise. Once the unquestioned political and economic leader of the free world, the United States is struggling to recover from the economic dislocation this loss of market shares and competitive advantage represents. The emergence of West Germany and Japan as major economic powers in their own right represents a formidable challenge. The days when American goods were synonymous with quality and desirability are gone. The urgent task for the corporate executive is one of preparing to meet the manifold challenges reversing the decline of U.S. shares in domestic and foreign markets constitutes.

The problem is that this challenge has not been met. The size of the crisis is readily seen in the trade balance figures, which reveal how ineffectual current strategic and portfolio planning have been at establishing competitive advantages (see Figure 1.1). A corporate officer, as Machiavelli advised his prince, Alonzo the Magnificent, "should therefore have no other aim or thought, nor take up any other thing for his study, but war and its organisation and discipline, for that is the only art that is necessary to one who commands."[1] The problem, however, is that the men and women who command the American firm in the latter part of the twentieth century have not been able to establish competitive advantages—the business world equivalent of warfare—in their firms. The inability to establish and sustain competitive advantages has

Figure 1.1
U.S. Trade Surplus
(1965–1986)

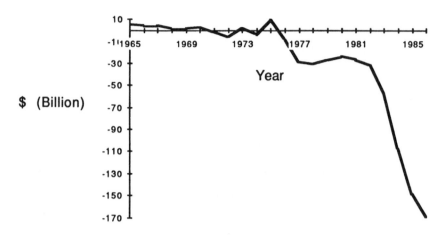

Source: U.S. Bureau of the Census, *Highlights of U.S. Export and Import Trade,* FT 990, monthly.

long been discussed in the business literature. Michael Porter in *Competitive Advantage* warns of firms who are, in his phrase, "stuck in the middle" and unable to muster the resolve to implement strategies capable of securing competitive advantage through cost, differentiation or focus.[2] There are many factors contributing to the frustrations encountered by corporate management as foreign firms make impressive inroads into domestic markets. Indeed, during the past quarter century, the emergence and implementation of strategic planning and portfolio management have not proved adequate in ensuring the success of the American firm in the fiercely competitive domestic and global marketplace. The single most important factor contributing to the demise of corporate America is the inability to manage corporate business units.

The failure to manage business units, implement portfolio strategies, and benefit from interrelationships among business units makes corporate America unprepared to seize opportunities. Despite the significant fall in the value of the dollar in 1987, for example, American firms have found it difficult to increase market shares. As the *Wall Street Journal* reported on April 27, 1987 in the wake of the dollar's decline, "Businesses are finding it difficult to win back export markets, and, increasingly, they are blaming foreigners' unfair trading practices. . . . Some critics also view the change in corporate attitudes as an effort to blame foreign trade barriers for the failings of U.S. corporate management." According to William Lilley, who heads the American Business Conference, a small group of high-growth companies that oppose import curbs, "There has been a greater willingness on the part of large corporate America to scapegoat our trading partners as a rhetorical device to minimize the inadequacies that corporate America has shown in competing abroad." "The uproar about the need for action," he continues, "is more of a political phenomenon than any kind of substantive, international economic phenomena."[3] This management failure, moreover, indicates that there is something amiss in traditional approaches and methods of strategic planning and portfolio management. The sense of crisis becomes greater as tensions rise and scapegoats are found. The slow drift towards protectionism underscores the managerial and political proportions of the dilemma at hand. Thus the proper management of corporate business units is necessary in order to secure market shares and increase profitability. The rest of the world continues to make significant inroads in all areas of business. Whether it is the domination of the micro chip markets or significant gains in the world of finance, corporate America is being displaced. The Japanese, for example, now dominate 85 percent of the world's memory chip markets, and in 1987 for the first time in thirty years, no U.S. bank ranked among the world's top ten in deposits. The goal of competing effectively in the world economy has not been met through traditional means alone. The avenues of the past two decades—strategic planning and portfolio management—have proved inadequate in arresting the economic dislocation or in securing market leadership positions. This inadequacy goes far in explaining why the American firm has declined in preeminence during the course of this generation. This section addresses this issue and identifies the fundamental flaws in the nature of strategic planning and the implementation of management systems for corporate business portfolios.

TRADITIONAL STRATEGIC PLANNING

As the 1960s drew to a close, the business community sought to establish a mechanism to manage the new-found complexity of the real world business environment. The preceding two decades constituted an era in which most American firms experienced rapid growth. Under the Marshall Plan, and assisted by the international arrangement governing trade and monetary policies, the *modus operandi* for the free world economies was collectively known as the Bretton Woods system. It was a series of financial, economic, and political agreements, which created a business environment that fostered stability and promoted growth. During this time of steady progress corporate America gained a dominant position in the global arena as the war-ravaged countries of Europe and Japan worked to restore their depleted economies.

A direct result of this stability was unprecedented growth by American firms. Indeed, as the 1960s drew to a close, cash-rich American firms embarked on programs to diversify their holdings and enter new markets. The world, however, was quickly growing complex as the other Western economies were rebuilt and began to assume the formidable positions they had enjoyed in the pre-war international arena. A system of managing the new complexity was devised to help American firms hold on to their market leadership positions. The intricate nature of the global markets meant that a preoccupation with managing a large multinational firm was no longer just an academic debate, but rather, a necessity. Thus strategic planning as a discipline emerged as the foremost approach capable of addressing the task at hand. The goal of strategic planning is a simple one. It is to create a vision, a set of goals, for the corporate entity and to orchestrate all corporate activities and functions to revolve around this end. An integral aspect of this mission is ensuring that a sustainable competitive advantage is firmly secured.

Managing corporate business units has become much more complex. Strategic planning was designed to meet the challenges of this new complexity and to help managers achieve corporate goals, but the proper implementation of strategic planning as described in the literature was difficult to achieve. The task of managing several different business units in the new, turbulent environment proved very demanding. It became evident that the transition from theory to practice was not to be a smooth one. Events affecting the economic environment entirely unrelated to the nature and purpose of strategic planning made matters worse. In 1971 President Nixon announced his New Economic Policy, and, independently, the Organization of Petroleum Exporting Countries (OPEC) imposed a series of price hikes on oil. These two events ushered in a period of economic turbulence. The rise of inflation and the slowdown of economic growth resulted in a period of stagflation, which saw the real value of investments collapse. Under these circumstances it was unclear what benefit the eager implementation of strategic planning had on business performance.

Thus in the early 1970s, as the perceived benefits a strategic approach to business planning failed to materialize, the effectiveness of strategic planning itself was questioned. The foundation for the widespread disappointment lay in the over-optimistic expectations about what is possible through strategic planning and portfolio management. New management tools are only as effective as they are understood by those who use them. Thus the perceptions of inadequacy subsided as strategic planning was given a broader role in the entire process of identifying the goals, mission, and methods a firm chooses when establishing its image and in targeting its market positioning.

Given this new understanding and purpose, the enthusiasm which characterized the initial discussions on the nature of strategic planning

Figure 1.2
U.S. Trade Balance with Japan
(1950–1985)

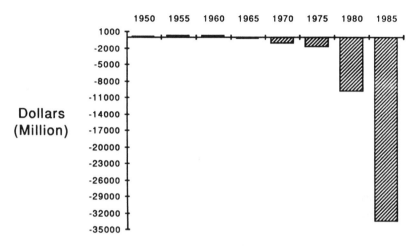

Source: U.S. Bureau of the Census, *Highlights of U.S. Export and Import Trade*, FT 990,
monthly.

was resumed. Thus during the past decade the discipline of strategic
planning has come of age in its own right. A concise, and precise,
planning process that extends beyond a budget year is recognized as a
valuable one. The contributions to corporate growth that can be realized
by having a medium- to long-term vision of a firm's goals and role in
the marketplace are great. In this way strategic planning has found a
place in business.

The question one has to ask, however, is how effective has strategic
planning been? During the time that five- and ten-year plans were being
implemented *en masse* throughout the business community, the U.S. has
seen its leadership position in global markets erode and the demise of
the market share American companies have traditionally held in the
twentieth century. It is ironic that an instrument designed to enhance
the flexibility and responsiveness of the corporate entity to the changing
conditions of the marketplace has failed so miserably to achieve these
goals. This irony makes the economic dislocation even more difficult to
accept. The trade imbalances and the cost advantages achieved by foreign firms—most notably Japanese and West German—constitute a major challenge to U.S. firms (see Figures 1.2 and 1.3).

Mismanaged corporate business units resulting in loss of world market
shares and profitability are the end result of two decades of strategic
planning. There is a basic flaw in the way strategic planning has been
implemented by firms. The economic dislocation of the past two decades

Figure 1.3
U.S. Trade Balance with West Germany
(1950–1985)

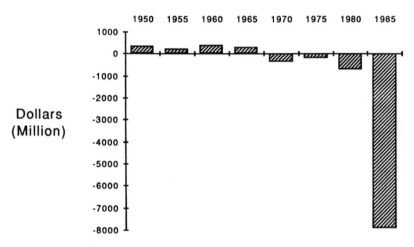

Source: U.S. Bureau of the Census, *Highlights of U.S. Export and Import Trade*, FT 990,
    monthly.

is a direct result of the failure of American firms to establish competitive
advantages or to adequately defend market positions. Indeed, too many
American firms have been stuck in the middle, stuck in neutral, if you
will, while foreign firms have roared ahead. The firm that is "stuck in
the middle," Porter laments, is one in "an extremely poor strategic
situation . . . [which] lacks market share, capital investment and the resolve to play the low-cost game, the industry-wide differentiation necessary to obviate the need for a low-cost position, or the focus to create
differentiation or a low-cost position in a more limited sphere."[4] This is
a crucial flaw, for it represents the inability to implement in an effective
manner a business tool with the potential to enhance a firm's competitive
advantage as it tries to secure a market leadership position. The question,
however, remains: how does a firm implement portfolio strategies that
result in a sustainable competitive advantage?

NOTES

1. Niccolo Machiavelli, *The Prince and The Discourses* (New York: Random
House, 1950), p. 53.
2. Michael E. Porter, *Competitive Advantage: Creating and Sustaining Superior
Performance* (New York: Free Press, 1985), p. 16.
3. *Wall Street Journal*, April 27, 1987.
4. Michael E. Porter, *Competitive Strategy: Techniques for Analyzing Industries
and Competitors* (New York: Free Press, 1980), p. 41.

≪ **2**

GENERIC STRATEGIC PLANNING AND
PORTFOLIO MANAGEMENT

In order to manage corporate business units through the implementation of portfolio strategies, the corporate officer must understand the purpose of strategic planning. Only then can the leap from portfolio theory to portfolio practice be made. In the simplest sense, strategic planning focuses corporate energies into thinking about its place beyond the single budget year ahead.

A natural response to the growth of the complexity in the nature of business that occurred during the late 1950s and 1960s, strategic planning attempts to consolidate a firm's efforts and resources as it analyzes its growth, profitability, market, and future. It this sense, then, strategic planning is intended to provide a direction to an established goal. In turbulent times, the implied goal of all strategic planning is the proper administration of business units. Achieving the perceived and desired result, however, has proved an elusive task.

The constant decline in the position of American firms *vis-à-vis* foreign corporations necessitates a complete reassessment of how managers implement strategic planning. It is not enough to rely on the traditional methods of strategy analysis, and growth planning for the record of the last quarter century clearly indicates that these methods have failed to produce the intended results. Although the world has faced increasing turbulence during the time in question, it must recognize that many foreign firms prospered during turbulence of equal magnitude. It can be argued that nations such as West Germany and Japan, for example, faced greater strains and difficulties during the oil crisis than did the

United States. Both these nations were more vulnerable to the effects of the oil crisis than was the United States. These two nations, however, were able to respond to the challenge the surge in oil prices posed and are today in stronger and sustainable competitive positions.

Their American counterparts, however, complacent in their historical ability to establish programs designed to secure and maintain leadership market positions, have not implemented strategic planning processes capable of establishing the conditions necessary to take advantage of adversity and use it as an opportunity to enhance corporate ability to prevail under the new conditions of a complex, competitive, and volatile global marketplace. The world is a global marketplace, and firms need to appreciate the strategic implications of this fact. The commitment to securing one of the three kinds of competitive advantages—cost, differentiation, or focus—has been lacking in the manner U.S. firms have approached the business world. This has proved a detrimental strategic tactic especially as multinationals capable of exploiting the economies of scale possible through the globalization of production and distribution become more commonplace. "Global industries," Porter observes, "require a firm to compete on a worldwide, coordinate basis or face strategic disadvantages. Some industries that are international in the sense of being populated by multinational companies do not have the essential characteristics of a global industry."[1] The rapid globalization of all industries serves as an impetus to formulate strategies from which a strong and formidable response to the foreign challenge can be mounted.

The corporate officer requires a thorough and intimate understanding of the three generic strategies which together constitute the three inroads towards establishing a market leadership position defendable in the long term. Without at least one of these strategies all corporate efforts to establish a significant presence in the marketplace will be difficult if not impossible. The three distinct strategies are:

Cost—A firm can work to become the lowest cost producer in its industry. The objective being to reduce production costs to a point where competitors are not able to match the costs of producing the same product or another product viewed as indistinguishable or comparable by the customer.

Differentiation—A firm with a differentiated product is one that offers benefits to the customer competitors cannot deliver because of exclusive processes or patents. Differentiation can also occur when the product offers unique benefits, which can command a premium price from the customer.

Focus—A firm can use either a cost or differentiation strategy aimed at a specific market segment. A firm that channels energies into a targeted focus can use either a cost focus or a differentiation focus to become dominant within the industry and market in which it competes.

One of these strategies must be embraced as the pace of globalization of industries throughout the world intensifies. As the end of the century draws near, however, it is important to realize that continuing revolutions in technologies and transportation now make *every* industry a global one. Thus, in the current environment, portfolio analysis of one's competitors is an integral part of the process by which explicit goals, missions, and strategies are developed. The economic dislocation of the current economic environment demonstrates that the corporate officer needs to adopt a conscious program that defines corporate goals and identifies the most efficient strategies to bring these goals to fruition. If you don't know where you're going, how will you know when you've arrived?

CORPORATE GOALS

To understand the obstacles encountered in traditional strategic planning, one must first examine the principles of strategic planning and the role it plays in assisting corporate management. As with other tools, strategic planning is of use only if the corporate officer is afforded a comprehensive overview of the various aspects of corporate life that strategic planning endeavors to improve. Only then can an objective appraisal of the success of traditional strategic planning be made.

First of all, strategic planning deals with the bottom line. Its orientation is financial in nature. It strives to quantify the growth, sales, revenues, market share, and position a firm's goods and services have achieved in the marketplace. In this way, an objective assessment of corporate progress can be achieved. The unforgiving market does not reward demonstrably inferior strategies. No matter how carefully laid out plans are, it is important to note that the final judge of the validity of a strategy is the client. The marketplace success or failure of corporate plans determine how sensitive corporate plans are to market realities.

Inherent in the proposition that strategic planning revolves around the corporate bottom line is the assumption that strategic planning plays a crucial role in the identification and evaluation of corporate goals. Not unlike other organizations structured for a specific purpose, a business corporation must have a goal, a direction in which all its energies are channeled. Whether the firm provides a specific and highly differentiated service to a customer or whether it manufactures a mass market product, the firm's survival and future integrity rest on its ability to stay one step ahead of market developments. To do this requires a strategy and a plan.

The strategist must devise a program for managing the firm's business units in order to maximize economic utility and profitability. Thus strategic planning evolved as a discipline necessary in the proper administration of business goals and objectives. There is no question that a coherent approach to the business world is necessary in order to maintain competitive advantage. Here lies the paradox, for here is the reason for the demise of corporate America's leadership worldwide: lack of a competitive advantage. The inability to implement portfolio strategies that can secure sustainable competitive advantages is caused by the relative strength of foreign firms' asset management. The problem is not that corporate America has bad strategies, rather, the strategies are good, but not good enough. While the absolute strength of any competitive strategy cannot be determined, the relative strength can. Thus while a strategy may be good, if another one is better, the good strategy is useless. The ability of corporate America to produce and market products is good, but Japanese and West German firms are performing better. Their relative strategies and marketing efforts are superior to those employed by domestic firms. The key to this nation's current dilemmas is that their management strength is our weakness.

The observation that foreign firms' superior strategies out-compete domestic firms bespeaks an internal organizational structure that is capable of producing superior strategies and an analysis mechanism that is capable of assessing accurately markets, industries, and economic trends. The demise of American firms in the global context is predictable in a market economy that rewards the superior performance. Those whose management abilities, portfolio strategies, organizational structures and business practices are inferior relative to their competitors' cannot expect to be successful in the marketplace. What aggravates the situation for the United States, moreover, is the unrealistic expectation established by officers for their companies. As will be discussed later, whether it concerns Sam Ginn's Pacific Telesis International or Richard Ferris' Allegis Corporation, unrealistic goals established by managers charged with managing firms outside their field of expertise undermine the chances of success. For managers who are inexperienced in managing diverse corporate business units and implementing sound portfolio strategies, success is ever so elusive.

CONTRIBUTING FACTORS

Managing corporate business units requires the identification of goals. An overall vision of a firm's future growth, purpose in the marketplace, and ability to build on its strengths is the first step to achieving a competitive advantage. Once goals are established, portfolio strategies must be selected. Important to selecting a portfolio strategy is an analysis of the factors that will contribute to the present or future success of the firm. The evaluation of market conditions, technological advances, customer preferences and needs, competitors, and political factors that af-

Figure 2.1
Contributing Factors for Successful Strategic Planning

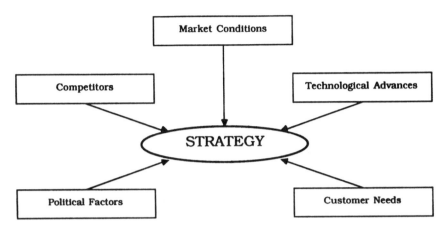

Source: International Credit Monitor.

fect directly or indirectly the firm is crucial to ensuring success. Without a reliable portrait of the prevailing status of these factors, the ability of strategic planners to define precise strategies is seriously impaired. In order to structure business units in optimal portfolio matrices, a sense of being in tune with the economy and in the political environment in which a firm operates is required. This relevance to the prevailing business environment is the foundation from which a program of competitive advantage can be erected (see Figure 2.1). The factors to consider are as follow.

Market Conditions—Analysis of prevailing market conditions is necessary to understand more comprehensively the current trends in a given industry or general market. The assessment of current trends, which may involve long-term or present cyclical factors, is necessary in order to evaluate with any degree of accuracy the real state of the market. The importance of understanding market conditions lies in the increasing globalization of industry. In a period where international monetary arrangements are absent, national economies move through the various stages of business cycles independent of other national economies. Thus the modern firm has to contend with the market conditions created not only by the product life cycles of their commodities but also by the different positions on the business cycle in which a multitude of nations might find themselves at any given moment.

Technological Advances—Technology plays an instrumental role in the success of a firm. The rate of increase of high technology and sophistication in the manufacturing process has been so great that technological considerations can no longer be divorced from the corporate planning process. As the century draws to a close, a significant advantage will be enjoyed by firms capable of capitalizing on the significant role technology will continue to play. This, however, does not imply that effective managers will be engineers. It does mean that managers will have to understand the role technology plays in affecting changes in the marketplace. As Mark Potts and Peter Behr argue, management need not understand how technology works, but "the best managers know how important technology is to their corporations' success."[2]

Customer Needs—In a time when the access to and importance of information has increased manifold, entire new markets, new needs, and new products have exploded on the scene. Identifying and satisfying these new customer markets, business and consumer, necessitates a coherent and methodical approach to tapping particular market niches. Gone are the days when a firm's customers could be satisfied with the same product or service. As the value chains of business and consumer customers have grown complex, so have the specialized needs to be satisfied along the various points of each customer chain. This, however, does not suggest that the world of tomorrow will be characterized by an endless stream of highly differentiated products. The same commodity may serve different needs of different customers at different points of their value chains; but unless there is careful research into the needs of the customer, the firm would not be able to identify the need/product match.

Competitors—Competing firms should be viewed as a real threat to the corporate customer base either directly or indirectly. Direct competitors market commodities that satisfy the same needs as one's own firm. Indirect competitors are firms capable of entering one's market or capable of marketing commodities that closely match the customers' needs. The substitution of one's firm's products or services for the commodities of another firm constitutes a threat to the existing customer base. Direct and indirect competitor issues must be reflected in one's corporate planning process. The entry of new competitors can also occur when a firm abandons a market niche in which it was firmly established. The vacuum created when Walt Disney stopped releasing its children's films based on fairy tales was filled by new entrants into the children's fantasy market such as the Smurfs cartoons. The erroneous conclusion that that market niche no longer existed created an opportunity for a competitor to supply a substitute for *Snow White* and *Sleeping Beauty*.

Political Factors—Government intervention in the marketplace is too often overlooked as a factor affecting business. Political risk exposure from the actions or inactions of domestic and foreign governments shapes the environment in which the market operates and constitutes a great influence. Indeed, while it is impossible to forecast the actions of governments, it is the corporate entity capable of analyzing "what if" scenarios and assessing the likelihood of certain actions that can gain a competitive advantage *vis-à-vis* competitors. The need to understand and tailor strategies to the sociopolitical realities of the economic environment is not reserved exclusively for firms operating abroad. Politics are everywhere human beings live; political positioning is an inescapable aspect of strategic planning. Currency revaluations, import quotas and tariffs are as important as local toxic waste laws and local cost-of-living considerations.

Together these factors affect the character and content of corporate strategic planning. Each plays an important role in assessing the realism of corporate goals and the avenues that will allow it to make its goals a reality. The purpose behind strategic planning is to take such factors into account when analyzing the financial aspects of corporate developments. It follows that good strategic planning attempts to direct a corporation's focus on not only next year's numbers, but on the numbers beyond the horizon, a few years down the road. Moreover, to demystify the estimates, it is necessary to evaluate and account developments outside a firm's control that may affect its future earnings potential and market position. The firm that understands how it is affected by these factors is in a position to control them, to respond to them, and to formulate sound strategies for managing the firm's business units.

REALIZING GOALS

Once corporate strategy reflects an adequate analysis of external factors, it can turn its attention to the evaluation of internal characteristics of the firm itself. The combining of both external and internal sources of information is necessary to define and adopt realistic corporate goals. It is the prudent firm that assesses its strengths and weaknesses in order to capitalize on its plusses while compensating for its minuses before tackling the real world. Only then can the company enhance its market position, thus increasing its chances of success.

The role of strategic planning, however, extends beyond the polishing of corporate objectives. Strategic planning can guide corporate officers to optimal policies for reaching goals. It is not enough to establish abstract goals; corporate planners must identify policies that will promote the overall corporate goals in general and a specific task in particular. This is where strategic planning plays a unique role in business: evaluating various policies and their ability to contribute to corporate goals.

Unless an analysis is able to identify the policies under consideration, its utility is limited. In the late 1960s this was one of the most pressing arguments made by the proponents of strategic planning. The promise of strategic planning was too enticing to resist. In a world where business leaders had begun to realize that the virtual monopoly in technology and manufacturing held by U.S. firms during the 1950s was eroding, corporate officers searched for a management tool that could hold the foreign advancement at bay. Strategic planning was this tool, and it was enthusiastically embraced.

PORTFOLIO MANAGEMENT

The mission of strategic planning is not a simple one. Managing the complex issues and many variables into a coherent plan of action requires a method of incorporating these separate issues into a broad view of a company: its identity, its goals, and its chances of success. The integration of these various concerns and the divisions of the corporate entity are served by a system of management that recognizes the separate business units within a firm as a corporate "portfolio."

The management of the firm's business units is complex. The firm must select appropriate portfolio strategies, implement these, and manage the performance of all the business units. These business units, moreover, should complement each other, building on the strengths of the firm, ameliorating the weaknesses. To accomplish this goal each division or subsidiary within the firm is identified as a strategic business unit (SBU), which is a subset of the corporate whole. Thus, the performance, mission, and commitment of any particular SBU is dependent on how it promotes the ultimate corporate goal. Unless an SBU helps achieve a goal or provides valuable support to other essential SBUs, the utility of that SBU must be scrutinized.

This is especially urgent in the face of fierce competition today. The firm is best served by a portfolio management system capable of integrating the various information and analytical requirements the modern world demands. Indeed, during the 1970s portfolio management was the buzzword as firms in every field implemented programs intended to exploit the benefits strategic planning promised.

The large-scale diversification of the late 1960s and 1970s, made possible by the previous decades' growth, resulted in great diversity of many U.S. firms. Portfolio management was designed to accomplish two goals. First, it was viewed as a system capable of managing the diversity of corporate business units. Second, it could assist the management of strategic planning, which was a complex process in and of itself. The mission of portfolio management, then, is an elusive one. The reason for this is basic. In order to design and implement a portfolio management program that can adequately accomplish these two objectives, corporate officers must be willing to redirect corporate thinking and attitudes in fundamental ways.

Short to Long Term—Emphasis must be placed on the bottom line years down the road and not simply on next quarter's earnings. The effects of a good portfolio management program takes years to be felt. This notion runs counter to the existing structure of business in America where investors and shareholders desire instant results and increased earnings every year. "Too often, it seemed," Potts and Behr observed, "executives would manage a company for short-term gains that would boost the price of their stock, and then take the money and run, leaving residual problems to the managers that followed."[3] The challenge is instilling a sense of long-term planning. This is a formidable task made more difficult by the trend of increasing transience among the top management at American firms. Never before have business executives changed jobs as frequently as they do now. This poses a serious threat to the ability of the corporate entity to initiate long-term programs. "Short timers" are not committed to results they won't be around to see or for which they will not be able to take credit.

Commitment—The total process of executing a portfolio management system throughout the entire corporation takes years to achieve. The process is slow, time consuming, tedious, and it requires patience. In much the same way that foreign competitors have exercised the discipline to see the results of their efforts come to fruition, so must American executives now be willing to realize the commitment necessary to make portfolio management successful. In short, firms must be in a position to envision and adopt programs that will consider a vast array of factors affecting commitment. The most important of these is the ability to balance opposing forces: shareholder pressure, resistance from the rank and file, and management's belief in the validity and relevance of the road chosen.

Resource to Management Efficiencies—The proper administration of human talent within the corporate structure is essential. Before adopting portfolio management programs, corporate officers need to elevate the priority of management talent allocation to the level of resource allocation. People blossom when they are given the opportunity to use their talents and to think. This is more urgent during a time in which the organizational interrelationships among management are changing. Cost considerations must temporarily give way to other factors, namely the marketplace. Unfortunately, this fact faces stiff resistance from the top management. Few CEOs are willing to consider dismantling the importance of cost control for even one quarter, and middle management often resists the idea of organizational changes which threaten to redistribute the existing, and comfortable, balances of power within the political structure of any organization.

STRATEGIC BUSINESS UNIT

The first step in preparing for the implementation of portfolio management is the definition of the SBUs of a business. An analysis of the markets, competitive edges, financial resources, lines of business, and investment opportunities is critical if the precise definitions and categorization of a portfolio's divisions are to be defined into strategic business units. An SBU can be a subsidiary company, a division, a product line, or a shared resource group.

Once all SBUs have been defined they can be assigned strategic missions. The missions are the SBUs' *raison d'être*. Their only purpose to the corporate entity is for them to accomplish their tasks in support of the overall goals of the firm. The position of the SBUs in relation to the goals of the corporation can be plotted on a grid (see Figure 2.2). The advantages of using graphical techniques is that it allows a firm the freedom of choosing a matrix compatible with its goals. Growth/share matrices are the most common, followed by industry appeal/business position matrices. This is only a partial listing of the possible portfolio grids. The visual aid of a graph is necessary in order to understand the concepts behind the purpose of assigning strategic missions to the various SBUs. It is also useful when measuring the progress achieved by the SBUs. More importantly, however, it offers a context by which to judge the performance of an individual SBU. The corporate officer must look beyond the bottom line when comparing two SBUs pursuing wholly different goals. The position of an SBU on a matrix is incomplete if not analyzed in light of the strategic mission assigned to the SBU. There are different criteria for different missions. The level of financial commitment to each SBU from management must reflect the degree of difficulty involved. SBUs must be given realistic goals, ample financial backing, and time to accomplish their strategic missions.

This implies a secondary purpose in defining the components of a portfolio as SBUs: it is necessary to think of an SBU as a stand-alone unit acting within the prevailing realities of industry economics. An SBU must be considered independent for strategic purposes. If an SBU, for example, performs a service whose benefits are common to all, such as legal, clerical, or mailroom functions, then the costs of providing these services must be charged to the SBUs drawing on these resources on a user basis. This allows for a paper profit and correct billings allocations throughout the entire portfolio. If it is demonstrably evident an individual SBU cannot operate as a viable economic entity, its structure and management must be evaluated. The advantage SBUs offer is that they permit the objective appraisal of how a unit's operations compare with current prices demanded by firms offering the same goods or services in the marketplace. This is invaluable information for the proper evaluation of the performance of an SBU.

Thus the stand-alone structure allows for the critical evaluation of the value-added end product of an SBU in the proper context. In addition, it offers the firm the opportunity to assess how an SBU is performing

Figure 2.2
The Portfolio Grid: SBU Position versus Corporate Goals

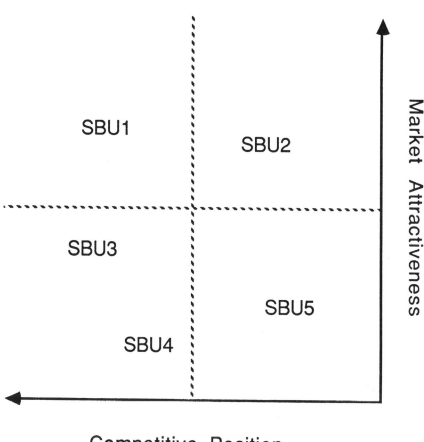

Competitive Position

Source: International Credit Monitor.

in the marketplace in any given time frame. Furthermore, if SBUs are classified as stand-alone entities, it becomes an easy matter to go one step beyond and allocate capital and human resources directly to each SBU.

Thus a firm is offered the opportunity to allocate resources directly to SBUs as their needs require various resource level commitments. In this way a firm is able to establish a set of policies that standardize procedures in a dynamic and responsive way in tune with market realities. Inherent in this proposition is the concept that the corporate entity must realize the benefits of interrelationships among the SBUs, each being allowed to contribute and to benefit from the resources of the corporate entity. Whether an SBU is funded on a per-project or per-task basis, the ultimate result is the same: an efficient resource allocation program that rewards results and maximizes profitability.

The ability of management to consider SBUs as stand-alone units and to allocate resources selectively, however, compounds the resistance and problems the implementation of portfolio management systems represent. If the complexities in designing and carrying out portfolio management programs weren't enough, the entire process by which SBUs are defined and evaluated in the context of the marketplace faces resistance from the rank and file. Despite resistance, it is valuable to strategically define corporate business units and establish the parameters of the divisions as SBUs. This organizational structure affords greater flexibility and more precise accounting.

WHY PORTFOLIO MANAGEMENT?

The appeal of a management tool capable of delivering on two fronts—managing diverse business units and the complexity of strategic planning—cannot be denied. This is one of the reasons why portfolio management was so widely accepted during the 1970s. The issue, however, is that portfolio management requires such redirection of organizational procedures and attitudes developed over the life of the firm—why consider implementing a program which can potentially cause an internal upheaval?

The answer lies in the vast potential benefits which can be exploited by portfolio management. Once a program for implementing a comprehensive portfolio management system is in place, the firm can expect to:

1. Understand the opportunities available in the various markets in which it competes;
2. Identify lines of business and investment options that maximize corporate interests and resources;
3. Achieve an accurate portrait of its divisions, its operations, and how each SBU contributes to the entire portfolio, which is indispensable to lowering costs and securing competitive advantage;
4. Enhance the quality of the strategies and appraisal of the prevailing market conditions;
5. Maximize resource allocation with the commitment allocations to SBUs and projects clearly defined;
6. Redistribute management talent allocation to strengthen the long-term goals of the firm;

7. Exercise greater control over its position in the marketplace and over its own destiny in the wake of increased competition; and,

8. Develop a common graphic and verbal culture that enhances corporate communications.

Moreover, since the corporation is best served by strategies that seek to deliver value to the customer's value chain, portfolio management is instrumental in identifying which activities and which businesses can best meet the needs of the customer. Portfolio management aids the corporate executive in determining which methods must be implemented in order to direct corporate energies to delivering differentiated products at the lowest cost. This is naturally complemented by the shifting from short- to long-term considerations.

The purpose of any economic activity is to realize optimal profitability. This is best served by building in the present with foresight. Portfolio management is an integral aspect of this. Despite the logic of these goals, in practice, portfolio management has failed to deliver on all fronts. The appeal of portfolio management is great—so great in fact, that the majority of Fortune 500 companies use portfolio management to deal with the complexity and intense competition of the marketplace.

Most firms using portfolio management systems operate SBUs that are interrelated on various levels. In such instances it becomes an easy step to engage in complementary activities benefitting the different SBUs within a portfolio. Increased interactions among the divisions of a portfolio allow for economies of scale as well as support services common to all the SBUs. The problem, however, has been that implementing programs needed to maximize the benefits possible by portfolio management has in many cases fallen short of expectations.

NOTES

1. Porter, *Competitive Strategy*, p. 275.

2. Mark Potts and Peter Behr, *The Leading Edge* (New York: McGraw-Hill, 1987), p. 79.

3. Ibid., p. 195.

ECONOMIC INFLUENCES ON PORTFOLIO MANAGEMENT

The economic developments of the last decade have worked to under-mine the implementation of portfolio management programs. Since 1979 the U.S. economy has been characterized by the accumulation of both public and private debt. The federal deficits of the last decade have been of such magnitude that the national debt of the United States has more than tripled since 1980 (see Figure 3.1). This debt places heavy burdens on an economy already reeling from the invasion of foreign goods into the domestic market.

The structural deficit economy undermines confidence in the ability of the government to exercise control over fiscal and monetary policies in a manner conducive to growth. As public and private debt has ex-ploded during this past decade, real interest rates have soared, private investment has been crowded out, the service burden of the national debt has acerbated the already strained fiscal demands, capital stock formation has lagged, and the currency markets have fallen into disarray.

Taken together these developments present a formidable challenge affecting the environment in which corporations must conduct business. A closer survey of the recent economic trends of the last fifteen years reveals the obstacles portfolio management implementation programs have had to overcome. More often than not these obstacles have not been handled in satisfactory manners. This does not necessarily imply that there are inherent flaws in portfolio management implementation programs, but rather, that the nature and magnitude of extraneous eco-nomic developments are impressive and pervasive.

Figure 3.1
Growth of the Federal Deficit
(1980–1988)

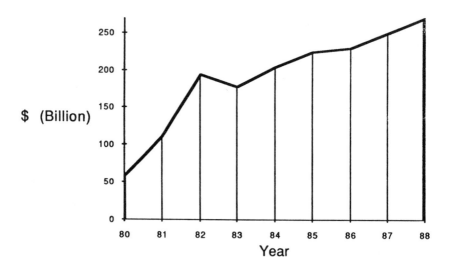

Source: U.S. Department of the Treasury and Office of Management and Budget, Historical
        Tables, Budget of the U.S. Government, 1987.

Since 1979 the U.S. government has incurred increasing fiscal deficits.
The tripling of the national debt poses serious problems, for the economy
cannot comfortably meet the service requirements. The accumulation of
so much debt in so short an amount of time undermines the economy
by increasing real interest rates and increasing the nominal price levels
as the debt is progressively monetized. Over the same period the U.S.
economy has been characterized by sluggish growth, high real interest
rates, capital inflows, and volatile exchange rate movements—all of
which culminated with the crash of Wall Street on October 19, 1987.
This is evidence that the federal deficits affect the direction of the economy.

Therefore it follows that strategic planners and portfolio managers
must have a precise understanding of the nature and effects of the
current structural deficits. A structural deficit is defined as a deficit that
occurs when government expenditures exceed government revenues
when the economy is operating at full employment. Full employment
is defined as an economy operating at full capacity and therefore higher
government revenue is not possible given the existing tax structure.
Thus, if at full employment there are federal budget deficits built into
the outlay requirements, economic developments will reflect the effects
structural deficits have on the economy.

The economic history of the past decade reveals the direct impact government actions have on the economic environment during any given time. The structural deficits have resulted in developments which undermine the ability of corporate executives to reap fully the benefits of portfolio management. Indeed, such characteristics as high real interest rates, private investment crowding out, overwhelming service burden of the national debt on strained fiscal demands, lagging capital stock formation, and increased volatility in the currency markets all work against the implementation of portfolio management capable of securing competitive advantage in a business world more demanding than ever.

INTEREST RATES

Real interest rates have risen dramatically since 1979. The idea that interest rates have fallen since 1979 is a myth. While nominal interest rates have fallen, real interest rates have risen. In fact, adjusted for inflation, interest rates are at their highest levels in the postwar era (see Figure 3.2). Unlike the 1960s when real interest rates averaged 1.24 percent, or during the 1970s when real interest rates were a negative 1.0 percent, in the 1980s real interest rates have soared to 4.93 percent through 1986. This is a direct result of the increased borrowing by the federal government to finance its deficits as well as the need to attract inflows of foreign monies to pay for government outlays. The U.S. has a foreign debt of over $200 billion dollars, larger than Brazil and Mexico's foreign debt combined.

For the business community the effects of the higher real interest rates affect corporate profit margins. The costs of servicing loans and incurring debt have never been greater in the postwar era. Capital is an expensive commodity and as such it is expensive to implement modernization programs of existing plants or invest in new ones. The high cost of upgrading or building state-of-the-art facilities undermines the ability of domestic companies to compete in the new global marketplace. The emergence of high real interest rates is a by-product of the structural deficits, which has alarming consequences for the entire business community.

CROWDING OUT

Increased government borrowing in the financial market to cover its outlays results in a gradual reduction of private savings in the economy. These funds—which were previously available to corporate firms in the private sector to borrow for investment in such areas as plant, equipment and housing—are no longer available. The structural deficits, therefore, absorb a large percentage of the private capital and consumer savings

Figure 3.2
Nominal vs. Real Interest Rates
(1948–1985)

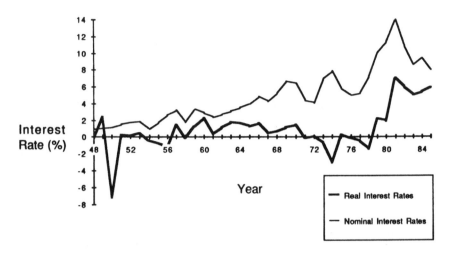

Source: U.S. Board of Governors of the Federal Reserve System, *Federal Reserve Bulletin,*
        Annual Statistical Digest.

available in the economy. The ensuing reduction in private sector investment results in slower economic growth.

Inherent in this proposition is the assumption that the nation will have to accept slower growth in the years ahead and a reduction in the real standard of living. Crowding out, therefore, not only leads to stagnation, but it results in an inefficient allocation of capital resources throughout the economy. Instead of financing investment and laying the groundwork for improved capital improvements for a period of future sustained growth, present resources are being spent on present government spending.

This portends dire consequences for business executives. In a time when foreign goods are flooding U.S. markets, the fact that there is a considerable withdrawal of funds available in the economy not only undermines the strengthening of the domestic infrastructure, but it increases the real costs for a firm to implement expansion plans designed to meet the challenge of stiffer competition. The reason for this is basic: government spends money on consumption while the private sector invests money in physical plants and job creation. Over the past decade as private capital has been redirected to government spending, the quality of the capital stock in the economy declines. This limits the ability of U.S. firms to compete.

The substitution of public services for private spending results in a

Figure 3.3
Percent of Labor Force Unemployed
(1945–1987)

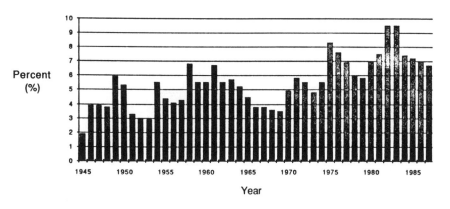

Year

Source: U.S. Bureau of Labor Statistics, *Employment and Earnings,* monthly.

reduction in the private use of the nation's economic potential. This is one of the reasons why economic growth has averaged a stagnate 2.2 percent for the years 1979–1987 while the unemployment rate has been stuck at a historically high rate of 7.1 percent for the same years (see Figures 3.3 and 3.4). Consumption and investment by business and consumers have declined as government purchases have crowded out the private sector.

As the quality of the capital goods and financing available in the economy has deteriorated in quality and increased in expense, it comes as no surprise to note that it is during this time that foreign nations have been able to penetrate domestic markets more thoroughly. The ability of Japan and West Germany to export goods to the United States is due in part in those nations' commitment to improving the quality of their capital stock and placing incentives for investment in capital goods by their respective nationals. Unlike the United States, where budget deficits have run unchecked, the Japanese and West Germans have been careful to ensure that their nations' firms are in a position to implement growth programs under attractive terms.

The most important result of crowding out during this past decade has been increased high real interest rates. As noted in the previous section, the high cost of money in real terms makes the implementation of comprehensive portfolio management difficult. In an environment where government actions reveal a lack of commitment to taking steps to strengthen the terms under which domestic business operates or improving the infrastructures, the resulting misallocation of resources creates another obstacle business must overcome.

Figure 3.4
Gross National Product
(1945–1986)

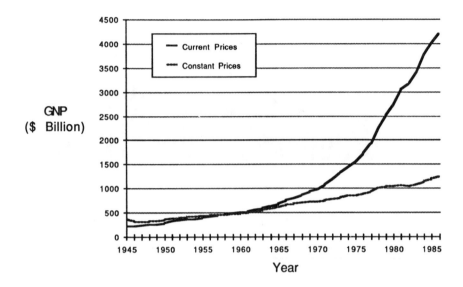

Source: Department of Commerce, Bureau of Economic Analysis, *The National Income and*
        Product Accounts of the U.S., 1945–1986, and *Survey of Current Business,* April and
        July, 1987.
1 January 1958 dollar = 100 cents.

DEBT BURDEN

The size of the federal budget deficit during the past decade has been
of such magnitude that the national debt of the United States has tripled
to an alarming $3 trillion. This debt explosion is without precedent in
this country, and its repercussions are only now being felt. The interest
service outlay requirements of this debt affects the basic structure of
government expenditure considerations and the business community at
large through secondary effects.

In the short term the service burden of the national debt requires
financial expenditures whose opportunity cost is great. In fiscal year
1980, for example, $52.5 billion was required to pay interest due on the
debt. In fiscal year 1985 this had jumped to $130 billion. The short-term
consequences of mounting debt servicing requirements are obvious; if
taxes are not raised to generate the revenue needed to pay interest
payments, then other government expenditures, including monies to
improve the nation's infrastructure, must be reduced. The reduction of
expenditures to maintain and improve the existing infrastructure hinders

the ability of American firms to compete with other nations. The other alternative, raising taxes, is ultimately reflected in the cost to consumers. Tax increases raise the costs of production, which are reflected in the prices quoted to consumers. This reduces the ability to achieve a cost advantage relative to foreign producers.

The long-term effects of the debt burden is more difficult to assess. The negative impact of these outstanding obligations is commonly called the "burden of the public debt." From an analytical perspective, incurring deficits raises aggregate demand in the economy. This, however, is not accompanied by a corresponding rise in the level of output. Thus there is a resulting excess of government-generated demand exerting an upward pressure on interest rates. As the level of net investment declines as a natural response to the higher real interest rates, the real "burden" of the national debt becomes evident: each year there is a smaller aggregate capital stock in the economy. In this manner a deficit-financed aggregate demand achieved through a marginal tax rate does lead to increased real output but at the expense of future real output. The long-term consequences of the debt burden is that the GNP will grow at slower rates in future years to pay for the deficit-financed growth of today.

The debt burden further undermines the ability of firms in this country to achieve competitive advantages. As the spectre of higher taxes looms on the horizon, especially in the wake of the stock market crash, it becomes increasingly difficult to reduce operating costs. More importantly, as there are structural changes in the economy, the ability of the U.S. to compete on a global scale is impaired. The more market-driven international business becomes, the more urgent is the need to upgrade a nation's infrastructure. For business, the squandering of national resources during a time of intense competition shifts additional burdens onto the shoulders of the business executive.

CAPITAL-STOCK FORMATION

The higher real interest rates, crowding out, and debt burden reinforce each other and magnify their effects on the economy. As a result, the rate at which capital stock is formed declines. Capital stock is defined by economists as producers' durable goods, producers' structures, and housing. Capital stock represents the available means of production of a national economy. Thus as the cost of borrowing money increases in real terms, the level of investment in capital stock declines, for the three component categories are interest-rate sensitive.

In addition, the recent changes in the tax code cast a certain cloud of uncertainty over how investment in capital stock will be treated under the new rules of the tax game. Despite the time lapse since the new laws went into effect, the full repercussions of the new incentives are still being felt. The net result of these events is a retardation in capital-stock formation in the economy. Not only does this result in maintenance difficulties for the existing capital stock, but the national economy runs the unwarranted risk of operating with outdated capital stock. The difficulties of the steel industry serve as a lucid example of the dangers of failing to keep up with changing technology. Other nations, most notably the Newly Industrialized Countries such as South Korea and Brazil, which enjoy low labor costs and favorable exchange rates, have invested in state-of-the-art steel production facilities, which have a clear cost and competitive advantage over American firms.

This, then, is the real danger in capital stock formation: as American firms attempt to implement strategic planning and portfolio management, economic policies beyond their control work to undermine businesses' best efforts. The continuing obsolescence and depreciation in capital stock results in an economy that is less competitive and viable. In the face of these conditions most firms have been forced to shift production facilities to the NICs, which offer tax incentives and a commitment to continued expansion of infrastructure. While in most cases this is in the best interest of an individual SBU or firm, the aggregate result is less than optimal for the economy as a whole.

CURRENCY MARKETS

In classical economics the absence of trade barriers results in an efficient specialization of productions across borders. It is obviously more economical to produce pineapples in Hawaii than in Iceland. Likewise, computers are more easily produced in California than Burkina Faso, formerly Upper Volta. Thus if each nation specializes in goods and services using inputs more readily found there, whether tropical climates or a highly trained labor force, then international trade is enhanced by the unrestricted movement of goods and services throughout the world.

For this to occur, sustainable exchange rates, fixed or floating, must be in place. The concept of purchasing power parity (PPP) explains why two countries' currencies must exchange at a rate that holds the costs of goods constant. Thus the aim of exchange rates is to price the same commodities at a constant price. If the exchange rate between the U.S. dollar and West German mark is 1 to 2, what costs 1 U.S. dollar should cost 2 Deutschemarks and vice versa. The concept of PPP further states that when there is a discrepancy in the exchange rates, unless there is intervention in the exchange markets, there will be pressure to rectify the exchange rates.

In addition to PPP, the concept of interest rate parity (IRP) predicts that the differences between nominal and real interest rates between nations are a result of expected future fluctuations in exchange rates and the perceived different levels of risk associated with operating in various countries. Thus if interest rates are adjusted to reflect the prevailing inflation rates, credit/political risks, and expected future exchange-rates, then the real interest rates are equal.

These observations predict that the volatile fluctuations in the value of the dollar in the last three years reflects the turbulence and effects of the structural deficits. From a high of 200 Japanese yen in the spring of 1985 the dollar fell to about 135 Japanese yen in the spring of 1987. More dramatic was the fall from 3 West German Deutschemarks in the spring of 1985 to a mere 1.6 West German Deutschemarks in the autumn of 1987. This volatility in the exchange rates and the currency markets plays havoc on firms with foreign operations. What could be a costly investment one month could very well seem like a missed opportunity, while the projected earnings from a foreign subsidiary could translate into a loss once the currencies are converted.

These developments, coupled with increasing concern over the long-term effects of the structural deficits and deteriorating balance of payments, caused alarm among political leaders. The volatility of the dollar proved so alarming that the Group of Five nations—the United States, France, the United Kingdom, West Germany and Japan—actively intervene in the foreign exchange markets on several occasions to support this currency or weaken another one.

The bottom-line effect of this on business is alarming. Strategic plans become useless in the face of erratic exchange rate revaluations. Portfolio management becomes all but impossible in the wake of crisis central bank intervention, and uncontrolled currency flows in and out across borders. The international monetary system is weakened by the volatile and unpredictable developments in the foreign exchange markets. The absence of an international monetary order capable of providing the liquidity needs of the developed world impairs trade. The troubles of the currency markets are acute enough without considering the tenuous conditions of the developing world. The debt problems of Brazil, Mexico, Argentina, Poland, and the Philippines, among other developing nations, threaten the stability of the international financial markets. This only compounds the problems faced by corporate strategic planners.

FORECASTING

The appeal of economic forecasting lies in its promise to reduce the degree of uncertainty inevitable in an unknown future. The dilemma, however, lies precisely in the fact that the future is an unknown. To pretend otherwise is wrong. Nevertheless, corporate planners must take measures to compile information that reduces the unknowns tomorrow holds.

In the postwar era the international arrangements among nations concerning monetary policies and domestic restraints on fiscal and monetary policy such as the gold standard, ushered in a period of sustained and disciplined growth. This collection of international arrangements, collectively called the Bretton Woods system, allowed for a more predictable analysis of economic policy. The dismantling of Bretton Woods in 1971, however, created a vacuum in the international and domestic political and economic arenas which increased the degree of uncertainty business faced when forecasting economic developments.

The turbulence in the real world has intensified in the years since 1971. To meet the challenge, more accurate and precise tools for forecasting the economic future have been sought. Unfortunately, their utility is questionable at best and dangerous at worst. Questionable at best because the absence of international arrangements, rules of the game so to speak, means that the barometers for gauging progress and development are now weakened. Dangerous at worst because the forecasting tools presently used create a sense of false security. There is no point in deceiving one's self by pretending to know what one does not know.

Nevertheless, forecasting, if properly managed, provides insights. The value and ultimate success of any forecasting tool lies in its ability to make reasonable assumptions and conservative assessments of future developments. It cannot be argued that forecasting is as reliable as it was during the 1950s and 1960s, yet its value can be enhanced. A more prudent approach is needed, especially in the wake of structural deficits. This cannot be stressed enough, for if viable portfolio management is to be implemented, it requires a more comprehensive approach to forecasting.

MARKET-CLEARING DIFFICULTIES

The structural deficits and the problems associated with them create a series of distortions about how business executives perceive the prevailing economy and how they act within the constraints of the world conditions as perceived. Since 1979 the United States' monetary policy has been aimed at controlling inflationary expectation and accommodating higher levels of deficit-financed aggregate demand. The Federal Reserve System, under Paul Volcker, has aimed at keeping inflation at bay through a controlled expansion of the money supply.

The very success of these policies, however, contributes to the distortions brought on by the structural deficits. In no uncertain terms, the individual actions of firms continue to reveal an unconscious assumption of the expectations of increasing nominal price levels. As actors in localized markets, the expenditure and consumption decisions of corpo-

Figure 3.5
Growth in Corporate Debt of Manufacturing Corporations (1960–1985)

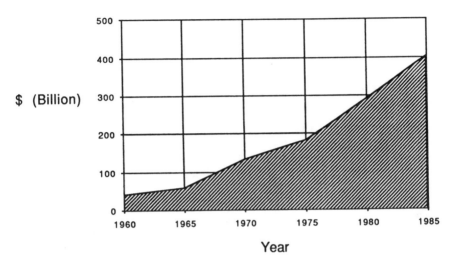

Source: Through 1981, U.S. Federal Trade Commission, thereafter, U.S. Bureau of the Census, "Quarterly Financial Report for Manufacturing, Mining and Trade Corporations," in *U.S. Council of Economic Advisers, Economic Report of the President*, annual.

rate entities reflect the lack of understanding of the changed monetary terms of trade that constitute the drop in nominal interest rates and inflation rates.

An example of this centers on recent trends in corporate debt policy. While money managers have focused on nominal interest rates, there has been an emphasis on the decline in nominal interest rates while ignoring the rise in real interest rates. Thus during a period when the cost of servicing loans has increased and is currently at historically high levels, corporate debt has increased dramatically (see Figure 3.5). Under the Carter Administration real interest rates were in the 2–3 percent range when adjusted for inflation. Under the Reagan Administration, however, while nominal rates declined, real interest rates rose to the 3–5 percent range—very high in a historical context. In this case, individual firms have not fully appreciated the difference between nominal and real interest rates. In real terms, the costs of borrowing funds is greater than before. The real costs of debt are great and the failure to grasp this fact results in an inefficient use of information and a misallocation of resources.

The firm intent on implementing a program to maximize its use of resources and achieve a cost advantage capable of placing it in a leadership position in its market niche must have a sound appreciation of the current economic conditions in order to make rational decisions. If portfolio management and strategic planning are to be important to the firm's value chain, an understanding of the market-clearing difficulties the distortions caused by the deficits is imperative.

PORTFOLIO MANAGEMENT LIMITATIONS

In addition to the economic developments of the last decade, which have increased the turbulence and volatility in the business environment, advocates of portfolio management have wrestled with certain limitations this management tool has yet to address. The national economic policies in place complicate matters for the corporate officer. For this reason there is a tendency to shrug one's shoulders, blame extenuating economic circumstances, and walk away.

This is misguided. Equally misguided, however, is an undaunted belief in portfolio management theory. There are clearly limitations which have to be addressed before an effective portfolio management system—regardless of economic conditions—can be implemented. If foreign firms facing the same conditions as U.S. firms can succeed, there is no reason why American firms cannot duplicate their success. Identifying the limitations inherent in portfolio management theory is the first step in finding a solution. Specifically, portfolio management today:

1. Lacks context;
2. Generates no new business;
3. Requires management and resource commitment not given; and,
4. Fails to maximize the SBU interrelationships.

Absence of Context

As earlier discussed, portfolio management has encountered unexpected resistance and has fallen short of expectations because of the prevailing economic conditions existing during the past decade. Indeed, portfolio management lacks context capable of tying the theory to the real world with great relevance. This limits the utility of this management system to the corporate executive. At present there is no mechanism in portfolio management that takes the existing economic conditions—whether structural deficits or the absence of an international monetary order—into account to fine tune corporate strategic planning and to increase the firm's chances of success.

Generates No New Business

The focus of portfolio management is on the internal organizational structure and on the interrelationships among the SBUs of a firm. As such, portfolio management does not actively set in motion actions that market goods and services to expand customer bases. Securing position and expanding market share are the highest priorities for business today. This means that portfolio management must address the concerns of the corporate officer in the newly competitive global economy.

Corporate Commitment

As noted earlier, a successful program of portfolio management requires a long term commitment from top management and the discipline necessary to incur short-term costs for long-term gains. Patience is crucial if a system is to be implemented that will refocus the attention and energies of the firm. Unlike strategic planning, portfolio management requires a redistribution of political power within the organization. This is perhaps the most difficult aspect of portfolio management to implement successfully.

Interrelationships

Traditional portfolio planning neglects the economies of efficiency possible through a horizontal organizational structure that exploits the interrelationships among the SBUs. The establishment of linkages to bind the SBUs in various capacities is necessary to harness the utility managing a portfolio represents. Thinking of a business portfolio as a combination of diverse enterprises independent of each other is inappropriate for the requirements of the present business environment.

Taken together, these four limitations of portfolio management cast a dark shadow over its utility in the face of the current business realities and the shifting of balance of power from the United States to its major trading partners. Efforts to address the inherent shortcomings of portfolio management are required in order to develop corporate hierarchies and structures whose integrity is sensitive to the real world dilemmas and realities of the 1990s. Gone are the days where the American firm enjoyed such competitive advantage that it could run the risk of mismanaging operations without endangering its market leadership position. When you're not the only game in town, you have to be good to survive and the best to thrive.

Thus, in this discussion we have identified the two areas that offer an explanation for the demise of the preeminence of the American firm in global markets during the time when strategic planning and portfolio management techniques became widespread throughout corporate America. First, there have been economic policies which have resulted in great turbulence and volatility in the economy. The emergence of structural deficits and the requirements necessary to sustain a deficit-financed aggregate demand run counter to the growth needs of business. The fiscal and monetary policies of the past decade have been geared at ensuring that the government has ready access to the capital markets to finance its outlays and to meet its debt-servicing obligations at the expense of maintaining and improving the national domestic infra-structure. In addition the taxes on the business community have in-creased, thus increasing the costs of production for American firms.

Second, traditional approaches to strategic planning and portfolio management are structurally limited because they lack a context that binds them directly to the real world and the current prevailing economic environment and incentives; they fail to generate new business and are too complicated and time consuming by their nature to be as responsive as required in the newly intense global economy; and, their proper implementation demands a high level of corporate commitment that has not been given by corporate management.

STRATEGIC PLANNING AND THE PORTFOLIO MANAGEMENT CRISIS

The underlying assumption in the discussion thus far is that the lack of competitive advantage and continuing loss of market shares worldwide, which characterize U.S. business, is to a large extent due to the limi-tations of portfolio management and turbulence in the economic inter-course across borders. The combination of the two threats to U.S. business on a world scale—the inability to ascertain prevailing economic conditions and the natural limitations of traditional portfolio manage-ment techniques—has resulted in three major trends posing grave con-sequences for the integrity and future prosperity of the United States in the global hierarchy.

These are: loss of market shares, higher costs, and the forfeiture of competitive advantage. The cumulative effects of these developments are easily discernable in the progressive deterioration of the balance of payments numbers during the past decade. The American firm has lost customer after customer in domestic and foreign markets to foreign firms. As fewer and fewer goods and services are sold to foreigners, the outflow of monies and of purchasing power to other nations signals a major redistribution of the global balance of economic power among the industrialized nations. This leads to a cycle in which the prospects of reversing the trends becomes worse and legislative measures aimed at protecting domestic markets, such as trade barriers or currency reval-uations, have limited effects on the overall balance of payment figures.

Loss of Market Shares

Foreign firms have made inroads into markets traditionally dominated by American companies. This holds true not only in domestic markets but also in foreign markets. As the case study in the next chapter will show, inferior strategies coupled with a lack of appreciation of the re-quirements of the global markets impairs the ability of U.S. corporate officers to initiate overtures capable of securing markets and making sales. Instead West European and Japanese companies have been ag-gressive and have been successful. While not too many years ago the American firm enjoyed an unchallenged leadership position in the most lucrative growth industries, other nations' firms command the respect of foreign buyers today. The result is one of eroding market positions and surrendering to foreign firms better prepared for the competitive struggle of making a sale.

Higher Costs

When companies implement strategies that have not been completely thought out, mistakes are made. More often than not these errors require drastic shifts in midstream, which force the reallocation of resources to address fundamental problems. Mistakes are expensive. This is one of the reasons why the final costs of American goods and services are out of line with foreign goods. While the discrepancies in the costs between goods made in this country and those made elsewhere have been at-tributed to higher labor costs in the United States, the disequilibrium in the exchange markets, and the imposition of tariffs on American goods overseas, the fact remains that in many instances it is management's costly errors that are responsible for the price differences. The American worker is productive and the terms of trade are equitable. As the case study shows, more often than we care to admit, the higher costs of American commodities are the result of inappropriate strategies.

Decreased Competitiveness

The net result of the loss of market shares and higher costs is that with disturbing frequency, American producers have been replaced with foreign firms. The commodities of the U.S. firm are no longer seen as adding enough value to the customers' value chains to warrant a pre-mium price for what is perceived as an undifferentiated product. The U.S. firm—in the eyes of American and foreign consumers alike—is not seen as delivering value. Few consumers buy Japanese cars because they want to enhance Japan's trade surplus; rather, consumers buy Japanese cars because they are perceived to be better values dollar per dollar than what else is available in the marketplace. Free actors in local markets, whether individual or corporate, foreign or domestic, seek to maximize the utility realized from the purchasing power of their income regardless of the origin of the producer. Consumers seek out the firms whose products enhance their own value chains. If a firm is unable to enhance a customer value chain by delivering a differentiated product, it cannot maintain market shares in an open economy.

4

PACIFIC TELESIS INTERNATIONAL: A CASE STUDY

The following case study centers on a firm whose experience is not unlike that of many other firms in the wake of recent developments in the global marketplace. This case study ties the arguments presented above together and applies them to a real-life situation. The disappointing results experienced by the firm in the case study stem from a fundamental lack of understanding of current economic realities. The problems associated with traditional strategic planning offer insights into the common errors made by American firms trying to secure market leadership positions while facing intense foreign competition.

Pacific Telesis Group (PTG) is the regional holding telecommunications company for the western United States (see figure 4.1). PTG, through its subsidiaries Pacific Bell and Nevada Bell, operates one of the most profitable regional telephone companies in the United States. A firm with more than $18 billion in assets and over 17,000 employees, it can draw from its vast capital and human resources for the expertise needed to ensure that they can enter any market with a formidable presence and not on an exploratory basis.

For this reason it comes as a surprise to learn that despite PTG's ability to draw on these resources it has been unsuccessful in its efforts to establish a portfolio of diversified companies in various lines of businesses. Despite its dominant position as one of the most profitable telephone utilities in the United States, all efforts to establish SBUs in a diversified portfolio enhancing shareholder value have been unsuccessful. Indeed, PTG's attempt at duplicating the success of Pacific Bell and

Figure 4.1
An Unbalanced Portfolio

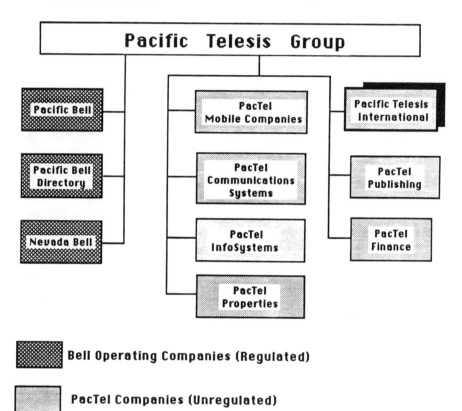

Bell Operating Companies (Regulated)

PacTel Companies (Unregulated)

Source: Pacific Telesis Group, *1984 Annual Report*.
    The Pacific Telesis Group companies represent a classic unbalanced portfolio. The
    Bell Operating companies, which are regulated by the California Public Utilities
    Commission operate in the black, while the unregulated companies operate in the
    red. The case in this discussion centers on Pacific Telesis International, the SBU
    charged with selling PTG expertise in the international market.

Nevada Bell in other lines of business can be called a complete disaster.
The reason for the inability of PTG to operate profitable firms in an
unregulated environment may lie in its own history. Pacific Bell and
Nevada Bell, like all other utilities in this country, operate in a regulated
environment in which state Public Utilities Commissions oversee investments, outlays and rates charged customers. Under this economic
context, in which the government guarantees a certain return on investment and authorizes rate increases to customers, PTG has proven

itself to be a leader providing excellent service to its customers at economical rates.

Thus with great confidence in its abilities, PTG embarked on a program of delivering the same value to customers in other lines of business within the framework of an unregulated environment. PTG sought to implement a portfolio management system designed to deliver value to its customers and to its shareholders. The Pacific Telesis group of companies identified several market niches in which to position themselves as market leaders. The portfolio envisioned by PTG would consist of firms duplicating the success of its regulated firms in an unregulated marketplace. Following divestiture, Donald E. Guinn, PTG's Chairman of the Board, President and Chief Executive Officer, announced in the 1984 annual report to shareholders that "any corporation, particularly one as new as ours, needs a clearly articulated and widely understood vision of the road to the future—and we have the strategy, the skills and the people to make sure we get there."[1] PTG was convinced that its SBUs could exploit the targeted opportunities in the unregulated market with as much success as the regulated companies.

The lines of business identified by PTG management were all in growing markets. The various subsidiaries were given the missions of securing market leadership positions in their specific niches. PacTel InfoSystems, for example, was to market personal computer hardware, telephone equipment, and accessories competing directly against successful firms such as Computerland and Businessland. Another subsidiary, PacTel Publishing, was charged with providing directory services throughout the country, from printing telephone directories for small communities to personnel directories for large firms. These two subsidiaries, like the others in PTG's portfolio, have failed to operate in the black, let alone establish themselves in market leadership positions. Indeed, PacTel Publishing was shut down as of January 1, 1987, after having lost millions of dollars.

The result has been that of the ten Pacific Telesis companies operating in the free market, all but one operate at a loss. Only Pacific Bell and Nevada Bell generate the monies needed to subsidize the remaining companies in the portfolio. Not only has PTG been unable to duplicate the success of its two regulated companies in an unregulated environment, but it serves as a classic example of the problems American firms have encountered during the last quarter century. The failure of PTG in the free market, moreover, is not unique. The problems encountered by PTG underscore the problems American firms have encountered time after time in the new global economy.

The case study centers on one Pacific Telesis company whose problems have been spectacular. Pacific Telesis International (PTI) is the subsidiary charged with marketing Pacific Telesis expertise overseas and exploiting investment opportunities abroad. The establishment of a firm designed to enter and exploit the global telecommunications market presents the opportunity to participate in a rapidly expanding field. As H. P. Gold-field, Assistant Secretary of Commerce for Trade Development, argued in March 1987 when addressing the Conference on International Tele-communications Market Opportunities in Arlington, Virginia, the world-wide telecommunications market is expected to become a $750 billion industry by 1990.[2] PTI's mission was to enter and use its ability to draw on the resources and experience of PTG to secure a market leadership position in a rapidly growing market. PTI was in the envious position of having all the technical know-how, an army of veteran professionals, and access to unlimited financing. From day one PTI was poised for an aggressive penetration of a fertile market.

Its history, however, is one in which all the classic pitfalls afflicting U.S. business in the new economic context were encountered. The cause of the problems PTI has faced stems from two sources: the inability to assess the realities of the current global economy and the natural limi-tations of traditional strategic planning and portfolio management tech-niques. A closer examination of these two areas reveals lessons for all U.S. businesses.

ECONOMIC REALITIES

PTI entered the telecommunications market at a time when aggressive marketing by foreign firms resulted in significant gains in both the in-ternational and U.S. telecommunications markets. The success of foreign firms in establishing a foothold in the United States is easily revealed. Whereas in 1981 the United States ran a trade surplus of $817 million in telecommunications, by 1986 this had become a trade deficit of $2 billion. PTI entered the market when established firms were gaining momentum and increasing their market shares at a healthy clip.

Their success was facilitated by the high value of the U.S. dollar. The strength of the dollar in 1985, PTI's first full year of operation, hampered efforts to price its bids for contracts as attractively as it would have otherwise desired. Nevertheless, good scenario and strategic planning would have foreseen that the persistence of the federal budget deficits and resulting rise in real interest rates would attract an inflow of foreign monies into dollar-denominated assets, thus alerting management to the disadvantage the high dollar posed for the young company. As expected, the rise in real interest rates and the need to finance the deficits exerted an upward pressure on U.S. currency and the dollar appreciated on foreign exchange markets throughout 1984, peaking in the spring of 1985.

In an economic environment in which the currency of one's firm's nation is overvalued and there is significant crowding out of domestic capital investment because of structural deficits, coupled with a falling consumer savings rate, it is only natural that a foreign firm is given a *de facto* competitive advantage. Under these circumstances, effective strategic plans call for a calculated and disciplined penetration of selected markets. If, as PTI clearly intended to establish, a presence in the Pacific Rim region is deemed necessary in order to build business in the growing economies of the nations in this region of the world, given the economic realities of the moment, the first office should be Hong Kong. No other city in the Pacific offers as sophisticated an infrastructure, a labor force educated in international business, geographic proximity to potential clients, and a currency whose exchange rate to the dollar remains attractive. Instead, PTI launched an extensive program to open in-country offices in Malaysia, Thailand, Japan, and South Korea without a single contract in any of these countries.

The prudent course of action, given the prevailing conditions of the world economy, would have been a step-by-step approach to establishing a presence in the international market. A reason for PTI's failure to see the obvious lies in its history. Its management was drawn from Pacific Bell. As a regulated utility, Pacific Bell is an economic entity used to operating in a high-cost environment officially sanctioned by the Public Utilities Commission. In the United States public utilities are organized along socialist principles. Pacific Bell and Nevada Bell are no exceptions. This contributes a management style that fosters fat and a "bail-out" mentality. If a utility makes an economic mistake, the Public Utility Commission inevitably authorizes a rate increase to compensate for the losses incurred by mismanagement. PTI entered the business world with its training firmly centered on the high-cost and insulated conditions of a regulated environment. Thrust into a free market environment, it was unable to grasp the fundamental realities of the domestic and global free-market economies.

PORTFOLIO MANAGEMENT

In the same way it was unable to assess the effects the emergence of a structural deficit economy would have on its business strategies, PTI has been unable to avoid the classic pitfalls of traditional portfolio management: lack of economic and political context, generation of no new business, lack of commitment, and failure to benefit from interrelationships.

Lack of Context

Not unlike the problems encountered in assessing the international economic scenario, PTI had no mechanism in place to channel its energies into a program capable of guiding its success. As a start-up it had insufficient international business experience in the global economy. Despite this, PTG was to compare PTI's performance to that of other corporations with vast experience such as British Telecom or Bell Canada. Expectations based on the performance of established firms with impressive track records, vast contact networks, and the ability to price their services in currencies with a marked advantage over the dollar is unfair at best. A newcomer needs a constant, real value reference that offers an objective measure of its success in economic and political terms.

Economic context requires a real value measure of performance in absolute terms across industry and across time periods. A level playing field measure will more accurately portray the opportunity cost of the operations of an SBU. In the case of PTI, the existence of context would have revealed earlier on what realistic expectations should have been. This would have lessened PTG's dissatisfaction with this SBU. A more efficient allocation of management resources would have then been possible. Instead, however, PTI was obsessed in channeling all management resources and energies into trying to survive management purges of the fall 1986. For over six months no efforts were directed into conducting business. An objective reference point is needed in order to establish realistic goals and to assess SBU performance. Had a realistic agenda for PTI been spelled out from the beginning, PTG would have been in a position to understand the time requirements mandated by international business. In the global arena where there are different levels of risks, varying economic growth rates and fluctuating exchange rates, it is necessary to establish mechanisms that allow for the assessment of real rates of return. If economic utility is to be accurately measured, real value context is necessary. This has not been the case with PTI. As a Wall Street analyst said, "I don't know how much more money PTI will be allowed to lose before the end comes." Where there is no system of checks and balances that tie the activity of a firm to the current events happening in the world, there is a loss of touch with reality and controlling a firm's activities becomes an almost impossible task. The excesses at PTI demonstrate that if left unchecked, a firm can quickly lose basic reference points necessary to assess progress.

Political context refers to the sensitivity to foreign cultural traits and political circumstances required in order to conduct international business. PTI has been viewed as a corporate ugly American—cash-rich and arrogant. This, coupled with the complete indifference to political risk assessment, impaired efforts to project a good image overseas. The experiences of PTI in Spain are a good example of its political lack of context. After working very hard to establish contacts with Spain's Telefonica, PTI was successful in securing a contract to build Telefonica's Centro de Investigaciones y Desarrollo (CID) building, which would be instrumental in placing Telefonica at the forefront of European research and development centers for new technologies in telecommunications. PTI's inexperience and ignorance of cultural subtleties, however, dashed hopes for a prosperous Spanish presence. Basic and ongoing disagreements with Neinver, PTI's Spanish partner, resulted in a multimillion dollar lawsuit against PTI by Neinver. While the suit dragged on for months in Paris at the International Chamber of Commerce's Court of Arbitration, PTI's Spanish office was all but paralyzed. No new business was generated as Telefonica expressed reservations about future dealings with PTI and few other Spanish firms wanted to join into agreements with the American firm. After months of fruitless efforts to secure any additional contracts in Spain, PTI effectively withdrew from the Iberian market in early 1987 by closing its Spanish in-country office. The gap left by PTI, moreover, was filled by AT&T. Telefonica entered into an agreement with AT&T to build a $200 million plant for advanced computer chips. Telefonica is negotiating further joint venture agreements with AT&T, which is capitalizing on PTI's exit from the Spanish market. Similar situations have been often repeated in countries ranging from Chile, where the representative office has been closed; to Venezuela, where the in-country office scheduled to open in 1986 has been canceled indefinitely, and from Malaysia, where the in-country office was shut down after incurring millions of dollars in losses, to India, where talks with Indian and American firms have been suspended. The history of PTI demonstrates that the importance of understanding the political context of the markets one enters is vital to the ability to secure profitable market positions.

Generates No New Business

A disproportionate amount of PTI resources have been spent on laying the organizational structure for a large firm without securing business. During its history PTI has been preoccupied with business plans, business projections, and determining in which geographic regions it would like to establish a presence, all at the expense of defining what lines of business it is in, what products and services it plans to sell, what its market niches are, and what differentiated products it will develop to offset the unfavorable exchange rates.

The emphasis of PTI efforts has been on form and style instead of substance. The absence of a coherent strategy for defining market niches, developing products to satisfy the identified needs, and aggressive market planning is the reason why there is no generation of business. An approach to world markets reminiscent of the 1950s, when the world eagerly sought out American products, is inappropriate for the aggressive 1990s. This is no longer the case, especially in an industry where the inability of U.S. firms to secure market shares has been a boon to foreign firms.

Without a realistic strategy of delivering products that enhance the value chains of international customers, PTI marketed itself as a potential jack-of-all-trades using the experience of Pacific Bell to compensate for the absence of a track record of its own. This strategy backfired; the California Public Utilities Commission (CPUC) made a strong case against the right of PTI to blur the distinctions between itself and Pacific Bell. An example cited by the CPUC was PTI literature suggesting it was responsible for providing the telecommunications requirements employed during the 1984 Los Angeles Olympic Games. In late 1986 this practice was abandoned. Perhaps this came too late. As the losses mounted and the prospects of income-generating ventures proved elusive, PTI, under a new president, embarked on a cost-cutting program resulting in a 75 percent reduction of its San Francisco headquarters personnel. The effort to cut expenditures, while necessary, is a time-consuming endeavor that shifts the focus away from the identifying of market segments and the development of products appropriate for the selected market. An emphasis on trimming losses does not have the potential of generating new business. Whether a PTI can launch an aggressive effort to gain business becomes more uncertain the longer it remains in a dangerous position of paralysis.

Lack of Commitment

The most grave pitfall PTI has encountered is the lack of commitment. Within PTI, there has been a major retrenchment from several key markets: Europe, Latin America, and Micronesia. With the closing of the Spain office, PTI has no in-country presence on the Continent. The closing of its Chile representative office and the decision not to open the Venezuela office as originally scheduled for the fall of 1986, implies that PTI has walked away from Latin America. As the PTI Director for the Americas, Eduardo Guzman, conceded, "When I came to this company I was told that there was a long-term commitment to Latin America. Now there's no interest in any of the business opportunities there. They've decided to walk away from the Latin market and I have no choice but to leave." The suspension of talks with several Indian and Australian telecommunications concerns and the closing of the Malaysia office signal a retreat from that region of the world.

The commitment to PTI from PTG, likewise, is unclear. The force reductions at PTI reveal the unwillingness of PTG to provide the funding to this SBU as originally planned. The fact that PTI management was replaced in late 1986, when Donald H. Sledge was replaced by S. Ross Brown as president, dispels the notion that PTG understands this SBU's problems—the prevailing economic realities, the failure to shift thinking from a regulated market to an unregulated one, and the absence of rational strategies. Rather, the replacing of management at PTI signals three things. First, it reveals a lack of loyalty to the individuals originally charged with the task of establishing the PTG name in global markets. Second, by choosing new management with no significant international experience, PTG demonstrates that it does not fully understand the root of the problems at its international SBU and is again poised for disappointment. As a consultant to PTI said, "The root of the problem at PTI was that management came from a regulated utility and officers had no training in the realities of the free market. The problem was further aggravated when they brought in new officers who also lacked the experience necessary. Ross Brown was PacTel Publishing's president—a firm which went bankrupt—before joining the international unit. In a sense Pacific Telesis was back at square one." Third, the new managers of PTI lack significant international experience. This is detrimental to achieving a corporate turnaround. In fact, at times the results of PTI management inexperience have been publicly embarrassing. On March 5, 1987, for example, the *Wall Street Journal* carried a front-page story based on a press release issued by S. Ross Brown, PTI's president, announcing that Pacific Telesis had agreed to join a consortium of investors on a transpacific cable for carrying long-distance service to Japan. PTG's chairman, Donald Guinn, learned of this in the paper and immediately retracted PTI's announcement, calling Brown's press release "premature." The next day the *Wall Street Journal* corrected the previous day's story with front-page coverage.[3] As a Bank of America officer said, "If this guy can't issue a press release, I seriously doubt he can run an international company." The lines of command and communication between the SBUs of the portfolio and the holding company are inadequate when the PTG chairman only learns of what course he has decided by reading the newspapers. Equally inadequate are the ongoing disagreements among the highest levels of PTG management. If, three years after these companies were created, PTG's President and Vice Chairman, Sam Ginn, and the CFO, John Hulse, are debating what fundamental measures and actions are required to accomplish their original goal—a prospering and prestigious presence in the international telecommunications market and a group of profitable firms exploiting the opportunities in the unregulated domestic telecommunications markets—then the implicit lack of commitment from PTG to their SBUs and to their original competitive strategies is revealed. PTG's official policy of not disclosing the revenues of the individual SBUs implies that the performance of their SBUs is not something of which they are proud or about which the firm can boast. The issue debated by top PTG management, then, centers on how to proceed to accomplish the original mission for PTI.

Interrelationship

The relationships among the various PTI in-country offices have not benefited from each other's resources and experiences to their fullest. The Bangkok office, for example, was successful in securing a contract to provide a digital paging service for the Thai capital under the trade name of PacLink. The personnel successful in securing this contract, however, were not given the task of trying to sell the same expertise to other Pacific Rim countries, such as Malaysia or Korea, where PTI in-country offices were seeking contracts of substance. The failure to recognize the fact that the marketing skills and technical expertise gained in Thailand could be transported to neighboring countries is unfortunate. The interrelationships possible are great: personnel could be transferred from one Asian country to the next, successful marketing strategies could be duplicated in similar countries, and the same lines of expertise could be promoted throughout the region. The experiences of conducting business in foreign countries was the key to success for PTI. Since most of its management came from a domestic firm which afforded its employees no international contact, knowledge of the ways of the international business world represented a significant factor in the firm's learning curve. In the case of PTI the ultimate goal is a simple one: build a reputation for being the unquestioned authority in a few selected capacities, thus offering a highly differentiated project with a solid track record. Instead, PTI is currently trying to sell PacLink and has withdrawn from efforts to market other digital paging systems anywhere. The Malaysia office has been closed, and no significant income-generating project has been secured in Korea.

From the start PTG failed to make a commitment to specific SBUs with predetermined parameters. Whether one looks at PacTel Finance, PacTel Properties, PacTel Publishing, or any one of the other SBUs in PTG's unregulated subsidiaries, the present turmoil at these companies seems inevitable given their approach. PTI's failure to make a commitment to a few selected markets and products, and to make its commitment firm, echoed PTG management style and ensured that grave obstacles would impede the realization of its goals from day one.

The result of these events is a discomforting one. Here we have one of the largest regional telecommunications holding companies putting its best efforts in capital and human resources to the task of creating a diversified portfolio of companies securing market leadership positions. After several years all the unregulated SBUs save one have yet to operate in the black. The only successful firm, PacTel Personal Communications, has done well, especially its cellular phone division. The other business units, however, are plagued by alarming revenue shortfalls. Some have been shut down after incurring millions of dollars in losses while others are in continuing turmoil. In the case of PTI, PTG's only SBU working in a global context, there is a major scaling down of operations at head-quarters: overseas offices are closed down signaling a withdrawal from major markets in Europe and the Pacific Rim, a multimillion dollar law-suit is still pending in Paris, there has been a corporate management bloodbath, and the top officers of the holding company are in sharp disagreement over the viability of the firm. Moreover, the SBU has no sense of strategic direction and no new business generation. S. Ross Brown characterized his firm's history as a "roller coaster ride" and it appears this ride is not over yet. Despite the experiences of the past three years, PTG remains at a loss about its unregulated portfolio. As late as June 1987 a spokesperson for PTG claimed that PTI's presence in the international market was only on "an exploratory basis." This contradicts the expressed mission as laid out in the 1984 annual report when the shareholders were advised that PTI "was formed to market telecommunications and information systems... outside the United States."[4] PTI's mission was reaffirmed a year later when the 1985 annual report announced that PTG was "now competing in the growing inter-national marketplace for telecommunications services." PTI, the report went on to boast, had secured "significant contracts during 1985," one of which was for the purchase of a firm with a presence in over forty countries.[5] This is hardly the mission of a business unit testing the waters. Here, again, we see a fault all too common in corporate America: top management refusing to come clean and level with shareholders when mistakes are made. Significant problems at PTI continue. Mr. Brown was replaced as president effective December 1, 1987. The ex-periences of PTI have chilling implications for U.S. businesses baffled by the loss of market shares to foreign competition.

LESSONS OF PTI

The result of this case study is a marked example of the perils too many American firms have been unable to avoid. The demise of the preeminence of U.S. industry on a world level during the last quarter century is attributable to many of the factors that have contributed to PTI's failure. If there is one lesson that can be learned from PTI, it is the need to find management tools to avoid the same pitfalls.

The shortcomings of PTI go far in explaining the difficulties afflicting every American industry. The strength of the dollar, while contributing to marketing difficulties during much of the 1980s, cannot be blamed for the loss of markets to foreign competitors. The real fault lies with the management tools used by corporate America. The role of proper economic assessment and political forecasting in order to create a context in which the chances of success are enhanced cannot be stressed enough.

The importance of rectifying the shortcomings of portfolio management is at the heart of avoiding the errors made by so many American firms. The challenge, then, is finding a way out of this vicious cycle.

While identifying the problems at the heart of the demise of the U.S. leadership position worldwide is of an urgent nature, it is not enough to leave it at that. Solutions must be offered. If strategic planning and portfolio management are to come of age and take their proper places as management tools, the areas of concern identified above must be addressed. In the second part of this book solutions are offered that provide the context necessary to establish realistic benchmarks by which corporate performance can be judged and the evident flaws of portfolio management can be corrected.

NOTES

1. Pacific Telesis Group, *1984 Annual Report*, p. 1.
2. H. P. Goldfield, Speech at *Conference on International Telecommunications Market Opportunities*, Arlington, Virginia, March 1987.
3. *Wall Street Journal*, March 5, 1987.
4. Pacific Telesis Group, *1984 Annual Report*, p. 23.
5. Pacific Telesis Group, *1985 Annual Report*, p. 25.

PART II

The Solution: Managing Business Units and Strategic Thinking

THE ROLE OF THE STOCK MARKET IN MANAGING BUSINESS UNIT PORTFOLIOS

In analyzing the problems encountered by American firms operating in the new global economy, two distinct contributing factors were identified: context and intrinsic flaws in portfolio management theory. If a program for increasing America's competitiveness and ability to secure market share in a global arena is to be recommended, it must be a program that addresses the issues raised by the identification of context and portfolio management theory as the Achilles heel of American business in the face of foreign competition. As Potts and Behr argue in *The Leading Edge*, "this is a particularly challenging time in American business history, an era in which the United States has lost its once-dominant position in many key old-line industries ... and is in danger of being outflanked in many newer areas. Years of inefficient management and manufacturing are taking their toll."[1] The present sense of urgency is growing more widespread as it becomes clear that the present economic dislocation threatens the long-term political economy of the nation. The problems identified in the previous section are real; the need to find solutions, even more so. In the discussion presented below, the two issues addressed center on one assumption: there is no substitute for sense. The discussion is presented in three sections. In the first section the issues of context are analyzed and a proposal is offered for providing corporate officers with relevant and objective measures capable of refining strategic plans and guiding management in efforts to size up markets and establish corporate policies. The second section concerns the shortcomings of portfolio management theory and how corporate officers can avoid the classic pitfalls. The third section introduces an approach that combines the various solutions offered into one program: strategic thinking.

THE IMPORTANCE OF CONTEXT

No firm operates insulated from the world. As a dynamic entity responding to supply and demand, it is a part of the environment in which it exists. For this reason the major themes and trends affecting a firm's economic environment are crucial to establishing a program designed to maximize utility. "The essence of formulating competitive strategy," Porter writes, "is relating a company to its environment."[2] Success, in short, can be achieved through a complete understanding of the economic context affecting the corporate entity and the ability of the firm to design strategies capable of securing competitive advantage. The ability to relate a firm's activities to its context is crucial for success. There are two kinds of context, internal and external. Internal context concerns the individual market in which a firm operates, its competitors, and its internal corporate culture. This internal context is addressed in the portfolio management discussion below. External context is the world that lies beyond the confines of the firm and the industry. It is the world where interest rates rise making debt unaffordable, or war erupts in the Middle East cutting off the supply of a primary material.

Defined in the broadest terms, this external context consists of the real world beyond the parameters of the firm or the industry in which it competes including the political arena. During the past decade the two single most significant developments affecting the economic context of business life were the emergence of a structural deficit economy in the United States and the inability of the West to establish an international monetary order to replace the Bretton Woods system thereby acerbating the Third World debt crisis. The former accounts for the surge in real interest rates, deterioration of the nation's capital and plant, and the intensification of trade imbalances. The latter contributes to wide currency swings, the impotence of GATT to facilitate trade and the prolongation of the debt crisis. The economic context is clearly a challenging one. For this reason the importance of context cannot be dismissed. In PTI's case the inability to tailor strategies to deal effectively with the realities imposed on it by structural deficits led to basic errors. The strong dollar and established firms in the international telecommunications market, for example, necessitated a calculated approach to foreign markets. The rules that applied at home did not apply overseas. Had a tool been available to determine what returns would have been acceptable, given the effects of the prevailing structural deficit economy,

PTI would have implemented different strategies and maneuvered itself into a position it could have defended.

The challenge lies in how to measure and assess the prevailing economic winds at any given time. The use of a measurement capable of rendering the economic context into quantifiable segments is necessary in order to develop more on-target strategic plans. Indeed without such an instrument a firm is placed at a competitive disadvantage. Too often in recent history has this been the case. The criteria that must be met before an economic context measurement can be selected are rigorous. The requirements with which a measurement must first comply to satisfy the criteria consist of being: a measurement whose nominal value can be easily translated into absolute numbers; a broad base indicator; an efficient information processor; an instrument reflecting wide global access; and a barometer whose performance can constitute a reference point in the strategic planning process of a firm. The stock market meets these criteria.

THE STOCK MARKET: CRITERIA FOR ECONOMIC CONTEXT

The stock market measures all available economic data and all available interpretations, rational and irrational, in the broadest economic index in existence today. It processes not only facts but opinions and expectations instantly. Therefore, if used properly, the stock market constitutes a measurement of economic context identifying the underlying trends in the economy while processing the significance and importance of all economic news. The fact that it reflects irrational human emotions as well is welcome. In this manner the stock market is able to constitute a sort of confidence index revealing apprehensions that may exist at any given time.

The stock market has the potential for solving the problems absence of context represents for corporate managers. It can reveal the underlying principles affecting the major trends and factors affecting the direction the U.S. economy will take. It also quantifies the opportunity costs associated with other investment options. In so doing it plays a key role in determining the acceptable rate of return that can be expected given the prevailing economic conditions. This is vital in establishing benchmarks and reference points for the returns realized by the various activities of a firm's SBUs. This is necessary information if decisions about resource allocation and end-game decisions are to be made based in fact.

In addition, the stock market satisfies the criteria established for an economic context indicator (see Figure 5.1). This, more than any other reason, is why the stock market was selected as representing the most

Figure 5.1
Requirements for an Economic Measurement Tool

o A Broad-based Indicator
o A Measurement Easily Translated from Nominal to Real Terms
o An Efficient Information Processor
o Reflects Wide Global Access
o Barometer Capable of Being Used as a Reference Point

Source: International Credit Monitor.

viable solution to the dilemmas posed by the absence of economic context. Upon closer examination it becomes easier to understand how the criteria are satisfied.

Constant Valuation

The price levels of the Dow Jones Industrial Average (DJIA) can be expressed in constant dollars. In this manner it becomes an easily referenced tool revealing the economic performance of an individual issue or the entire market in absolute dollars for reliable comparison purposes across time. This is necessary because an effective economic context indicator must also be an inflation deflator. The distortions caused by rising nominal levels are thus eliminated and a sensible approach to determining the real value and real returns available is possible. In addition, the valuation of the DJIA in constant dollars offers a historical perspective. This is necessary in order to have a more thorough understanding of the effects macroeconomic policies have on the returns available on various investments in the economy.

Broad Base

The stock market is the most broad-based economic indicator available. It represents all economic sectors and industries. In this manner it functions as the most reliable general measure of economic activity in the nation. This ability to include and reflect developments in the entire economy enhances its ability to indicate changes that may affect the whole spectrum of economic life in the nation. In addition to the wide range of domestic concerns represented, it also includes major foreign firms thus offering a more complete appraisal of the economy. This is because many of the foreign firms listed on the exchange have a major presence in the United States, and as such their performance in the economy is of fundamental significance as well.

Efficient Information Processor

The market reduces all available information to a price. This is a result of the market's ability to translate all developments into supply and demand changes, which affect prices. The stock market adheres to the theory of perfect information more reliably than any other instrument. In this capacity, the market is able to process information continually, reflecting the constant flow of information characterizing the business world today. Furthermore, the ability to process all data enables the stock market to minimize distortions. Factual errors or irrational behavior have transitory effects on prices. In other words, the random nature of news generation may result in daily fluctuations or even secondary movements, but the primary trends—bull or bear markets—will not be affected by any single individual news development to a greater extent than it merits. In this way the market is continuously working towards achieving an equilibrium between the news and its implications for the economy as a whole; this is important. Its ability to turn facts, opinions, and expectations into prices instantly enhances the appeal of the stock market as a barometer of what effects economic trends will have on the returns on investment.

Wide Global Access

The sheer number of participants and the volume of shares traded on the stock market is overwhelming. The huge number of participants, both individual and institutional, on a worldwide basis guarantees the independence and integrity of the stock market. While the few institutional actors large enough to affect an individual security's price are barred from doing so by law, there have been instances when a security's price has been manipulated. Fortunately, these cases are rare and, not unlike the effects of information, transitory in nature. Thus while a specific security may be affected, the overall performance of the market remains immune to distortions caused by the actions of any individual actor. This freedom from manipulation and distortions is of great importance for only when these conditions are met can firms rely on the stock market as a relevant indicator of the prevailing economic trends. One of the factors contributing to the independence of the market is the use of state-of-the-art technologies that link individual and institutional investors throughout the nation and throughout the world into a highly responsive market that executes orders in seconds.

Performance as Reference Point

The overall performance of the market offers the opportunity to establish expected standards of return on investment. In much the same

way that rising interest rates funnel monies into money markets and
bonds, the overall return possible in any given time period is a function
of the opportunity cost as measured by alternative investment instruments. The returns prevailing in the securities markets act as reference
points. This results in a realistic perspective by which to judge the performance of a specific SBU. If, for example, the return of the stock market
over a two-year period is 25 percent, and an SBU is returning only 15
percent during the same period, then we have an efficient barometer
for measuring opportunity cost and SBU performance. This offers management a tool to measure the performance of the SBUs within a portfolio
in an economic context. Only by using external reference points can the
returns of an SBU be judged. In addition to industry standards or the
corporate history, the use of external reference points offers management
the ability to adjust industry, corporate, and SBU returns to reflect the
alternative opportunities available in the current economic scenario.

STOCK MARKET PERFORMANCE

Given that the criteria established are met, the next step is to review the
stock market in the postwar era to determine what the historical performance in constant terms reveals. The utility of using the inflation-
adjusted returns of the stock market as an objective reference point is
beneficial to corporate strategic planners. The question, then, is whether
the stock market constitutes a tool that can stand the scrutiny of analysis
to determine if it reflects the major underlying principles affecting economic developments since the end of the Second World War. In this
discussion the role of the Dow Jones Industrial Average is reviewed and
its ability to act as an objective reference point is examined. While the
Dow alone is not a complete reflection of the performance of the market,
it serves the purpose of meeting the criteria for constituing an objective
barometer of the economy's direction. Corporate executives, like investors, should examine a broad range of indexes, such as the Standard &
Poor's 500, the New York Stock Exchange index and the NASDAQ
indexes for a more diverse and complete picture the markets' activities
for taken together, these indexes are subject to less volatility.

HISTORICAL STOCK MARKET PERFORMANCE

Consider the performance of the Dow since 1945 (see Figure 5.2). From
its humble beginnings at the end of 1945 when the Dow stood at just
under the 200 point level, to the summer of 1987 when the Dow soared
past the psychological 2500 barrier. During these intervening years, the
steady rise in the Dow reflects the economic growth experienced during
the 1960s. The 1970s, however, proved a trying time for the stock market.

Figure 5.2
The Dow Jones Industrial Average (1945–1985)

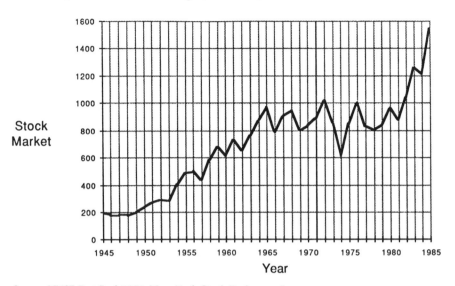

Source: NYSE Fact Book 1986, New York Stock Exchange, Inc.

The dismantling of the international economic arrangements stemming from the Bretton Woods system, coupled with the impact of the oil shock crisis led to a period of rising interest inflation rates coupled with recession. The stagflation created a period of turbulence for investors, and this was reflected in the market.

The stock market fell as the 1960s drew to a close and hovered around the 700 point level for several years before rebounding. Throughout the balance of the decade the stock market vacillated within the 700 to 1000 point range, often reacting to the economic developments with great trepidation. It was not until the end of 1981 that the present bull market began. The minor corrections of 1982–1983 did not foreshadow the steady climb of the stock market to its present level. The bull market, in fact, has been characterized by the establishment of new records, in prices and volumes of shares traded, on a regular basis.

The picture that emerges from the historic performance of the stock market is one in which we see the gradual rise in the level of the Dow as the economy has progressed. The 1970s proved to be a trying time for investors, as the economy reeled from the effects of unprecedented inflation. In fact, over the course of the decade investors left the market in droves, signaling the lack of confidence and apprehension about the economy, feelings which permeated the business community. From this vantage point, it is an easy step to propose that the recent rise in the

level of the Dow reflects improved economic conditions and prospects
for the future performance of the economy.

The importance of the stock market performance is so great that over
the course of its existence several theories have been proposed that are
designed to explain and predict future behavior. All these efforts revolve
around various means of measuring supply and demand in the market.
These theories, however, imply that there is a time lag between the
moment information is known and the moment it impacts the stock
market. This is incorrect. To argue that the lag exists and that certain
patterns in how information is processed can be detected in the price
variations of the stock market is to say that there is a mechanism available
for beating the market. This has never been shown.

In fact there is no theory on the performance of the stock market that
can give an investor an unfair advantage. The only "theory" which can
be of use is the Dow Theory, which states that the changes in the prices
of securities occur in patterns that reveal shifts in supply or demand
over the long period. Individual price changes are called Daily Fluctuations and are not revealing in and of themselves. Trends that last from
two weeks to two months are called secondary movements and reflect
changes in supply or demand that may prove significant. Patterns that
last for over four years are called primary trends (bull or bear markets)
and these reflect a significant shift the economy. It is easy to see that
the Dow Theory is more a mechanism for categorizing stock market
performance than it is a theory for predicting future performance.

The reasons why it has not been possible to create a theory for anticipating future prices lies in the nature of the stock market itself. As the
Dow Theory suggests, the behavior of the stocks reflects, rather than
creates, shifts in supply and demand. The market reacts to developments
as they occur without initiating shifts in supply and demand. The process
by which the market continuously processes information as it is ran-
domly released and takes into account the interpretations of the significance and implications these data have is characteristic of market
economies promoting great levels of efficiency. In this respect, by looking at the stock market, an objective and instant appraisal of the world
outside the firm and its industry is possible.

In many respects, the integrity of the stock market is guaranteed by
three factors:

First, supply and demand are determined by economic, political, and
market developments that reflect the rational and irrational interpretations of the entire body of investors. News is processed instantly. The
absence of a time lag assures that manipulation or the opportunity to
beat the market is diminished.

Second, the market is an efficient instrument in continuous equilibrium. For this reason daily fluctuations are immaterial to the overall

performance of the stock market. The random dissemination of information in society is instantly reflected in stock prices, but the nature of the market eliminates the opportunity for lasting distortions.

Third, major shifts in directions signal medium- to long-term shifts in supply and demand. The prices of the stocks will react to changes in supply and demand as they occur. The movements in price behavior occurs according to each economic sector, industry, or firm over a period of time in which the reasons for a shift in supply and demand exist.

Throughout the decades the stock market has performed in compliance with the conditions mentioned above. The historic performance of the stock market is one in which there has been a steady appreciation in values since the close of World War II. Throughout the 1950s and 1960s the stock market increased in price level in predictable business cycle patterns. This is in keeping with the underlying conditions prevalent at the time caused by the Bretton Woods system. The 1970s, however, ushered in a period of commodity and currency volatility as well as economic turbulence. The stock market remained within the same range during most of this time of uncertainty. It was not until the end of 1981 that the present bull market began. During the years since then there has been a dramatic rise in the price level of stock markets. Unprecedented in its rise, the present stock market reflects technical factors contributing to its rise; deflationary pressures in the economy from 1981 through 1986, high real interest rates, the inflow of foreign monies into dollar-denominated assets, high levels of liquidity in the economy, and the impact of program trading on the price level. The bull market, however, ended abruptly on October 17, 1987. The continuing effects of the deficit economy erupted in late October when the Dow dropped an unprecedented 508 points in a single day. Stock exchanges around the world came tumbling down, demonstrating the global interdependence of national economies.

CONSTANT-DOLLAR DOW

A different picture of the Dow emerges, however, when the stock prices are adjusted for inflation (see Figure 5.3). The steady long-term appreciation of the stock market shown in the first graph disappears when the Dow is represented in absolute terms. This inflation-adjusted representation of the price level of the Dow reveals a market characterized by turbulence and a significant loss in value. The Dow peaked in 1966 at a high of 306.38 in 1913 dollars. It declined thereafter before rising briefly in 1974–75. The decline in the aggregate price level continued for six more years until late 1981 when the present bull-market appreciation began. All the gains made since 1981 were eliminated in a

Figure 5.3
The Constant-Dollar Dow (1945–1985)

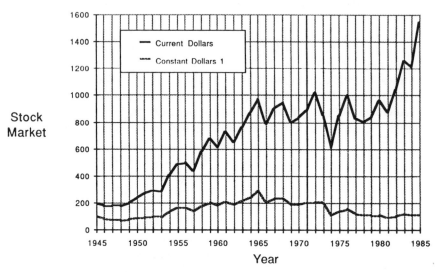

Stock
Market

Source: International Credit Monitor.
         1 January 1913 dollar = 100 cents.

single day. The crash of the stock market has placed the Dow back to its pre-1970 levels as measured in constant dollars.

The graph, moreover, reveals that the Dow presents an accurate portrait of the impact of current macroeconomic policies on the economy. The significance of the decline in real values after 1966 indicates there is validity to the contention that the market assimilates the effects of the current macroeconomic landscape in the prices of the stock market. Moreover, the vacillating values of the market throughout the 1970s reveal the great turbulence the oil shock and stagflation caused the economic environment. The oil crisis resulted in a large withdrawal of purchasing power from the United States to a small group of Arab nations. The problems associated with efforts to recycle the petrodollars are reflected in the constant dollar valuations. Of equal importance is the political turmoil that engulfed the nation during the Watergate episode. From a constant dollar level of 242 points in January 1973, the Dow declined to a low of 109 in December of 1974. This was the sharpest decline in the postwar era, representing the turbulence afflicting the economy and the uncertainty of the sequence of events. The Dow recovered by September to a level of 172 points before beginning a new series of declines, which were aggravated the by 1980–1981 recession. The Dow fell to an all-time low in the postwar era in mid-1981, hovering around the 85 point level.

The analytic significance of the constant-dollar Dow is that it reveals how the market performs in different kinds of environment. The rollercoaster ride of the Dow demonstrates a curious observation: In times of inflation the Dow depreciates in real terms, while in times of deflation the Dow appreciates in real terms. Thus a mechanism for identifying and quantifying the expected rate of return available within the economic parameters of the day exists. The historic performance of the Dow shows a consistency in the ability of the Dow to be free of distortions when represented in constant terms. As an indicator of how business is doing and how it is expected to do in the future, the Dow mirrors underlying strengths and weaknesses in the economy.

1966 Constant-Dollar Peak

The Dow peaked in real dollars in 1966 reaching a level of 306.38 in 1913 dollars. Even though the years since have been characterized by increasing volatility and rising volume, the 1966 high has not yet been reached. The 1966 high underscores the ability of the Dow to reflect the impact of macroeconomic policies on the business environment. As the 1960s drew to a close, events in the beginning of the decade laid the groundwork for the turmoil which was to explode in the 1970s. As the economies of the Western European nations and Japan strengthened, the international monetary arrangement proved inadequate to meet the liquidity necessary for international trade and finance to operate smoothly. As currency runs and revaluations became increasingly familiar, the strains on the Bretton Woods system became apparent. These ongoing developments, coupled with President Johnson's decision to finance the Vietnam War and the Great Society by increasing the money supply, created conditions which invited inflation.

The oil embargo and the unilateral dismantling of Bretton Woods by President Nixon in 1973 resulted in an uncontrollable situation as inflation exploded in the economy. The dollar was devalued, currency markets fell into disarray, precious metals soared, commodities shot up, and a recession began. These events were anticipated by the Dow because the rising money supply and periodic disagreements with other Western nations resulted in revaluations and currency runs. The underlying principles affecting the business community signaled a turn of the tides. The days when a steady and continuous pattern of growth was to be expected were over. The new economic landscape was one in which shocks were common, primary goods were scarce and expensive, currency markets were volatile, national price controls proved ineffective, and the rising nominal inflation and interest rates blurred calculations on returns. The ensuing period of turbulence further eroded the prices of the stock market.

The events of the 1970s reinforce the notion that the market serves as an indicator of the probable returns on investment. The overall performance of the market demonstrates that in time of inflation, the opportunity costs of engaging in business are significant. Higher utility is possible by either investing in individual firms which perform well during periods of inflation, such as oil companies, or investing directly into areas that appreciate rapidly in periods of rising nominal prices, such as real estate or gold. The implications for a corporate portfolio manager are important ones; during times of continued turbulence, a portfolio should shift focus and determine the impact of prolonged rising prices on the business portfolio. A firm has to identify how its SBUs can relate to the changed environment and anticipate which markets will become more attractive as inflation affects the economy. A construction company, for example, would do well to develop its expertise in ways that will allow it to enhance the value chains of oil companies over manufacturing companies. The purpose is that in an inflationary environment a firm whose plants are used in some capacity to extract, process, or market oil products will do better than firms that cater to the needs of steel mills.

The emphasis then lies in using the opportunity costs as revealed through the stock market performance for targeting which markets and products to enter. During the 1970s, for example, manufacturing firms and firms producing consumer goods fared poorly contrasted with real estate and oil companies. Had a portfolio manager considered the implications of the constant-dollar Dow, the 1966 peak would have signaled the long-term consequences of the policies of the late 1960s and the 1970s. The declining returns of the market suggest an underlying weakness in the economy and suggest a period in which real estate and commodities industries will fare well. This proved to be an accurate assessment.

The 1966 peak was a turning point; the economic incentives of the previous generation disappeared. The growth industries of the 1950s and 1960s—consumer appliances, automobiles, heavy equipment, steel, defense, and high technology—the foundation on which the nation established and secured a world leadership position—were endangered by the declining price levels of the constant-dollar Dow. The following years confirmed the continuing economic turbulence and uncertainty as inflation erupted and the growth industries in constant dollars were in the real estate, construction, and primary-materials sectors of the economy. The market has shown an uncanny ability to unveil the changing directions of the economy.

1981 Bull Market

The direction of the economy has once again changed. A major appreciation of the Dow has been underway since the second half of 1981.

The constant-dollar appreciation experienced a slight reversal in 1984 before resuming its present course. In nominal points the rise in prices has been unprecedented. In constant dollars, however, the rise is there, but it is less dramatic. The fundamental shift in direction can be caused by a number of factors.

The first reason for the increasing appeal of the stock market lies in macroeconomic policies adopted in 1981. The government had enacted a series of policies designed to reduce the inflation rate and allow for a controlled increase in the money supply. The macroeconomic policies of President Reagan resulted in a period of deflationary pressures on nominal price levels. These policies were complemented by a glut in the world oil market. The net effect was a period of falling prices for oil, in real estate, and precious metals. The fortunes for the market, moreover, encompassed the new economic currents and began to reflect the new incentives. The falling returns available outside the market and the stabilization of the nominal price levels brought an infusion of capital into the markets. The macroeconomic policies of the Reagan years have created an environment in which the economic sectors, battered by the turbulence of the 1970s, are in positions to realize improved returns.

The second reason for the appreciation of the market is the absence of inflation. The constant-dollar Dow reveals a pattern of behavior in which the Dow appreciates during times of deflation. The 1980s have been such a period. As a result the 1981 bull market can be viewed as a major correction. The losses incurred during the 1970s are being restored. The market, it seems, is making up for lost ground and lost time. The surging market, however, does not signal better times ahead or renewed confidence in the future returns. Rather, the market is indicating an absence of deflation. There is some validity to this argument. The Dow has yet to reach its all time high of 1966. Even at its 2722–point peak in the autumn of 1987, the Dow had far to go to reach the 306–point level in 1913 dollars. Indeed, for the Dow to reach the level of 306 in 1913 dollars, it would have to surpass the level of 3100 in 1987 dollars. There is a long march ahead before any real gains are made. Although those who bought into the market in 1982 when the Dow stood at a mere 85 level in 1913 dollars have made considerable gains, it must pointed out that the long-term investor has still not recouped losses.

The third reason for the bull market centers on the flow of foreign monies into the U.S. economy. Since 1979 the emergence of structural deficits has occurred simultaneously with a major overextension of debt by all sectors of the economy. The debt capacity of the government, as for many private individuals, has been reached. As a result, the United States is now dependent on the infusion of foreign monies to maintain a deficit-financed aggregate demand. The implications are serious ones; the surge in real interest rates is necessary to attract foreign currencies into dollar-denominated assets to finance consumption. The bull market, then, can be viewed as a result of the $100-billion-a-year inflow of capital into the U.S. economy from abroad. This debt exposure to foreigners fuels the bull market without indicating increased confidence in the economy. This process can feed on itself for only so long. Time ran out on October 19, 1987 when the stock market crashed, ending the bull market.

The Crash of 1987

The wide-held belief that the market was poised to surge past the 3000 point level came to an abrupt end on October 19, 1987. The effects of the structural deficits, both budget and trade, resulted in the worst crash since the Great Depression. The loss of confidence throughout the world in the ability of U.S. officials to demonstrate fiscal restraint and monetary responsibility have contributed to the unprecedented developments in Wall Street. On that single day over $1.15 trillion worth of wealth evaporated from the economy. Investors around the world were affected by the crash. The loss of confidence can be expected to affect consumer spending during the coming years. The crash of the stock market, moreover, signals the dire consequences the deficits pose for the economy if left unchecked. The renewed efforts to balance the budget and address the trade deficits have resulted in two events. First, Washington has once again focused its attention on raising revenues and cutting spending. During the autumn of 1987 investors remained sceptical that these efforts would prove effective. Second, the dollar reached record lows against major currencies. The problem, however, is that it will take months before exports are stimulated by the weaker dollar.

The job of Alan Greenspan, Paul Volcker's successor, is now more difficult. If the dollar falls further, it will become increasingly difficult to finance the U.S. budget deficits for the simple reason that foreigners will become reluctant to invest their money in a depreciating asset. To avoid this, Mr. Greenspan should raise interest rates to stablize the dollar and attract foreign monies. If he does this, he stands to slow down the economy, contributing to the chance of a recession now that consumer confidence has been shaken by the crash. If he fails to do this, however, he stands to fuel inflation because the lower interest rates will contribute to money supply growth and the weaker dollar will increase the price level of imports. This is a very difficult dilemma which means difficult political choices must be made and trade-offs accepted.

STOCK MARKET AND POLITICAL RISK EXPOSURE

Whichever reason accounts for the stock market appreciation during this decade, and its subsequent crash, the analytical results in this discussion are the same. If the stock market is an acceptable barometer of the direction of the economy, then the significance of its behavior as documented in constant dollars offers insights into the internal workings of the economy during a time of structural deficits. An integral part of signaling the direction of the economy entails assessing political risk considerations. The 1981 bull market, then, has two profound implications for the business world.

The first lesson is that this period of price appreciation underscores the power deflationary macroeconomic policies has in affecting the returns available in the industries represented by the markets. The decline in the inflation rate and the rise in real interest rates shifted the economic incentives throughout the economy. The economic sectors that perform well during periods of stabilized price levels, such as automobiles, consumer goods, major appliances, and the information industry stand to gain from the elimination of turbulence in the business environment. During the 1970s the effects of the persistent inflation and commodities shocks opened up the economy to the threat of sudden withdrawals. Policymakers were preoccupied with the short-term effects sudden outflows of petrodollars invested in dollar-denominated assets would have on the economy. The introduction of a predictable nominal-price level allows for the markets to assimilate information while maintaining equilibrium. The implication is that in the short term the market is able to quantify the real returns possible in inflation-adjusted terms.

The second observation is that the market's behavior underscores the infusion of monies. Since late 1984 the surge in real interest rates relative to the interest rates prevailing in the other industrialized nations have introduced an unprecedented level of liquidity in financial markets in this country. The appreciation experienced this decade is unwarranted by the performance of the economy. It can be inferred by the lackluster growth rates of the current business cycle that the driving force in the upward trend in the nominal and constant prices of the markets is fueled from the deficit-financed aggregate demand. The significance of this observation is a basic one: the bull market is a result of technical factors associated with the emergence of structural deficits and not a result of improved growth rates. In this manner, the constant-dollar Dow reveals what few market analysts have been able to detect. The dangers of the debt are not evident in a nominal representation of the Dow. The constant-dollar price levels, however, as well as the information about the economic record of the past few years, suggest that the overextension of debt by all sectors of the economy have consequences not fully appreciated by the standard interpretations of the market during the current bull market. For this reason the political risk exposure of the market is increased during times when the Dow's appreciation is not supported by comparable economic growth rates. This is now more evident than ever before. The frailty of the 1981 bull market is a result of the powerful effects of the budget and trade deficits on the national economy.

STOCK MARKET PERFORMANCE IN TURBULENT TIMES

The importance of the stock market as a barometer for assessing the direction of the economy lies in the historical perspective offered by using the constant-dollar Dow for identifying the underlying currents in the economic landscape of the nation. The ability to quantify the opportunity costs and the turbulent effects of inflation is necessary if strategies which enhance competitive advantage are to become a reality. The nature of the financial markets to remain in continuous equilibrium in the medium and long term offers a much-needed stability. While the day-to-day fluctuations in the securities prices have become increasingly volatile, the overall ability of the stock market to constitute an objective reference point remains undaunted.

The introduction of new technologies, however, poses questions. There is increasing concern over the role of computer trading and the high nominal levels of the market. There is no reversing technological advances, and the fact remains that managers charged with large stock portfolios, usually pension plans, have to rely on computers to fulfill their obligations. The widespread use of computer trading is a part of the market that will not go away. While these new technologies contribute to the new volatility, investors will have to accommodate this new fact of life. Furthermore, as we have seen, while the nominal level of the stock market is at record levels, in real terms, the Dow stands far below its 1966 peak. Nevertheless, even though the real prices of the market are represented in inflated dollars, there has been much concern about the wide swings in daily fluctuations. The new volatility and the wide price swings cannot be avoided when the price level is as inflated as it is currently. The volatility that contributes to the feelings of anxiety about the direction of the market can be eased by a constant-value presentation of the Dow.

The uneasiness caused by the increasing volatile behavior of the market can be alleviated through an understanding of the nature of the markets. Understanding the inevitable introduction of new technologies, the increasing nominal levels in prices, and the surge in volume all work to create wide price swings. The stock market includes millions of individual investors and thousands of institutional investors. Institutional investors and professional traders account for about 75 percent of all trading while individual investors make up only 25 percent of the market. Institutional and professional investors, like individuals, make split-second decisions trading large blocks of stock based on information as it is released—information consisting of news, rumors, interpretations

Figure 5.4
Reported Average Share Volume on New York Stock Exchange (1945–1985)

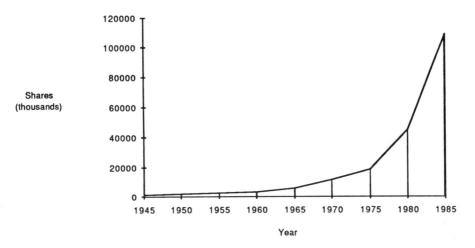

Source: NYSE Fact Book 1986, New York Stock Exchange, Inc.

of news events, and gut feelings. Although it may appear as an irrational and undisciplined approach, together the decisions of each individual contributes to an aggregate interpretation of what the future holds for the economy and the nation. Thus, not unlike Adam Smith's invisible hand, the market reflects the composite actions of each party trying to do what is in his best interests. Taken together, however, the market's figures constitute a measure of the heartbeat of the economy.

The volatility of recent years will not go away. In fact, it will increase in the decades ahead. The reason for this is twofold. First, the number of players in the market is growing at as rapid a pace as the proliferation of computer trading programs (see Figure 5.4). As the volumes of shares traded and the effects of programs rise, there will be wide price swings that will surpass the records set in 1987. Second, the effects of the structural deficits will be more inescapable in the years ahead. The mounting debt by all sectors of the economy will create a scenario in which the pressures to monetize the debt—inflation—will be too enticing to resist.

The combination of these two factors will result in more people trading more shares, a growing reliance on computers to execute buy and sell orders, and the emergence of higher inflation rates, which will push the nominal value of the prices of the securities even higher. While the effects will be to diminish the constant value of these securities, the nominal volatility of the stock market, which is of concern to many investors, will increase. During the week of October 19, 1987, moreover, the market's volatility became so uncontrollable that computer trading was suspended. Had trading been allowed on October 20, 1987 it is almost certain that the strains on the exchanges would have been so great that the New York Stock Exchange would have been forced to close down. The future of the market is a volatile one.

THE STOCK MARKET AS ECONOMIC CONTEXT

The lessons for corporate planners are important ones. The use of a constant-dollar Dow reveals three observations vital to the planning process of corporate strategies. The historic performance of the stock market reflects the then-current macroeconomic policies of the government. In so doing the constant-dollar Dow represents an objective reference point allowing for more precise strategies and the establishment of more realistic benchmarks. The use of the stock market as a point of reference for measuring the available returns in the economy will allow a company the opportunity to "relate," as Porter terms it, corporate activities to the prevailing economic context.[3] At a time when the overriding objective of corporate plans is to achieve competitive advantage, this comes as a welcome development.

The lesson which makes a strong case for using the stock market as a tool for determining economic context is significant: the real value of returns are dependent upon the prevailing inflation rate. In times of inflation, the stock market depreciates in real terms, while in times of deflation the stock market appreciates in real terms. This is an important revelation. As discussed above, the stock market peaked in 1966 and has declined steadily until 1981. The present bull market has resulted in a rapid appreciation of the securities, although the current levels are nowhere near the 1966 peak. The bull market, seen in this light, becomes more of a correction compensating for the high inflation of the 1970s than a raging market.

The more persuasive argument is that when adjusted for inflation, the stock market reflects the effects of the structural deficits. In a time of increasing debt, rising real interest rates, and currency revaluations, the resulting period of deflation and the unprecedented inflow of foreign monies into dollar-denominated assets allows for a period of correction. The stock market in the 1980s is recovering from the losses of the 1970s. The evidence for this interpretation is stronger than the conventional argument that the economic growth of recent years and expectations for higher earnings are driving the market. The bull market which began in 1981, the evidence suggests, speaks of a technical appreciation of stock prices following a period of high inflation and not of a period of confidence in the direction of the structural deficit economy.

The observation that the stock market loses value in real terms during times of inflation while it appreciates during deflation allows managers to view corporate strategies in a new light. The macroeconomic policies of the past decade speak of an economy living beyond its means and threatening to create distortions that are out of touch with reality. There have been distortions. The environment in which U.S. business has operated during the past decade has been one which does not fully reflect the shifting balance of economic power among the industrialized nations. The result has been a dramatic one: deficits at home and abroad. The decline in market shares and the deterioration in the balance of payments are the price paid for the luxury of living in a dream world.

If a program for reversing this trend is to be implemented, the first step is in introducing the concept of economic context into the business strategic planning process. The measurement of stock market performance in absolute terms is strategically sound. The prevailing return on investments in the stock market constitutes an objective measure of the acceptable return given the existing economic conditions. An analysis of the stock market performance in the post-war era reveals a consistent pattern in the behavior of the stock market that mirrors the effects of the current macroeconomic conditions during given time constraints.

By reflecting the economic context of the times, the stock market becomes an appropriate context to use when establishing reference points by which to establish benchmarks. In this manner, corporate strategic planners can add the stock market reference points to the growth/share matrices and share/momentum charts in determining strategies. As discussed in detail in the third section of this book, the growth/share and share/momentum matrices deal with firm and industry developments. The use of stock market reference points enables corporate planners to link an individual firm or an entire industry to the economy as a whole.

The relevance of growth rates and SBU performance have more meaning when compared with the opportunity costs possible as measured in constant terms. Only then can precise benchmarks be established to reflect the impact of macroeconomic policies on the business environment. A measure of relevance has been lacking. Thus, if the stock market constant return is accepted as an objective reference point for determining the return on investment possible in a given economy, then an economic portrait is available allowing a firm to analyze its market interactions in view of the prevailing economic context.

This, in turn, allows a firm to develop strategies and set goals within the parameters dictated by the existing economy. The benefits to corporate planners are manifold.

• Allows for accurate analysis of the economic environment;
• Measures the appropriateness of corporate goals;

- Refines strategic planning;
- Enables for realistic expectations in SBU performance;
- Makes possible a "big picture" view of corporate role in the marketplace; and
- Resolves the first major shortcoming of traditional portfolio management-absence of economic context.

The next step is to address the flaws in portfolio management theory. The benefits derived from using economic context in the formulation of strategic planning is limited unless the issues identified in the first section are not fully explored and resolved. The problem areas portfolio managers have encountered must be addressed and the issues resolved before the use of the stock market as an objective measure of the prevailing economic context can enhance the ability of corporate executives to manage a business portfolio.

PORTFOLIO MANAGEMENT THEORY

A fundamental grasp of the issues affecting the economic scenario in which a firm operates is the first step to avoiding the pitfalls encountered in the international business arena. Beyond the economic context lie the questions raised concerning portfolio management. If strategic planning is to be an intricate aspect of management, then the flaws identified in portfolio management theory must be addressed. Here we turn to these problems.

The nature of the problems identified stem from a complacent world view and historical isolationist tendencies in the American character. While the United States is nowhere as xenophobic as some other nations, such as the Soviet Union, it is nonetheless a nation perhaps too disdainful of business practices in foreign countries. At times American overconfidence in home-grown business techniques has placed U.S. firms at a disadvantage. The social and cultural emphasis on teamwork in Japan, for example, is responsible for the discipline and cooperation necessary to fuel economic growth. The American emphasis on the virtues of the individual—the maverick business entrepreneur who goes against the odds—is too often romanticized and, thus, it overshadows the equal importance of teamwork. For every Steven Jobs there is a NASA team of engineers and technicians who make a satellite launch successful. The work of team effort is as important as the work of an independent maverick.

Given the realities of the intense competition characterizing the international business world, the three flaws of portfolio management must be addressed. These are the absence of context, the inability to generate new business, and lack of commitment. Each of these problems represent a group of dilemmas corporate officers face. Taken together they can undermine the overall corporate strategies and erode market positions. In the PTI case study, the absence of a mission in the international telecommunications market made it difficult to channel corporate energies and resources into specific efforts and optimal market segments. As a result PTI was unable to generate sufficient business to comply with its growth projections as stipulated to PTG. The continuing losses at this SBU, in turn, resulted in great dissatisfaction at the holding company. As a result PTI management was replaced and corporate resources were withdrawn from this SBU.

The history of PTI is typical of many American firms ill prepared for the complexities of the global economy. This need not be so, however. There is no reason why corporate officers cannot recognize the errors of others and learn from them. The economic dislocation of the past two decades can be reversed provided measures are taken to address the critical failings of American business. The resolution to the dilemmas posed by current portfolio management theory lies in method. In the same way that corporate thinking must shift from the short to the long term, the conceptualization of the purpose of the firm, the nature of the industry, and the interplay of market forces must also reflect the changing influences brought about by the emergence of a structural deficit economy. The solutions proposed below reflect this need.

NOTES

1. Potts and Behr, *Leading Edge*, p. 3.
2. Porter, *Competitive Advantage*, p. 3.
3. Porter, *Competitive Strategy*, p. 3.

≪ **6**

THE ROLE OF ECONOMIC CONTEXT

Each SBU must have a specific mission around which its activities are centered. All corporate activities must center on fulfilling the needs identified that are required to accomplish the mission. A purpose, then, gives a context to the meaning of corporate interactions. Without an end, the purpose of an SBU's existence is unclear. Unless there is a goal to reach, a mission to accomplish, the reason for existence is unclear. The more clearly defined a mission is, the easier it is to establish standards that can measure the success of the SBU serving its purpose.

It is wrong to assign an open-ended and broad mission to an SBU. PTI, for example, should not have been sent out by PTG into the "international telecommunications markets." As subsequent events demonstrated, this mission was too broad for the managers at PTI. A *carte blanche* license to enter a rapidly growing field was inappropriate for managers who had no previous international business experience. Had PTG instead charged PTI with a more clearly defined mission with predetermined parameters, success would have been more within reach. Had PTG, for example, charged PTI with marketing Pacific Bell's 1984 Olympic expertise in South Korea for the 1986 Asian Games and the 1988 summer Olympic Games, the ability to measure PTI's success would have been a more objective and quantifiable one. It is clear that a specific mission, specific markets, and specific products must be identified to give context and purpose to an SBU's existence. A broader mission is more appropriate when a track record is established and benchmarks have been proven to be effective measures of progress. When this is done, broader missions can be handled efficiently provided the system of checks and balances plays its role.

In the same manner as an SBU requires a mission, so must a portfolio serve a clearly defined market. If a firm is to be successful, it must engage in related lines of business and establish benchmarks to facilitate aggressive marketing. These two activities ensure that, like planets revolving around the sun, all the SBUs in a portfolio revolve around the purpose for the portfolio's existence.

RELATED LINES OF BUSINESS

The large diversified corporation engaged in widely divergent industries of the 1970s is no longer appropriate. The vast holdings of ITT, for example, have been progressively sold off as ITT has narrowed its focus. The lines of business to which a firm is committed, moreover, must reflect the benefits that can be derived from related lines of business. When the SBUs in a portfolio engage in complementary activities, it becomes possible to maximize the benefits derived from economies of scale. This applies not only to common activities, such as a common legal division, which can service the legal needs of the various SBUs, but also to the experience and know-how of human resources. SBUs engaged in businesses complementary in nature allow for the easy transfer of human talent among SBUs without recruiting from outside the corporation.

Furthermore, it eliminates the need to have new talent acclimate to the corporate culture. It follows that if the SBUs are charged with working within related lines of business, integration is a more ready option. The portfolio is afforded the luxury of growing either vertically or horizontally—or both—with much more ease. At the same time all the SBUs can benefit from the new additions equally. This is also true for the consolidation of existing SBUs. If it becomes apparent that more than one SBU is engaged in an activity that can be done more efficiently by one, integration of the various functions into one SBU is facilitated. The purpose, then, is one where the portfolio is a flexible and responsive one. As the marketplace changes and as the varying effects of the economic context become apparent, the firm is poised to respond in a manner that will increase its chances of success.

The corporate entity is afforded flexibility when it approaches its portfolio from a related-lines-of-business viewpoint. The economies of scale possible from sharing various common activities of benefit to all the SBUs, coupled with a sharing of the various experience backgrounds of its personnel, result in a program where the addition of new SBUs and the consolidation of existing ones all work to enhance profitability and the likelihood of success for the firm as a whole. The net result is a portfolio able to maximize its position on a growth/share matrix. As discussed later on, the number of high-performing SBUs can be increased considerably by using a related-lines-of-business strategy.

BENCHMARKING FOR AGGRESSIVE MARKETING

Once the markets in which a firm is to concentrate have been identified, benchmarks to indicate progress can be established. The entry into predetermined market segments and related lines of business allows the SBUs to concentrate resources on highly differentiated products. More important than decreasing costs, as outlined in the learning curve, the ability to funnel efforts into creating differentiated products is instrumental in securing competitive advantage. Whether through advertising or quality a differentiated product, perceived or factual, has been more effective in increasing market share than price advantage. Corona beer, for example, has a highly differentiated image in the consumer's mind, and its market share is higher than other Mexican beers, such as Dos Equis, which have lost market shares even though their quality is equal if not better than Corona's.

Thus if an SBU concentrates its efforts on differentiation, the firm is in a position to allocate resources to the SBUs whose performance merits increased resources. The ability to respond to market developments quickly allows for an optimal distribution of resources to the SBUs as they require support. When a firm engages in activities that use resources to their optimal degree, efforts at achieving competitive advantage can be sustained. This permits for a forceful marketing program designed to secure leadership position. The use of specialization of efforts enables the creation of a well diversified portfolio serving the manifold needs of related lines of business. In this context optimal benchmarks can be established offering the flexibility and objectivity needed to determine the progress each SBU is making as the firm strives to realize its goals.

Aggressive penetration of segmented markets will succeed if the portfolio can be devised to assign specific missions to the various SBUs with the purpose of allowing each to pursue its own mission. The dual nature of related business lines and aggressive marketing of differentiated products allows for realistic benchmarks. Under these circumstances, the development of all the units within the portfolio is facilitated. If a portfolio is to prosper, it must be well managed and this entails a clear sense of purpose, a defined meaning to the context in which the SBUs operate. Success lies in a carefully conceptualized vision of corporate identity and purpose for being.

BUSINESS GENERATION

The next flaw to be corrected is the inability of the strategic planning and portfolio management processes to generate new business. The solution is the implementation of lines of expertise to support the lines of business actively pursued. Lines of expertise are areas of specialization. This gives a firm the status of being uniquely qualified to serve a need or provide a product in the customer's eyes. Not unlike product differentiation, the goal of lines of expertise is to implant in the customer's mind the belief that one's firm stands out from the competition in being able to satisfy a need. This approach creates an image for the corporate entity as being in a position of superior expertise in the customer's mind. The process by which these lines of expertise are identified with the firm consists of two parts: the SBUs must secure quality market shares, and the corporation must achieve a high-technology mix.

Quality Market Share

A firm in the position to recognize its strengths and weaknesses is in a position to capitalize on its strengths and compensate for its weaknesses. This is the first step in establishing quality market shares. A quality market share differs from a regular market share in that a firm whose SBUs are engaged in related lines of business and who can market related lines of expertise knows itself very well. As an authority in its targeted market, it can concentrate its efforts on serving all the various aspects of the needs it tries to meet. This is important when trying to satisfy the several needs of a customer's value chain. Only if the firm is capable of identifying the spillover needs it can meet, can an approach designed to be an important supplier for several value-chain needs of the customer be implemented to maximize the quality of the market shares.

This requires, in part, specialization. A corporate portfolio in which the SBUs are devoid of the jack-of-all-trades syndrome can avoid the errors of PTI. With no track record and no field of specialization, PTI presented itself as a firm that could as easily build R&D facilities as design telephone networks, provide the telecommunication requirements for transmission of the World Cup soccer games, design intelligent buildings, build a cellular phone network, and so on. All things to all countries proved to be a misguided approach.

For this reason, specialization in lines of expertise is instrumental in assuring a balanced allocation of resources. The benefit from specialization is a basic one; once lines of expertise come of age, their cash flow can be reinvested in the basic lines of business to enhance differentiation and transfer any surplus cash to strengthen the positions of related SBUs.

This is a superior marketing strategy: identify a market, become a known expert, aggressively pursue a leadership position, reinvest in the SBU and in SBUs engaged in related lines of business.

In the real world, managers find that identifying a market niche and establishing appropriate benchmarks to record progress is more useful than placing an emphasis on the learning curve. Indeed, obsession with low-cost production is often times of secondary importance when compared to product differentiation. This is the most convincing reason for the emphasis in this discussion on capitalizing on a firm's strength in order to specialize in key markets that can generate cash to reinvest in related lines of business to achieve superior lines of expertise. A quality market share is the key to reversing the decline of American business.

High-Technology Mix

The future belongs to those who are able to recognize technology as a weapon. The role automation and technological advances are playing in revolutionizing business is a fundamental one. The firm who can employ technological innovations can write its own ticket. IBM's introduction of System 360 series in the late 1960s, for example, incorporated technological advances that made all other existing systems obsolete, thus giving IBM a competitive advantage upon which it has been able to capitalize. The problem, however, is the rising costs of R&D today (see Figure 6.1). The development time for new products and new processes is longer than in the past. Also, due to the rapid nature of technological advances, the lifespans of new products are much less than in the past. High-tech products become obsolete within months of introduction. Therefore, a successful program designed to maximize the benefits technological advances promise requires a degree of commitment both in resources and in time. Resources must be allocated to R&D activities related to the production processes. Only when there is a committed amount of revenues slate marked for the necessary R&D functions can a firm justify incurring short-term sacrifices for benefits down the road.

The emphasis on changes, automation or entirely new processes, is the first step in examining the manner in which technology promises to change the way customer needs are met. The economic dislocation of the past two decades can best be met through a concerted effort aimed at fine-tuning existing production processes. Competitive advantages secured through technological advances represent major challenges to competitors. There is always a time lag before the new technology is available for their use. The resulting discrepancies in implementation time offers the firm pioneering the new technology an opportunity to become dominant in the marketplace. Polaroid's exclusive right to use

Figure 6.1
Research and Development Outlays (1955–1985)

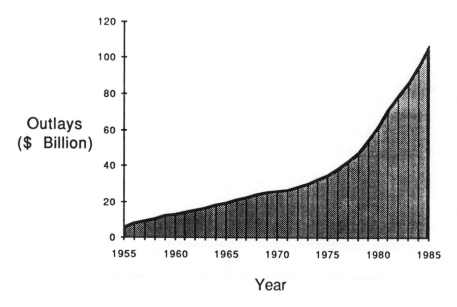

Source: U.S. National Science Foundation, *National Patterns of Science and Technology Resources*, annual.

the instant photography technology enabled it to become so closely identified in the consumer's mind with instant photography that other entrants, even Kodak or Fuji, face formidable obstacles in trying to gain market share from Polaroid.

Technology, however, works best when it is tied into the marketing and distribution divisions of a firm. In efforts to establish a strong presence in the market, it is necessary to complement R&D with resource allocation to achieve economies of scale in distribution. A strong network can best get the new products, or technologically differentiated products, throughout the customer base. Zenith's impressive distribution networks allow it to distribute new products or differentiated products within a short time frame. This allows the customer access to the products as their notoriety is still newsworthy. Lag time between introduction and customer access is a crucial aspect of marketing if brand loyalty is to be established. The best product in and of itself is insufficient to produce a competitive advantage if the customer must wait while the product makes it through an obsolete distribution network.

THE ROLE OF COMMITMENT LEVELS AND PORTFOLIO STRATEGIES

The final shortcoming of portfolio management theory concerns management's lack of commitment. In a world accustomed to next-quarter results, portfolio management theory does not place due importance on the role management commitment plays in fostering success. The business world is filled with short-term maneuvers that gloss over problems for the benefit of quarter-earnings announcements and annual reports. These methods of smoothing over structural problems, however, are inadequate for the competitive world in which we live.

The only way sound strategies and a carefully designed portfolio is to be successful is through a concerted effort that demonstrates commitment. The nature of the commitment is twofold: managerial and financial. The two kinds of commitment work together to strengthen corporate positions. The strongest strategy is insufficient to guarantee success if there is inadequate follow-through. The demanding nature of global markets is one in which the present is an opportunity to lay the foundations for future growth. Indeed, a successful portfolio is one that reflects long-term strategies and the willingness to incur short-term losses. The logic behind this is simple: short-term losses become nominal if real long-term gains are realized. Efforts to address the economic dislocation of the past decade and to deal with the continuing effects of a structural deficit economy have to include a renewed level of commitment to portfolio management.

Managerial Commitment

Managerial commitment stems from a sense of confidence. Confidence, in turn, is only possible where a conscious, long-term, and comprehensive view of the corporation's place in the marketplace is well defined. The establishment of multiyear business plans that outline goals and set the tone for all corporate activities allows for confidence in a firm's future. The defining of goals and adequate strategic planning reflective of the economic context of the prevailing business conditions is of foremost importance. Each SBU must know what corporate attitudes towards risk are and what latitude they are afforded in undertaking risks. The corporate culture that increases the likelihood of success is one in which failure after earnest attempts at calculated risks are forgiven.

Management cannot throw in the towel at the first sign of adversity. If strategic plans are valid, they will instill confidence by the weight of their own merits. Thus, should sound strategies coupled with educated risks meet with initial adversity, these obstacles must be viewed as the short-term phenomena they are. A firm capable of anticipating change and whose strategic planning process allows for evolution is better able to react to the changing conditions of the marketplace without losing a beat. As we saw with PTI, their holding company had little commitment to either the original mission of that SBU or to the management. This dissatisfaction stems, in part, from the failure to create an organizational structure compatible to the local environment. McDonald's, for example, does not organize its restaurant menus in foreign countries along the same structural lines as it does for domestic restaurants. The indifference to the foreign idiosyncrasies would make it difficult to engage in as profitable operations abroad as it does in the United States. McDonald's overseas operations demonstrate that sensitivity to cultural, historical, and political realities is instrumental to ensuring success.

The end result is ominous: when firms do not respond to the local differences, the chances of success decrease, thereby eroding commitment to the original strategies. To minimize the chances of this, SBUs must be headed by experienced managers with proven track records. The cultural subtleties, political differences, and business complexities of international markets are such that many American firms are at a competitive disadvantage *vis-à-vis* foreign firms. Unlike the United States, where there is a long tradition of isolationist tendencies coupled with a history in which foreigners searched out American firms, foreign companies have long been accustomed to international trade. The Pacific Rim countries, as well as Europe, have significant trading traditions. With the exception of Japan, the other major trading partners have pervasive traditions around trade. The shifting balance of economic power away from American firms can only be reversed through leadership from managers knowledgeable in the international marketplace.

Financial Commitment

Managerial commitment, however, must be supported by financial commitment. Resources—human, capital, and plant—must be allocated to the SBUs as dictated by their specific missions. Each SBU must receive resources, in the words of Marx, "according to his need." The problem, however, lies in identifying what the needs are. The proper determination of needs depends on the SBU's mission, the experience, or lack thereof, of the corporate entity in that market and the role that SBU plays in the entire portfolio. This requires financial commitment on three fronts: resource allocation, benchmarking standards, and time. A thorough understanding of the financial requirements for the completion of a specific task is the first order. No SBU can be expected to achieve results without appropriate funding. Different missions have different resource needs. A realistic assessment of the financial requirements for a particular project is the key to making sure an SBU is not left in a position where the money stops halfway through a project.

The commitment of resources may be withdrawn when goals are not met on time. This suggests that the benchmarks by which the progress of an SBU are judged must clearly reflect a degree of realism. It is unfair to compare an SBU new to a market by the same standards one uses to measure the performance of an established competitor. As a new entrant aiming for highly contested market shares, it is inevitable to assume that established firms have the experience and connections necessary to secure and defend market positions. In the same manner each SBU must have benchmarks it can realistically hope to achieve. The establishment of benchmarks, therefore, must reflect an understanding of the marketplace and of the reasonable abilities of an SBU. Given a fundamental grasp of the nature of the business environment in which an SBU operates, the firm must be willing to allocate its most precious resource— time. Consider an SBU which is in the process of entering a new market. As a new entrant it is in a vulnerable position testing the waters of that specific market. This requires leadership encouraged to take calculated risks as it tries to position itself in an optimal market niche. The only way a portfolio reflecting strength is to be realized is if each SBU knows that there is sufficient patience when entering new markets, a promise of continued resources as needs change, and encouragement from the portfolio managers to take educated risks. Time measures opportunity costs. Thus there must be a willingness to be patient and have follow through if benchmarks are not to produce unfavorable opportunity cost analyses. More often than not, unless there is an explicit financial commitment, SBUs are reluctant to take the often-necessary risks entry into new markets requires.

INTERRELATIONSHIPS AMONG BUSINESS UNITS

The history of portfolio management is plagued by the tendency of its practitioners to consider each SBU as an independent unit. The result is that too often a business portfolio resembles an individual investor's portfolio. The individual investor aims to hedge possible losses by including a diverse array of investments that perform well under different conditions. In this way, the investor is afforded the opportunity to realize gains in some investments while enjoying some sense of security in the fact that the portfolio contains investments that, should the first set of investments do poorly, will offset losses. The purpose, then, is to achieve an optimal balance of investments that enhance the overall returns of the portfolio.

While this is an advisable approach to an individual's portfolio, a corporate portfolio has a different objective in mind. The aim in considering corporate portfolio strategies, as Porter writes, is "based on competitive advantage, not financial considerations."[1] It is to harness the economies of scale and of scope possible through the interrelated nature of SBUs within a business portfolio. The horizontal organization Porter advocates is designed to reduce costs and promote differentiation through the various SBUs engaged in related lines of business.[2] There is much to be said in favor of benefits that can be realized through the implementation of horizontal links maximizing the use of participating in related lines of business.

There are obstacles to a horizontal organizational structure for a portfolio. These are manageable, however, if the portfolio engages in "lines of expertise" as a management approach. This requires a significant commitment to the long-term goals of the firm and the place it hopes to occupy. A formidable barrier that must be overcome is the identification of what needs a firm is to satisfy for the customer's value chain. The ability to exploit the economies of scale within the SBUs of a portfolio can only go so far before there is a dangerous blurring of the distinction within various departments or divisions. A good example is the experience of Bausch & Laumb. The pooling of various activities such as strategic planning and marketing departments of several SBUs into one effort resulted in a chaotic situation. Sales personnel were confused about the products they were selling, and strategic planners came up with conflicting strategies for a continuously changing list of products. Eventually this attempt at horizontal structuring was abandoned for a more traditional portfolio management arrangement. The experiences of Bausch & Laumb, however, need not be the rule. A careful program designed to encompass the related lines of business with the vision of marketing the entire lines of expertise can be successful.

The ability to maximize the benefits from interrelationships pivots on how the firm sees its identity and its place in the marketplace. A clear mission in the marketplace is necessary in order to build the horizontal links among the various SBUs which harness the benefits of a common management pool capable of transferring expertise and know-how from one SBU to another. A horizontal structure that balances the opposing needs of sharing common economies of scale and maintaining independence is necessary for the SBU to remain a limber player responsive to market changes as they occur. Thus while recognizing that interrelationships exist, it is not an easy step to create an organizational structure that can exploit the benefits that enhance total portfolio utility.

Nevertheless, if the SBUs within a portfolio are to function in unison, existing interrelationships must be recognized and horizontal links must be established. It is, of course, necessary to recognize that a major impediment to the widespread implementation of horizontal organizational structures throughout American industry is the cultural history of the United States. Other countries, such as France and Japan, which have different traditions concerning the role of the individual in the family and in society, have easier times organizing firms along lines that give these firms strategic advantage when implementing programs to enhance the benefits promised by the ability to exploit SBU interrelationships. This is not to discourage efforts to implement programs designed to establish links among SBUs, but rather, it is important to assess the task at hand if the chances of success are thereby enhanced.

NOTE

1. Porter, *Competitive Advantage,* p. 319.

≪ **7**

STRATEGIC THINKING

Thus far in this discussion our efforts have centered on the clinical examination of the various aspects of traditional strategic planning and portfolio management. The attempt to offer solutions to these flaws widely explored in this discussion is not enough by itself. Rather, the solutions must be presented together constituting a program for management that offers managers appropriate techniques for dealing with the complexity of the new competitive nature of global markets and the continuing effects of the structural deficits on the business environment.

In *Competitive Advantage*, Porter calls for the implementation of "horizontal strategies" that affect the relationships among SBUs within a portfolio that cut "across divisional boundaries . . . [thus resulting in] a coordinated set of goals and policies across distinct but interrelated business units."[1] The purpose of these horizontal strategies is to maximize possible benefits through interrelated links among the SBUs. The purpose of a horizontal organizational form is to help the diversified firm evolve in its effort to meet the challenges of the competitive environment. As Porter writes:

The principles underlying horizontal organization imply a new organizational form for diversified firms. The concept of decentralization has revolutionized the way diversified firms are managed, bringing with it a wide range of practices and management expectations. Many leading companies have successfully made the transition to decentralization.

Diversified firms must undergo further organizational evolution if they are to respond to today's competition. Because of the importance of interrelationships, there is a growing need for a new corporate organizational form that recognizes both vertical and horizontal dimensions. Decentralization in diversified firms is still a necessity, but must be overlaid with mechanisms to achieve the important interrelationships. The balance between vertical (decentralization) and horizontal dimensions in the organization of the diversified firm is an ever changing one, and the ideal is perhaps a constant shifting of the balance as the need to emphasize different activities changes. However, a balance that combines significant elements of both vertical and horizontal will be increasingly necessary. The balance must also reflect differing interrelationships from business unit to business unit.[2]

While the ability to harness the efficiencies available through shared resources and strategies is great, Porter offers no strategy for "relating the company to its environment"[3] beyond the internal organizational structure of the firm and its relationships within the parameters of its industries. Thus there is a real need for the corporate entity to become a dynamic participant in its market with a firm grasp of the realities affecting the prevailing economic landscape. The introduction of the notion of strategic thinking into the currency of business life is an attempt to address the observed fundamental shortcomings of strategic planning, traditional portfolio management, and the economic context (see Figure 7.1). No one in business can argue that the United States can continue its present course of massive trade and fiscal deficits, declining market leadership positions worldwide, and great volatility in the currency markets. These threats pose as great a threat to the economic survival of the nation as do foreign firms' ability to increase market shares at the expense of domestic companies.

Strategic thinking not only reflects the recommendations for horizontal organization made by Porter but it offers a mechanism for determining objective reference points that can be used to gauge the progress an SBU makes. This, then, becomes a systematic approach of addressing the economic dislocation caused by loss of market shares and profits to foreign firms. A systematic program capable of allowing firms to grasp their own destinies is instrumental in shifting the balance of eroded economic power. The continuing decline in sales of U.S. goods both to domestic and foreign customers constitutes a structural change in the economy. The ability of the American firm to create value for the customer's value chain is thrown into question when deficits persist and an overextension of credit characterizes the economy.

The history of recent decades represents a major economic dislocation. Whereas in the past the United States was a net exporter of goods and services to the rest of the world, today the United States is dependent

Figure 7.1
Benefits of a Strategic Thinking Approach

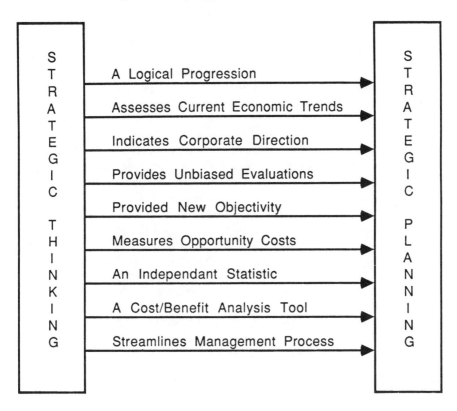

Source: International Credit Monitor.

on sovereign foreign economies to supply our basic requirements. This shift in economic power away from the United States, moreover, has been accompanied by a corresponding transfer of net purchasing power to foreigners at the expense of the American consumer. Loss of market share is closely linked to loss of profits. For this reason, it is of national importance to incorporate the solutions offered in this discussion into a sound program.

LOGICAL PROGRESSION

The next logical step in the evolution of management requires the incorporation of economic and political context. Thus, through a sound program identifying the significant external factors, the analysis of context and industries can be conducted. This allows for the incorporation of key factors into corporate strategies. The benefits derived from a management system that considers the current economic context as well as the evolutionary process in the horizontal organizational structure within a firm are manifold.

The inability to keep pace with the more sophisticated organizational structures of our global competitors is one of the contributing factors in the United States' present economic dislocation (see Figure 7.2). As briefly alluded to, the fundamental shortcoming of present management techniques is its reluctance to accept a less parochial view of the world. Current strategies and portfolio management approaches lack a global strategy. Firms must see their products in a global context, competing for a global market position. Strategic planning confined to a more limited sphere more often than not results in a set of policies that undermine the long-term goals of the firm. The effects of America's parochialism are nowhere more evident than in the balance of trade figures. The outflow of monies to pay for imports is unsustainable. As Alfred Malabre argues in *Beyond Our Means,* the present overextension of debt by all actors in the economy is unsustainable and portends of serious consequences for this nation as the day of reckoning nears.[4]

A factor which contributes to a myopic perspective of the business environment is an excessive emphasis on the short term. A clear goal around which activities can be centered is a way of managing the present with the future in mind. The long-term viability of the firm must be borne in mind when strategies are decided upon. A logical progression in tools of management reflects concern for the global implications of today's actions. Firms must be in positions in which they can anticipate change and react to market developments. Considering the global implications in the management of corporate portfolios broadens management's field of vision. A firm is no longer in a position of weakness, but rather, it now becomes a responsive, limber player capable of anticipating and responding to the changing markets by capitalizing on corporate strengths. This is one manner in which to choose the most appropriate road to competitive advantage. A global perspective on the place a corporation occupies in the world is the first necessary step in reversing recent losses and making up lost ground.

CURRENT ECONOMIC TRENDS

The flow of economic data generated by government and private agencies here and abroad is overwhelming. To assimilate the implications of

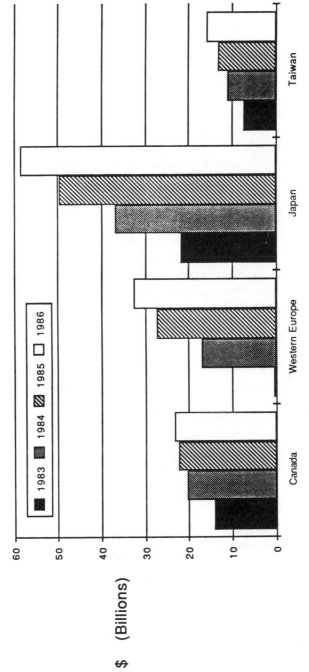

Figure 7.2
U.S. Trade Deficit with Major Trading Partners

■ 1983 ■ 1984 ▨ 1985 □ 1986

$ (Billions)

Canada   Western Europe   Japan   Taiwan

Source: Commerce Department, *Commerce America*, Bi-weekly.

these data in order for it to have relevance to the firm, a mechanism must be in place to represent the data in constant values. The ability of strategic thinking to have a constant-value measure offers a historical perspective that aids fine tuning strategic planning. Current economic trends shape the face of the economic environment. If for no other reason than this, a mechanism that assures a measure of current economic events free from distortions is a welcome tool to the strategic managers.

Using the stock market as an objective reference point to prevailing and expected return on investment is an integral aspect of the market area planning (MAP) process making the analysis of key markets and the role competitors are playing more reliable. The use of the constant-dollar Dow adds a fresh perspective capable of producing an accurate picture of the economy in order to identify and quantify the significance of current economic developments. By the same token, the firm's competitive position is enhanced by a tool that offers new insights into the observed behavior of one's competitors.

Inherent in the proposition that there is a need for an economic indicator that will reflect real, constant value is the idea that such a measure will facilitate establishing benchmarks by which SBU progress is rated. The critical difference is one of comparable performance. The returns of a portfolio can now not only be measured against the performance of competitors or on factors affecting the industry, but these numbers can be given a broader meaning when presented in the context of the economy as a whole.

The ability to make precise comparisons is instrumental in shaping the way strategies relate to the realities of the marketplace. Which markets should be pursued? Should funds be channelled into the manufacturing process? How much commitment is there to automation and technology? To product differentiation? To certain market segments? What are the opportunity costs of remaining in this industry? Is the most optimal utility being realized? An inflation-adjusted indicator makes possible precise answers concerning how the corporate entity is performing now and how it will perform in the future. The insight offered by an accurate measure of the current economic direction of the economy is an integral part of enhancing the ability of the firm to anticipate and react to market changes.

Corporate Direction

Implicit in the contention of improving corporate ability to anticipate and react to the market is the argument that a hierarchical ordering reflecting utility of the SBUs within a portfolio is possible. The objective referencing of each SBU return makes possible a divisional assessment of the performance of an individual unit and its contributions to the portfolio as a whole.

The corporate executive is in a position to assess three distinct factors affecting the bottom line:

1. *Direction of the firm*—Participants in the same markets face similar conditions, and the ability to determine constant-dollar returns constitutes a basis for comparison enabling the firm to size up its own performance. This objective external reference point allows for *a priori* analyses of the internal functions of the various SBUs as they interact in the marketplace. Thus the direction of the firm *vis-à-vis* competitors is revealed as is the direction of the firm in the economy of the industry.

2. *SBU focus*—The performance of each SBU reveals its progress in accomplishing its strategic mission. Moreover, it is possible to estimate the contribution each SBU makes to the value of the portfolio as a whole. SBUs that do not measure up can be analyzed to determine the cause of their underperformance. The early detection of problems is the key to their early correction. A new cost, differentiation, or focus strategy may be necessary to reverse lackluster performance. The most appropriate course of action can best be determined by analysis of the successful SBUs: what accounts for their ability to perform well? What is required for the other SBUs to duplicate this success?

3. *Corporate strengths*—Considering the different returns of the various SBUs within a portfolio identifies where corporate strength lies and strategies that meet with more success. It is imperative to determine whether investing in new production processes or in advertising will create a more differentiated product. Identifying successful tactics is necessary if the firm can embark on a program to take measures which ensure that a competitive advantage can be sustained. Building on strategies that meet with success is the only way a firm can compete from a position of strength.

Opportunity Cost

In a competitive environment the ability to secure unbiased information is of critical importance. The traditional reliance on the internal generation of statistics is no longer an adequate means by which to make decisions. The need for continuous comparisons to the economic environment belies the problems encountered with traditional internal systems of measurement. Internal reports tend to be biased in one of two directions: they either overstate the ability of their firm to deliver a product or service given certain time and costs parameters, or they overstate the ability of the competition to secure and defend market conditions. The effects of either of these biases on strategic planning is significant. Biased reports can cause a firm to enter a market for which it is unprepared thus undermining the chances of securing a position, or it can discourage entry into a market in which it can establish, sustain, and defend a market position.

This constant vigil against biased information allows for measuring the opportunity costs of staying on present course. As a result, strategies can be defined for an optimal portfolio matrix. There are significant opportunity costs that can ultimately determine the utility of the activities of any SBU. The pros and cons regarding acquisitions, investments, and corporate operations present foregone opportunities that constitute a real cost. The failure to quantify the opportunity costs incurred by pursuing various policies interferes with the longer-term goals of the firm by not identifying potential markets and appropriate segments. The result is a misallocation of resources that undermines the ability of the firm to create an efficient system of response to the volatility of today's markets.

Objectivity

The analysis of opportunity costs as an external consideration plays an important role in identifying the many options open to the corporate entity. The proper use of external reference points, however, allows for the identification of calculated risks the firm is willing to incur. The experiences of the past two decades demonstrate that the consequences of such unwillingness to encourage educated risks are great. Foreign firms, such as Honda and Fuji, have taken the lead in innovating new marketing strategies and implementing massive advertising campaigns. In neither case was success guaranteed, but the willingness to take the risks that American firms have so often been reluctant to take, has paid off handsomely.

The question, then, centers on the identification of what criteria must be met before a risk can be backed. The fact is that risk is an inherent aspect of market economies. Risk, however, can be quantified and contained. The ability to rely on objective measures facilitates the task of risk containment. An objective measure, such as rendering external economic data in absolute terms, accomplishes two goals. First, objective measures are unbiased and in so being they allow for the early identification of problems. Early detection of a trouble spot and deficient performance generates feedback necessary to modify strategies. Early detection, furthermore, points out areas where forecasts are incorrect, suggesting that this serves as a mechanism that will help a firm avoid the same errors in the future. Corporate managers capable of identifying problems when they start can use this to gain a competitive advantage, for the response time between the emergence of a problem and the time when corrective measures are taken is reduced. The competitive advantage this represents lies in the fact that a firm with an established procedure for identifying problems can then concentrate resources on the progressive fine tuning of strategies rather than on crisis managing.

Second, objective measures allow for the easy identification of solutions. The same objective reference points used to establish benchmarks and identify problem areas can be used to evaluate potential solutions. As strategies evolve to reflect changes in the marketplace, they can incorporate solutions determined to be appropriate and adequate. As the corporation confronts the pressures from the fiercely competitive environment, it must encourage mechanisms that can search, identify, and evaluate solutions in an efficient and systematic manner.

Strategic thinking offers the objectivity that has been lacking in traditional portfolio management. With the ability to present reliable and objective measures that can be quantified and the real value of which can be determined, the firm is in a position to create a mechanism for the continuous processing of information in an orderly way. This is required if firms are to keep an eye on the future without being obsessed by the day-to-day affairs of conducting business. A precise understanding of the big picture must remain foremost in the consciousness of the firm.

Cost-Benefit Tool

The use of the stock market as an objective indicator of anticipated economic performance enables a firm to have an independent statistic. There is a strong need to have a reference point that is not influenced by corporate politics and that is entirely open to public scrutiny. Fudging numbers here and there, overstating strengths, and dismissing structural flaws has undermined the objectivity of management. People Express Airlines, for example, failed to understand the degree to which its customers were price elastic. Their customers represented certain market segments who could be satisfied with a basic service: no-frill air service to and from certain cities. By expanding service to cities that were of marginal interest to its flying public, adding unwanted services, and blurring its image by trying to lure the demanding business traveler, it expanded too rapidly while losing its customer base. The consequences of losing sight of the corporate objective in the marketplace can be dire. Thus the need for a statistic uninfluenced by internal, biased corporate pressures which is also beyond manipulation by any single player is real. The use of strategic thinking as a cost-benefit tool is enhanced by the object nature of deflating nominal numbers generated by the Dow.

Defining a portfolio matrix requires budget constraint considerations. The selection of projects and SBU acquisitions depends on whether the budget is variable or fixed and on whether the SBU in question is stand-

Figure 7.3
Criterion for Portfolio Matrix Classifications Using Cost/Benefit Analysis

Complementary SBU/ Fixed Budget	Complementary SBU/ Variable Budget
Positive net cash flow.	Positive net cash flow.
Stand-alone SBU/ Fixed Budget	Stand-alone SBU/ Variable Budget
Equal marginal benefits.	Equal marginal benefits.

Source: International Credit Monitor.

alone or complementary. The executive must distinguish among the varying degrees of horizontal linkages among the SBUs when determining budget commitment requirements. The corporate officer needs to analyze the components in a cost-benefit approach to acquisitions or projects. The proper classification of a portfolio matrix must be examined and reviewed before an optimal combination of related SBUs is found (see Figure 7.3). The guidelines strategic thinking requires are:

1. Variable budget, stand-alone SBU: Continue SBU activities until the marginal benefits equal funding requirements, thus becoming zero.
2. Variable budget, complementary SBU: Select all SBUs that yield a positive net flow.
3. Fixed budget, stand-alone SBU: Distribute capital allocations throughout a portfolio to achieve equal marginal benefits from each SBU.
4. Fixed budget, complementary SBU: Net benefit considerations prevail and the portfolio mix must reflect the ability to achieve net benefits.

The classification of SBUs according to established horizontal links enables the firm to assess performance in a new light. In any business portfolio in which there is a stand-alone SBU that cannot be linked through horizontal structuring, the firm must be able to realize marginal benefit from the last dollar spent to justify keeping that SBU. The remaining SBUs are those which are complementary and enjoy the benefits of links, thus exploiting their interrelationships. The corporate officer's mandate is to acquire a mix of SBUs whose benefits are greater than their costs as a whole.

In this manner the firm is able to quantify the performance of both an entire portfolio and an individual SBU in terms of costs and benefits. This is a requisite to establishing an optimal combination of SBUs capable of ensuring the firm is in a position to secure a sustainable market position. The integration of a coherent cost benefit analysis reflecting distributional considerations of the nature of individual SBUs to meeting the objectives of the portfolio is possible through a disciplined implementation of strategic thinking. Once cost benefit analysis becomes an integral aspect of corporate management, more precise missions can be assigned to an SBU. In addition, weak interrelationships can be strengthened and the proper place an SBU is to occupy in the portfolio can be determined.

A more rigorous strategic agenda is now possible. This conscious effort to determine cost benefit analysis impact on the portfolio matrix is of high priority. A cost benefit program has not always been a conscious activity of management. In many instances the notion of cost benefit plays a peripheral role in various management activities. As a result, when there is no established policy to consider the direct and indirect or the tangible and intangible costs and benefits of various portfolio matrices, the hidden cost benefit results can be inferred through revealed preference. Not unlike a consumer who states one preference but whose observed actions reveal another, business decisions, or indecisions, constitute an accurate tool of revealing true preference. Thus a firm runs the unnecessary risk of having its preferences identified by competitors through its unconscious activities. This diminishes the ability of the firm to secure competitive advantage.

MANAGEMENT PROCESS

The inability of traditional strategic planning and portfolio management to allow more firms to capitalize on the weakened dollar and recapture export markets lies, in part, in the fact that these management tools have been administered in a cumbersome and time-consuming fashion. Indeed, many strategic planners have become obsessed with the processes of strategic planning and portfolio management to such a degree that they lose sight of the ultimate goal of these tools: securing a sustainable competitive advantage for market leadership and higher profitability. This is readily seen in many firms where strategic planning departments come into existence as a matter of course.

Too often data collection, research activities, contemporary state-of-the-art laser-printed graphics and charts, brainstorming management meetings, and retreats have replaced more substance than corporate America is willing to concede. More efficient data collection and analysis methods have been passed up by management too concerned with their frequent-traveler mileage awards than anything else. The seduction of the current strategy generation processes, however, must not diminish the importance of an efficient and logical manner for arriving at strategies required for the sound and insightful portfolio management American business needs. Style and decadence are no substitutes for real substance, powerful strategies, and sustainable market leadership positions.

These goals are best served by a management process that is an efficient method of data evaluation. The very abundance of information today becomes a liability at times. The proliferation of statistics and information means that valuable time and management resources must be allocated to separate the wheat from the chaff. In the past two decades this has proved to be a formidable task and seemed like an end in itself, rather than a tool aiding the proper management of business portfolios. The introduction of the concept of context expressed in absolute terms in the formulation of strategies, however, is necessary in order to assure that sustainable market positions are secured. The world today demands a system of streamlining the management process. The firm that is to defend a clear market position is one that can reduce the laborious nature of strategic planning and move on to the business of portfolio management. The goal, the executive must remember, is to use information to anticipate and react to changing conditions with the benefit of reliable information and a system in place capable of delivering strong strategies for strong management.

STRUCTURE OF STRATEGIC THINKING

The success of any strategy rests on a firm's ability to seize opportunities in the marketplace. Shifts in supply and demand, coupled with the evolution of markets and products, create an ever-changing spectrum of opportunities. Moving forward, however, requires looking backward. This means that as the firm assesses its ability to excel in today's competitive environment, it needs to implement a management system capable of delivering on several fronts. The firm that is in a position to analyze the internal and external conditions of its environment increases its chances of success. Strategic thinking is structured to reflect these needs. Equal importance must be placed on both the internal and external factors affecting a firm. This is especially important for the American firm since U.S. cultural history does not show the traits necessary to facilitate the smooth integration of horizontal organizations.

In this discussion it is argued that strategic thinking is the tie that binds the separate units within a firm and a portfolio into a dynamic entity. In a complex world of a turbulent nature, it becomes imperative to have a comprehensive vision of the firm's place in business and a set of strategies geared to making the vision a reality. The past experience of many firms demonstrates the importance of having a long-term vision for the firm. Without a defined goal formal strategic planning systems undermine their own purpose. This is where the absence of ties have failed to bind formal planning to the overall management process. The notion of strategic thinking is to establish concrete linkages among the various management functions in order to establish a fluid system capable of delivering on several fronts: streamlining the internal functions within a firm, increasing portfolio economies of scale through horizontal linkages, affording planners the context necessary for the realistic establishment of goals, and finally, identifying which competitive advantage strategy is best for each SBU and for the portfolio. This is no small order. Ambitious as it is, however, the contention that present management systems fail to stand up to the requirements of today's competitive environment is not without merit. The task lies in addressing the shortcomings of traditional strategic planning and portfolio management.

To this aim strategic thinking consists of two parts. The first, lines of expertise, centers on the internal organizational structure of the firm and how the SBUs interact within the portfolio. The potential economies of scale and economies of scope that exist through linkages among the portfolio's business units are considerable and efforts to capitalize on these must be made. The second, market area planning, incorporates current economic context into an SBU's, or the firm's, competitive strategies and on the components required for an aggressive marketing program seeking a cost, differentiation, or focus advantage. The use of context is necessary to determine how to allocate resources among the SBUs and how their performance compares with the opportunity costs available. The analysis of the marketplace is in order if the most opportune lines of businesses are to be identified and pursued.

The combination of addressing the firm's internal structure and external interactions in the marketplace results in a broader view of the firm, how it operates, what role it plays in the market, and how it can enhance economic utility. Strategic thinking, moreover, links the past to the future for a reassuring sense of continuity. The firm that can look into the historical performance of its SBUs is in a position to anticipate threats, recognize opportunities, and determine what its strengths and weaknesses are. This is the only way to capitalize on technology, innovations, and changing markets while building on strengths, compensating for weaknesses, and staying one step ahead of competitors. It is surprising how few American firms have done this.

Thus it appears that the solution lies in a strategic thinking process as outlined in this discussion. This is long overdue, for while commentators have argued for the need for more widespread familiarization of the strategic planning processes, little has been done to make more executives comfortable with corporate planning. In the broadest sense an officer should realize that the strategic process centers on an understanding of the firm's identity and how it envisions itself in the future. With this foremost in mind the planner works on devising a specific sequence of actions and policies designed to make the long-term goal a reality. This requires channeling energies into working towards the same goal. Each SBU activity must support the overall portfolio and fill a strategic need.

This is not an impossible task. The case study presented in this section focuses on the success of Digital Equipment Corporation (DEC). Through a concerted effort, DEC has been able to make great strides in realizing its long-term goal. Unlike the fiasco at PTI and the mess at PTG, comprehensive strategies have been implemented by clear-thinking executives. An accurate assessment of the economic context of the industry, of competitor threats, and of the resource commitment required has paid off. The success of DEC, moreover, suggests the power that strategic thinking represents for corporate America. At a time of increased volatility and intensified competition, the firm with a competitive advantage is the one committed to the identification of long-term goals and the implementation of specific, detailed actions required to turn a goal into an accomplishment.

NOTES

1. Porter, *Competitive Advantage*, p. 318.
2. Porter, *Competitive Advantage*, pp. 414–15.
3. Porter, *Competitive Strategy*, p. 3.
4. Alfred Malabre, *Beyond Our Means* (New York: Random House, 1987).

DIGITAL EQUIPMENT CORPORATION: A CASE STUDY

This following case study best exemplifies the benefits inherent in a conscious effort to implement sound strategic thinking. The solutions offered in the previous chapters are at work at Digital Equipment Corporation. Unlike many firms throughout corporate America, DEC's ability to rely on managers with a singular vision of the firm's role in the marketplace and a broad understanding of the forces shaping the economic landscape in which the firm operates is the reason why this firm has been able to defend its market leadership position and exploit the opportunities in its industry (see Figure 8.1).

Founded in 1957 by Kenneth H. Olsen, DEC is the third largest producer of data-processing equipment in the world. The ability of DEC to manage its growth and maintain its momentum has resulted in an impressive record: during the past nineteen years its sales have grown at a 30 percent rate, compounded annually. In 1987 its total revenues exceeded $9.3 billion worldwide, an increase of 24 percent over the previous year's earnings. Net income for that year rose 84% to $1.14 billion. More impressive, however, is DEC's explosion in share earnings, which grew in 1986 by almost 81 percent. Today DEC is positioned for an aggressive increase in market shares both domestically and internationally. In the summer of 1987 DEC announced major price reductions aimed at increasing market shares in the United States and abroad. This campaign, designed to increase DEC's market share of the computer work stations, is important to its overall strategies as international operations account for 64 percent of profits.

Figure 8.1
A Balanced Portfolio

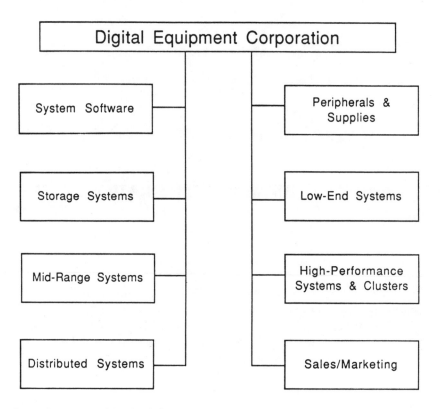

Source: International Credit Monitor.
Digital Equipment Corporation represents a classic balanced portfolio. Organized
along traditional lines, DEC's portfolio of SBUs are partitioned by functional lines
of expertise. Each SBU complements the other, enabling DEC to realize economies
of scale that promote a strategic advantage. The case study examines how DEC's
portfolio of SBUs and strategic planning process is used to maintain profit margins
and continued market growth.

The secret of Olsen's and DEC's success lies in the emphasis placed
on the channeling of corporate resources into well defined related lines
of business that complement each other. DEC manufactures, sells, and
services computer hardware, software, peripheral equipment, and related supplies. The computers range from the MicroVAX II, a low-cost
entry-level computer, to the VAX 8800, DEC's most powerful computer
system. The genius of Olsen lies in his insistence from the outset that
all of DEC's equipment be compatible. All of the computer systems DEC
markets are compatible with each other, allowing the firm the ability to

grow and to use DEC's equipment without encountering any of the difficulties associated with program conversions or upgrading to new technologies. In this respect DEC stands apart from the competition. This affords DEC two key advantages: first, it can offer new systems to its customers that will meet the more complex needs of growing companies, and second, it fosters a customer dependency on DEC through the unique value DEC offers its customers. This is one of the reasons why DEC, for example, is considered the leader in high-speed computer networking systems with its VAXcluster network. These networking systems are capable of tying together many VAX systems to one database, providing mainframe power at a fraction of the cost. Moreover, all VAX systems use the same underlying architecture and operating system, allowing customers to move products from one DEC system to another without modifying any software. This ability enables DEC's VAX line of unified micro-mainframe software to be the fastest selling software in the industry.

The success of DEC epitomizes the ability of corporate America to realize its goals. The history of Olsen's firm is one of a company run by corporate officers with a singular commitment to the vision they have for their firm. In the case of DEC it is a vision of creating a major computer firm whose business is driven by technology. The reliance on fully integrated, easy-to-use, high-speed computer networks is the cornerstone of DEC's success. "Our goal is to connect all parts of an organization— the office, the factory floor, the laboratory, the engineering department— from the desktop to the data center. . . . We propose to connect a company from top to bottom with a single [computer] network" Olsen informed shareholders in the firm's 1986 annual report.[1]

The future envisioned by Olsen is comprised of a series of goals that were significant in and of themselves. The most formidable challenge, however, lay not in the goals, but in the implementation of a corporate strategy that could use the firm's resources in a management system. The turning point for DEC came when it realized that it could expand the market segments targeted. In its early history DEC had concentrated on producing highly precise equipment for the scientific and engineering research markets. Its unequaled superiority and subsequent domination, however, led Olsen to realize that DEC's role in the marketplace could be a larger one. Thus armed with a broader vision for the firm, Olsen implemented a sweeping new corporate strategy called the "New Digital Marketplace." The purpose was to define DEC's future marketplace through a committed effort to reshape the computer industry.[2]

The next step in realizing its vision of the future centers on expanding DEC's compatibility to competitors' computer systems. Its recent introduction of the VAXmate line of computers allows a Digital product to communicate with an IBM computer for the first time. This portends

Figure 8.2
Digital Equipment Corporation: Sales Growth (1975–1986)

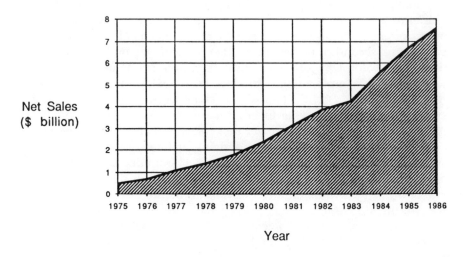

Net Sales
($ billion)

Year

Source: DEC Annual Report, 1986.

the future emphasis of DEC's lines and is a natural outgrowth of its history. DEC's relationship with its competitors has been one of intense rivalry. In twenty-nine years DEC grew from nothing to an almost $8 billion enterprise (see Figure 8.2). Its stellar growth has resulted in its ability to shoot past its competitors, such as the pre-merger Burroughs and Sperry, as well as NCR Corporation, Control Data, Wang, and Hewlett-Packard. This growth extends to the industry giant of International Business Machines. Ten years ago IBM was over twenty times the size of DEC. Today it is only seven times as large. Olsen's commitment to a set of sound strategies designed to create excellence in the long term is paying off.

DEC's ability to surpass all major competitors and make significant ground against the industry's giant firm is firmly rooted in its unwavering commitment to using a single, standard VAX architecture for all DEC products. This competitive strategy—and the resulting technological lead in computer networking—has made DEC "IBM's most serious challenger in 20 years," according to Morgan Stanley security analyst Carol Muratore.[3] In the summer of 1987 DEC's hard work and patience had paid off, for it was then positioned to make significant inroads into IBM's bread-and-butter markets: large financial services companies and corporate dataprocessing centers. The emphasis on compatibility with IBM equipment, plus the cost reductions that make it the cost leader in the industry, promise to increase its recent successes. In 1986 a full year before the price cuts and IBM compatibility were announced, DEC secured over $2 billion worth of orders for office systems from existing IBM customers.

The future for DEC is a bright one. While IBM lost market shares to every business with which it competed with DEC in 1986, DEC made strategic gains in the same markets. In 1986 IBM's overall U.S. revenues for midsized systems dropped, whereas DEC's grew by an astounding 33 percent. As Paine Webber's Stephen K. Smith noted, "[there's the] strategic direction for the industry, and DEC is taking the lead."[4] Indeed, DEC's future is firmly based on its past. That past is one in which a comprehensive and thorough analysis of the marketplace, the industry, the economy—domestic and international—and the underlying factors shaping the business environment in which DEC operates was the foundation from which the competitive strategies implemented were developed. The result is the creation of a formidable company that is able to compete and win at home and abroad against domestic and foreign competitors. As evidence, in the summer of 1987 IBM introduced the new 9370 line of mid-range computers. Targeted to compete directly with DEC's offerings, these products were hailed by IBM as the "VAX-killers." Despite these claims, IBM was unable to penetrate DEC's stronghold in the mid-range computer market. In 1987, DEC had its strongest year ever. Net income rose 84 percent and sales were up by more than 25 percent. This ability to create superior strategies rests on DEC's sensitive understanding of its environments and the realities of the real world.

ECONOMIC REALITIES

DEC's performance during the past decade is astounding in light of the economic realities in which it has had to operate. Since 1985 the computer industry has faced an unprecedented slump. The rush of entrants into the market that occured with the popularization of the personal computer resulted in an increase of supply that dwarfed existing demand, resulting in a market that was quickly saturated. The slump toppled giants like Osborne and left no firm unaffected. In 1986, for example, industry-wide revenue grew only 7.4 percent, a dramatic plunge from the 30 percent annual rates for the years 1980–85. This, coupled with an earning-per-share drop of 35.3 percent, created a business environment that presented major obstacles to firms wishing to grow in this depressed market.

With the computer power of every product increasing and prices falling, the industry was downsizing. Osborne was not the only casualty; during a five year period over two hundred firms went bankrupt or had to reorganize under the protection of chapter 11. The firms that remained

did so through an aggressive campaign that entailed fundamental restructuring and company-wide cost-cutting campaigns. There are numerous examples of unrest in the computer industry. The recent merger
between Burroughs and Sperry, the restructuring of Control Data, and
AT&T's retreat from the PC market are key indicators of the turbulence
throughout the industry. Even the formidable IBM, hurt by the proliferation of lower-priced clones, has reduced its work force in 1986 through
company-wide programs, which included a hiring freeze and attrition
among the rank and file.

The prevailing economic principles of the industry undermine growth.
In a time when companies have been overwhelmed by the rapid rate of
technological advances and the speed with which new products enter
the market, many firms have altered their purchasing patterns to reflect
their anticipation of the new technologies and new products. Throughout the end of the 70s and early 80s, for example, many firms spent
more heavily on computer equipment and software systems than in
previous years. As a result, most businesses are reluctant to budget large
outlays for the purchase of more computer systems, especially when
they believe these will soon become obsolete. This, coupled with the
fear of having to shoulder the burden of pioneering new computer technology, has exerted a marked downward pressure on the purchase of
new computers and software in recent years. The resulting slump has
come at a time when foreign firms have made substantial inroads among
the market shares of domestic firms. The penetration of domestic computer markets by foreign firms, most notably the Japanese, represented
a major obstacle for domestic computer manufacturers. The trade figures
of recent years reveals that while exports of electronic equipment and
software increased at a 20-percent rate from 1979 to 1983, imports increased by more than 50 percent during this same period. In terms of
total market share, foreign firms increased their presence in the domestic
markets from 7.3 percent to just over 20 percent.

PORTFOLIO MANAGEMENT

The challenge for Olsen at DEC was charting a winning course given
the turbulence his industry faced. The general slump that mandated
across the board cuts, the slowdown in capital equipment expenditures
by customers, the inflow of foreign products, and an economy whose
strength was drained by the persistence of the structural deficits presented a series of obstacles DEC had to overcome. This, coupled with
the natural growth limitations of a maturing industry, made the task of
managing the firm's portfolio more difficult.

The task at hand for DEC has been to post real revenue gains in a
time when nominal gains have been achieved throughout the industry

through short-term fixes, such as cost cutting and earnings manipulations faciliated by currency revaluations. Olsen's efforts have met with success, for DEC has realized a 20 percent increase in revenues in fiscal years 1985 and 1986. These recent gains stand apart from the performance of other industry players that have been plagued by substandard performance and a deterioration in market shares at the hands of foreign competition. DEC has been able to avoid the classic pitfalls in portfolio management by instituting a management system that revolves around the act of thinking. Strategies are well planned, clearly thought out, and forcefully implemented. The state of strategic thinking at DEC is the envy of corporate America, for these are the policies that not only stand up to domestic competition, but are able to make significant inroads into foreign markets.

Presence of Context

The ability of DEC to hold its own rests on Olsen's careful consideration of the underlying economic principles affecting the economy in general and the computer industry in particular. Building on DEC's analysis of how these economic forces impact the firm's chances of success, Olsen has formulated a sweeping set of strategies that reflects the context of the prevailing business environment in which DEC has found itself. The incorporation of economic and political context in the formulation of competitive strategies allows for a more rigorous application of strategic planning theories. In this manner the firm is able to create a series of plans that, when set in motion, facilitate the realization of the firm's long-term goals.

Economic Context—The implementation of competitive strategies at DEC reflects the economic context in which the firm operates. To tackle the challenges represented by the entrance of foreign firms into the marketplace at a time when significant downsizing pressures are being felt throughout the industry, DEC embarked on a program to address four key issues. Under Olsen's direction, strategic plans addressed the economic challenges posed by the intensified competition, the uncertainty of DEC's markets, the entire industry's direction, and the need for an internal restructuring of the firm's organization. The bottom-line effects of these concerns threatened the long-term prospects of the firm in the changing and complex marketplace.

Competition—Despite the presence of new entrants in the marketplace, the most formidable threat remained IBM. To diminish the threat, DEC chose to avoid direct competition with IBM and instead follow a "parallel" strategy. DEC's realization of its similarities and dissimilarities with IBM has afforded it the option of growing parallel to IBM without competing directly with the industry giant. In this manner Olsen's firm can claim that it "does not compete with IBM."[5] The strategic freedom this allows is psychologically significant. Instead of concentrating on the far-reaching implications of every IBM move, DEC can funnel resources into an aggressive strategy that treats itself as an industry leader. In this manner, DEC can see itself as the firm others wish to emulate. DEC realized that IBM was so large no other competitor could seriously contemplate overtaking it. Thus DEC is the next competitor in line. DEC's aggressive strategies set the pace for all the other competitors. Its strategy has worked; DEC's nonchalant attitude and disinterest in IBM have paid off. In 1987 DEC enjoyed a two-year technology lead over IBM in networking. More significantly, it is expected that by 1992 DEC will dominate the markets in which it competes, displacing IBM.

Market Benchmarking—DEC's strategy has been to follow market trends and help shape them. The trend in recent years has been towards networking and smaller sized systems. Companies want to automate the factory in order to become cost competitive with other countries who have enjoyed lower overhead and labor costs as well as considerable currency advantages. As firms strive to restore their competitive advantage, they have relied on smaller, more powerful systems. They want to integrate the office so that documents and information may be mailed instantly. The technological and organizational revolution requires firms to adopt systems that benefit from the ability to network information through computer systems. DEC's technological lead in computer networking gives it an impressive advantage over its competitors.

Industry Benchmarking—DEC has been sensitive to the importance market position plays in ensuring the success of a product line. Its business unit, the Rainbow line, is an example of this. Although the line was profitable, it was not performing as expected, that is, gaining significant market share in the PC market, and becoming the industry leader in its niche. DEC decided that the Rainbow was a mature product that would not meet expectations without a disproportionate allocation of resources. As such it shut down the SBU to redirect the resources Rainbow used towards its more important goal, a unified corporate strategy centered on computer networking based on a standard architecture. The void left by Rainbow in the PC market has been filled by the VAXmate, an IBM-compatible unit that connects easily to DEC's VAX computers.

Internal Restructuring—The incorporation of economic context into the firm's strategies was complemented by an internal operational and financial restructuring. To streamline financial operations in an effort to reduce operating expenses, DEC began a company-wide cost cutting program in 1985 when the market began softening. An integral part of this effort focused on reducing inventories, lowering accounts receivables, scrutinizing the creation of new staff positions, and reducing expenses. In 1986, for example, DEC trimmed inventories 32 percent, although equipment sales rose 9.4 percent during the same time. The firm's business units were also structured to benefit from the many interrelationships possible. The net effect of these changes is a leaner and meaner firm that is better positioned to make efficient use of its vast resources.

Political Context—The savvy navigation of DEC through foreign waters speaks of a firm aware of the cultural and economic differences that distinguish not only countries but also markets. DEC is responsive to differences in markets. Thus it reorganized its European sales force. Its overall strategy in the global arena is to develop an effective and unified international sales force. To this aim it has decentralized by country responsibility for product line sales. Each sales region is allowed to tailor its business strategies and methods to reflect the individual character-istics of the business sector targeted. This allows for a higher success rate. It comes as no surprise that DEC has been taking away from IBM's meat-and-potatoes markets in Europe. The success of DEC's "outbound" approach allows for a customized sales force that allows for a more focused marketing strategy.

The success in Europe is being duplicated on a global scale. DEC has made impressive inroads into Japanese markets. International opera-tions accounted for 35 percent, 40 percent, and 42 percent of total op-erating revenue in 1984, 1985, and 1986 respectively. For the fiscal year ending June 30, 1987, European sales were up 25 percent over 1986. Its manufacturing operations include plants in Canada, the Far East, and Western Europe. Its worldwide customer support organization of over 30,000 maintenance and software support personnel is spread over fifty-four countries on five continents. Its customer support was rated the best among major computer vendors by an independent survey. DEC, then, demonstrates that it can grow while maintaining a high level of quality.

This success is facilitated by two factors: sophisticated managers who are comfortable with the ways of international business and excellent products that enhance customer value chains. As Michael Bobrowicz of the Gartner Group marketing research firm says, "It comes down to one thing. DEC has the only products that work."[6] Its elegant software interfaces are compatible with all other DEC products. Its strategy of developing unified VAX system architectures enable all of DEC's prod-ucts to be used interchangeably. This, coupled with its leadership po-sition in networking technology, make DEC's products highly differentiated. DEC has emerged as the only company capable of effec-tively tying together all aspects of the computerized office—putting DEC way ahead of anyone else.

New Business Generation

The incorporation of economic and political context facilitates the generation of new business. As John F. Smith, senior vice president of engineering, manufacturing, and product marketing, has noted, "Having one target to shoot for made our engineers more productive. They could go off and do their own thing, and as long as they followed a certain level of discipline, they could come back and plug their part in . . . and it would work."[7] One unifying corporate goal and one VAX architecture aided in the generation of new products, and led to an entrepreneurial spirit. This allows for superior products that sell themselves.

The rigorous quality-assurance testing programs at DEC, for example, require sophisticated equipment that is made by DEC for DEC. In fact, many products that are developed for internal projects prove so useful that they have been tailored to meet the needs of customers and are marketed. Many unique software and hardware equipment, such as the DTM (DEC Test Manager), the MMS (Module Management System) and the CMS (Code Management System) began as in-house testing tools. This approach improves product quality while generating new products and new business. As Alan Willett, of Scientific Calculations, said at a recent Digital users group convention, "It must be great to be able to work for a company where you know that every project you work on matters. . . . If the software is good enough it could become a product. In many ways, it is as if they are all a part of new product development."[8]

Presence of Commitment

The significant strides made during the past decade are the result of long-term plans and an ongoing program that analyzes the long-term effects of short-term decisions. In this respect DEC remains unmatched in its commitment to itself. DEC, for example, first became committed to the VAX project in 1979, investing billions of dollars in R&D. The long-term goal was to develop a new generation of VAX superminicomputers. These computers would range from small PCs to computer clusters with mainframe power. The firm envisioned these computers to be fully compatible with each other. The project was completed in 1984, five years later, ahead of schedule. DEC could have easily cancelled this project, for during the early 1980s it faced unexpected turbulence and a revenue shortfall. It remained committed to the original project, however, and pushed forward. The investment in this project was considerable for it required the mastery of new engineering disciplines, the building of new microprocessors and disk storage units, and the creation of new networking software. DEC even reorganized its sales and marketing forces to better market the new products, which were only a dream away. Its faith in its people and program remained unshaken, despite the industry-wide slump. And it paid off. As soon as the VAXes were introduced into the market, they began to crush the competition. DEC's commitment and investment in itself paid off as sales surged in 1985, 1986, and 1987 while the overall industry was still reeling from the ongoing slump.

Interrelationships

The success at DEC was complemented by the new links forged not only among DEC's portfolio's business units, but also between DEC and its customers. DEC has used the expertise from its sales and technical SBUs to develop an "Electronic Store." This device was developed to allow customers to order products and supplies via their DEC computers without leaving the office. Once the customer has access to the "Electronic Store," he can browse through an electronic catalog for the product, obtain the price, determine availability, and place an order. The order is then sent via a modem to DEC's appropriate sales office and processed. The customer can also secure demonstration software without leaving the office. This allows the customer to test desired software while establishing an ongoing business relationship with DEC. The advantages to DEC in using this system are that it decreases turnaround time and frees up the sales force to the task of selling larger ticket items and targeting new markets.

Internal interrelationships have also been forged. All SBUs have been linked together via networks. In the words of Olsen, "Progressive companies analyze their organizations, understand their goals and then completely change the way they run their business in order to make them more competitive and more effective in pursuing their goals. They recognize the benefits of tying their entire company together with a single computer network that is as accessible and easy to use as a telephone system. . . . The free flow of information creates excitement and motivation and enthusiasm, and helps unify the company. The information becomes a strong internal catalyst and a powerful competitive tool."[9] These horizontal linkages have allowed greater freedom; each SBU can concentrate on its strategic mission.

The interrelationships allow both the product development and the manufacturing business units to benefit from economies of scale and economies of scope. The whole concept behind DEC's VAX architecture allows different SBUs to share ideas, develop in parallel, and transfer personnel to where it is needed. In this manner, there is great diffusion of expertise and know-how among the business units, thus strengthening each SBU. The result is a more dynamic company whose em-

ployees operate in a wider context, allowing for the entrepreneurial spirit
that is a requisite to success in today's competitive environment. In
addition, DEC stresses using the same basic computer parts for all product lines as opposed to redesigning each product. This serves to reinforce
a pattern of consistency that reduces uncertainty among managers. The
development and manufacture of products becomes an evolutionary
process that links the past to the present and the present to the future.
Few firms can boast of such an achievement.

LESSONS OF DEC

The success of DEC is not casual. It is the result of hard work by
dedicated men and women who are talented, experienced, and sure of
themselves. It is the product of superior competitive strategies that are
well defined and of focused strategic plans that are competently implemented. The importance of a clearly articulated vision of the future,
capable managers who consider the context in which they must operate
within the realities of the business environment, and strong leadership
cannot be dismissed lightly. The creation of competitive strategic plans
that are sensitive to the demands of the marketplace and the need for
highly differentiated or low-cost products is the foundation on which a
sustainable success is built.

The on-target analysis of the market is half the story. While a complete
understanding and appreciation of the markets and industry forces is
necessary to ensure success, it must be complemented by an internal
structure that considers the implications of the new competitiveness.
The firm's portfolio must seek to unify its business units into horizontal
links that exploit economies of scale and economies of scope. The firm
must emphasize the advantages possible by maintaining either a low
cost position or a highly differentiated product. This structure endears
a strong entrepreneurial spirit that facilitates the formulation of superior
strategies and superior performance. DEC demonstrates that an appreciation of the market is as important as an internal organizational structure that fosters excellence. DEC's policies set it apart from other firms
in corporate America that are completely wiped out not only by the
marketplace but also by internal decay.

The differences between DEC and PTI are of no small importance.
DEC's ability to thrive in a hostile environment stems from the clear
strategies, the sound plans, and the competent execution of corporate
plans. In this respect, then, DEC stands out among American corporations as a firm that has been able to seize opportunities, recognize
threats, and exert a controlling influence over its own destiny. Recognizing that, as with individuals, there is power inherent in will, makes
progress possible. Andy Warhol, whose sardonic wit captured the spirit

of Americana in the latter part of this century, once noted that "they always say that time changes things, but you actually have to change them yourself."[10] This is an appropriate observation, for this is precisely the case with DEC. Finding itself facing mounting foreign competition at a time when the industry faced negative growth, it devised a plan to implement aggressive strategies to position itself in a formidable position. DEC's effort to change its destiny by controlling the present has proved successful, thus securing its future.

In the next section, the discussion will focus on the steps necessary to allow a firm to secure the future. There are other firms whose success has matched that of DEC in its ability to seize opportunities and shape its prospects. Whether it is Heinz or Bears Stern, there are common patterns in the strategic thinking process of the top management in these firms that accounts for their ability to rise above the common mediocrity that is all too pervasive in corporate America today. The discussion will also focus on firms that, like PTG, have leaders lacking in vision, commitment, and courage to forge the future in their own image. Eastman Kodak and General Motors, for example, are two other firms that come to mind when one thinks of mediocre performances. Not unlike PTI, these firms have sabotaged their futures through an incompetent execution of strategic plans. In a market economy such as ours, the bottom line is all that matters. It is the marketplace, that unforgiving continuous interplay of supply and demand, that separates the winners from the losers, and superior strategies and superior managers from the mediocre strategies and mediocre managers. It is the market that passes judgments, that alters the terms of trade, that determines futures, and that distributes profits among competitors. The market is relentless in its treatment of faulty reasoning, faulty strategies, and just plain faults. Firms like PTG, Kodak, and GM have failed to understand the dangers the fault of *hubris* represents. Arrogance without talent is a fault. It is a fault punished by forces that shape Adam Smith's invisible hand.

The purpose of the next section is to offer detailed instructions on how to avoid *hubris* and use strategic thinking to proceed through that ever-so-complex labyrinth of today's competitive environment and in the process to achieve a sustainable competitive advantage. The incorporation of the recommendations offered here should become a *modus vivendi* for corporate America. There are certain evident truths about the business world that transcend industries and can be applied across time. The singular realization that emerges again and again in these case studies is that success depends on able managers with proven track records, who have a sense of history and know their strengths. It is the corporate officer who obeys the ancient Delphic command and knows himself that can help his firm seize its own future. If corporate America is to rise to the occasion, it must also rise above the complacent mediocrity of the unenlightened simpletons that populate the business world today. It can best accomplish this by emulating Olsen's fine example at DEC.

NOTES

1. Digital Equipment Corporation, *1986 Annual Report*, p. 3.

2. International Credit Monitor, "Digital Equipment Corporation's Competitive Strategy: An Analysis of Revealed Policy," 1987.

3. Peter Petre, "America's Most Successful Entrepreneur," *Fortune*, October 27, 1986, p. 24.

4. Marc Rosenthal, "The IBM-DEC Wars: It's 'The Year of the Customer,' " *Business Week*, March 30, 1987, p. 86.

5. "Digital's High-Tech Coup," *Dun's Business Month*, December 1986, p. 28.

6. Ibid.

7. Ibid.

8. Telephone Interview, April 1987.

9. Digital Equipment Corporation, *1986 Annual Report*, p. 3.

10. Andy Warhol, *The Philosophy of Andy Warhol*, (New York: Harvest Books, 1975), p. 107.

PART III

The Application: Managing Corporate Business Units and Strategic Thinking in Turbulent Times

≪ **9**

IMPLEMENTING STRATEGIC THINKING

The challenge, then, lies in working strategic thinking into the management style of corporate America. Although it is a formidable challenge, it is one task the American executive can handle. The past decade has seen a proliferation of critics attacking complacency, inefficiency, and loss of competitiveness as the cause of the economic dislocation afflicting the United States. The implicit criticism has been that the American executive is to blame for the loss of leadership positions in many markets worldwide. While there is much validity to these claims, few critics have come forward and proposed concrete solutions that can produce tangible results and effect improvements over the current situation. This section, moreover, takes the solutions earlier in the discussion and applies them to real-world situations for real-world results.

The challenges, as noted, are great, but they are not overwhelming. The critics of the American business community underestimate the abilities of this nation to rise above obstacles. Indeed, after a while the constant flow of criticism becomes, as T. S. Eliot said, "a tedious argument of insidious intent." The reason for the criticism is obvious; the economic dislocation of the past two decades has resulted in a new phenomenon for the United States: the current generation of Americans entering the work force will face a lower standard of living than the generation of their parents. The maturing of the American economic system is discomforting for it inspires uneasiness. Furthermore, as the balance of economic power has shifted away from the United States there has been a renewed surge of severe criticism, casual introspection, and disturbing resignation. This need is not inevitable, for while "men are much more taken by present than by past things,"[1] and the criticism of corporate America is a valid one, the decline of the American firm can be reversed. There is no reason why a successful strategic thinking program cannot be instrumental in turning the current situation around. The secret lies in a concerted effort that is committed to achieving goals that are firmly based in the new global realities. The economic power of our major trading partners must be recognized as must be the fact that the road to restoring this nation's eminent position lies not in erecting trade barriers but in recognizing the shortcomings of past and present management practices and going on from there—going on to the future.

SUCCESSFUL STRATEGIC THINKING

The firm that is to enjoy success in the 1990s is the one capable of implementing competitive strategies that secure competitive advantage. From there, strong portfolio management arises and the internal integrity of the firm is assured. Thus armed with internal cohesion and efficiency, the firm can embark on an aggressive campaign designed to realize corporate objectives. The cognitive process required for this to occur, however, is complex. Too often, for example, consultants argue that management must recognize its strengths, identify its weaknesses, and see threats and opportunities as they arise. The problem, however, is that the identification of strengths and weaknesses and the ability to recognize threats and opportunities requires two mutually exclusive functions: analyzing the past and predicting the future. One's strengths and weaknesses have meaning only when compared to the relative abilities of others. Comparisons, moreover, are possible only when examining past performance for an insight to the historical trends demonstrated by the competing firms. The ability to recognize threats and opportunities likewise rests on one's accuracy at projecting present trends and developments into the short- and medium-term futures. The firm skilled at analyzing the likelihood of future deviations from the documented historical market trends can recognize emerging markets and declining niches and can identify competitors capable of securing positional leadership.

The implementation of a successful strategic-thinking program centers on embracing the past in order to see the future. The result is a focused corporate strategy with a sense of purpose and an intimate knowledge of historical trends. If a firm is to organize itself along iines of expertise in order to have the internal cohesion and efficiencies necessary to compete in today's environment, and if a firm is to have strategic market area planning leading to competitive advantage, it must be willing to initiate the organizational changes described. Foremost in the conscious-

Figure 9.1
The Application of Strategic Thinking to Management Structures

Source: International Credit Monitor.

ness of the corporate executive must be the realization that the circumstances of the day require the firm to take measures to increase the control over its own destiny.

Management Structure

The transition towards a program that uses the operational techniques of strategic thinking requires a shift from a static to a dynamic management structure (see Figure 9.1). The tasks of management are more efficiently processed through the incorporation of dynamic structures. The proper role of management in the business world centers on processing information, implementing strategies and policies, controlling the activities of subordinates, approving budgets, assessing progress towards realizing the corporate vision and evaluating SBU and portfolio performance relative to reference benchmarks.

Throughout the post-war era, while the Bretton Woods system prevailed and a consistent pattern of stability was evident, static management was the order of the day. The *static management structure* sought to assign specific tasks along defined lines of authority to individual managers responsible for the successful completion of tasks. The top-down chain of command was manifested in one of two distinct techniques: control and implementation management.

Control management is based on the notion that the future stems from the past. Therefore the evaluation of present performance is based on what the historical quotas and standards have been. The task of each SBU is determined by historical considerations and not on perceived future market demands. This, however, implies there is a low degree of turbulence and volatility in the marketplace, for it suggests that tomorrow is not unlike today. In this manner, control management gears standards of success according to the past and not the future.

Implementation management, likewise, is a backward-looking approach to goal setting and performance evaluation. Based on the individual line manager's own assessment of performance, the historical experiences of the firm are at the foundation of expectations for the future. The result is a system in which standards and quotas are the basis of evaluating performance and utility to the portfolio as a whole. The problem, however, is that this approach assumes there is low development of inter-relationships among SBUs.

Moreover, both control and implementation management techniques are appropriate for firms choosing to rest on their laurels and operating in an environment with low turbulence. These techniques inhibit aggressive marketing programs and interfere with a firm's attempt to focus on the future. As the name implies, static management structures assume an unchanging world that can be expected to progress along discernable patterns of behavior with few threats or opportunities on the horizon. Unfortunately this is not the world of today. Firms unable to identify threats and opportunities, develop new markets, and innovate will be faced with shrinking market shares. Thus, before a firm is in a position to implement a comprehensive strategic thinking program, it must adopt a more responsive, flexible, and appropriate management technique for meeting the challenges of a turbulent world.

Dynamic management structure, then, is the most appropriate approach to management in the wake of a post–Bretton Woods world. The advent of structural deficits, economic dislocation, and volatility has coincided with the emergence of formidable competitors from abroad. A dynamic management structure is one in which there is a fluid processing of information and a flexible management style. The result is an efficient mechanism for determining how tasks are assigned and completed. This is accomplished through extrapolative or entrepreneurial management techniques.

Extrapolative management rests on the assumption that the firm must look to the future to seize opportunities and prepare for threats. This forward-looking approach is based on assessing the significance of historical performance in order to determine the context in which the firm operates. From this information trends are identified from which forecasts are drawn. Within the context of the given environment and the expected growth and profitability trends, a series of objectives are identified. These goals are prioritized in accordance to the firm's long-term schedules. The next step is to determine the resource allocation requirements, the profit margins for each SBU, and the optimal matrix of goals that each SBU can be assigned in order to maximize interrelationships within the portfolio and benefit from complementary lines of business. The firm stands to increase its ability to anticipate change and react to unexpected developments through a continuous assessment of the future through extrapolation.

Entrepreneurial management is based on the assumption that the future is discontinuous and random. Therefore, the ability to analyze the future implications of present trends and to identify how various forces stand to affect the economic context is crucial to firms capable of capitalizing on opportunities. These analyses are necessary in order to determine the internal resources of the firm as well as the firm's prospects for capitalizing on perceived future developments. The constant matching of identified trends and emerging markets with the firm's capabilities and SBU prospects is necessary to create an environment that encourages innovation and creativity. The flexibility created when activities can be channeled into new products and new markets as they are evaluated allows the firm to use its resources in ways that are responsive to random and discontinuous market developments.

The dynamic management structure allows the firm the freedom to choose strategic postures as markets change. In times of high turbulence and volatility the ability to correct deficient performance, modify SBU missions, and review competitive strategies is necessary if a firm is to achieve an optimal SBU matrix and to coordinate all activities towards realizing the corporate vision. The role of management structure changes and becomes more responsive to the demands found in economies, industries, and markets where there is a high degree of uncertainty. The result is a management system capable of balancing the needs for short- and medium-term revenue generation and the need to support resource and commitment allocation necessary for the portfolio's strategic development. The give-and-take nature of a dynamic management structure enables the firm to exploit opportunities presented by product innovations, new markets, technologies, and contextual changes.

The careful reader cannot help but notice that static management systems are top-down while dynamic management structures are bottom-up. This is correct, but it is not the complete picture. The importance of instituting a dynamic management structure lies in the ability of these techniques to help the executive manager employ the changes necessary. For the duration of the century their economic context will be affected by the effects of the structural deficits and the intensification of competition in global markets. Thus, as firms strive to harness the benefits of lines of expertise and institute market-area planning, the functions of management will be affected by the new circumstances. The traditional management functions are by necessity affected by the introduction of strategic thinking.

Information

The mechanisms in place for the collection of external and internal data take on a new importance as singular events are carefully analyzed to determine the specific characteristics of random events. At the same time, the importance of historical information declines as the level of turbulence rises. Along the same lines, extrapolative and internal information remains equally important. The use of contextual information, however, rises as the firm tries to identify the underlying currents affecting economies, industries, and markets. The role information plays in shaping competitive strategies becomes a crucial one.

Implementation

The policy decisions emerging from a thorough review of the information can be implemented throughout the portfolio in various means. In stable environments specific tasks can be assigned to individual SBUs. As the degree of uncertainty rises, similar tasks can be assigned to complementary SBUs who can exploit the economies of scope possible through close interrelationships to bring their efforts to fruition. In markets characterized by high volatility, however, the best course of action is to implement policies as subunits of an individual SBU. This allows for the policy in question to be considered as an entrepreneurial effort, testing the markets while minimizing harm to the overall performance of an individual SBU.

Control

The distribution of assignments throughout the portfolio creates certain levels of expectations that are to be satisfied. The control for all activities within a portfolio rests with top management and their evaluations of performances are influenced by the input of SBU managers. The constant flow of feedback from the SBUs shapes the content of control decisions and their effects on the activities of an SBU or a specific project. The lines of control and the delegation of responsibilities reflect the progress made towards realizing the strategic goals of the firm. In this discussion the control decisions need to move away from a historical context to a forward-looking strategic one. In periods of greater turbulence a firm's need to develop interrelationships necessary for extrapolative and entrepreneurial management structures becomes commonplace, there is a tendency to blur the direct lines of command—and responsibilities—within the portfolio. This must be avoided.

Budgeting

The budget planning process has to reflect the long-term goals of the firm. While there are pressures to please shareholders and analysts through short-term considerations on budget allocations, the long-term strategic goals of the firm must take precedence over other issues. Thus budgets need to reflect the overall needs of the firm years down the road. The long-term considerations, furthermore, must be reflected in the budgets of specific projects. The corporate officer needs to establish commitment levels and the resource allocation parameters for specific SBUs, projects, and the identified long-term strategies in order to determine minimum profit level expectations from the various activities.

Vision

The portfolio matrix changes as threats and opportunities are identified and evaluated. The continuing turbulence requires an ongoing evaluation of the timeliness and feasibility of corporate goals. New markets and products may radically affect the perceived role of the firm in the marketplace. At the same time the threat of entrants and maturing markets may shift the firm's incentives. Thus competitive strategies are in a continuous process of thesis, antithesis, and synthesis not unlike Hegel's vision. These constant modifications to the firm's original vision, moreover, are welcome. As the world changes, so must the corporate vision evolve to reflect the new context and new needs. This, however, presupposes the existence of a flexible management system capable of fostering more precise visions of itself.

Benchmarks

The progress of a firm's progress is ultimately measured by benchmarks. The objectives of specific projects, the goals of certain activities, and the missions of the SBUs constitute the ultimate test of how salient and successful a firm's competitive strategies are. The use of benchmarks affords corporate officers the opportunities to see how the best laid efforts stand up to the forces of supply and demand. The success or failure of an SBU, a project, or a program is an unforgiving appraisal of the firm's capabilities. When SBUs fail to reach expected milestones, the firm can analyze the sequence of events in order to locate the shortcomings that account for the disappointment. In turn the firm can search for a set of alternative choices and actions capable of delivering the original objectives. The use of benchmarks is important if the viability of competitive strategies is to be determined by the marketplace.

Thus the business environment of today requires a dynamic management structure that can respond to the changing marketplace with vigorous competitive strategies. The functions of management also need to reflect the new realities of the competitive environment. For this reason the corporate officer has to facilitate the evolution of management systems that are tailored to the unique requirements of one's firm. The development and implementation of competitive strategies mandate a management approach that is sensitive to the individual needs of each

Figure 9.2
Components of Strategic Thinking

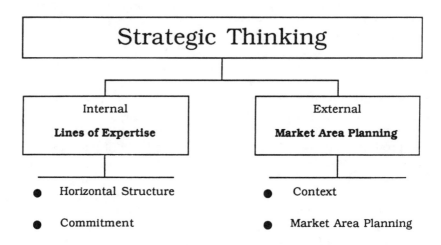

Source: International Credit Monitor.

SBU and the vision of the entire portfolio and that respects the integrity and utility of entrepreneurial projects designed to open up new markets and exploit innovations. The low turbulence of the Bretton Woods system is gone and the structural deficits' role in increasing the dangers of monetizing outstanding obligations precludes a reduction in contextual turbulence in the immediate future.

The management process is complex. The business environment of today requires a transition from static to dynamic management structures. The national and international macroeconomic issues facing the business community signal greater turbulence in the years ahead. Thus, the current environment supports the contention that the circumstances in which business operates today requires the implementation of strategic thinking in order to develop the competitive strategies American business needs. The issues for the executive lie in balancing the needs of the internal structure of the firm and the external interactions of the firm with the marketplace (see Figure 9.2). The internal considerations center around the development of lines of expertise designed to maximize the portfolio's utility and the relationships among the SBUs with each other and to the firm. The external considerations revolve around the need for market-area planning. The incorporation of context into competitive strategies is crucial to the success of the firm. After industry analysis, the competitive strategy—be it cost, differentiation, or focus—requires a high degree of vigilance as opportunities and threats emerge during these turbulent and volatile times. A rigorous market area planning program affords a firm the opportunity to build on its strengths, anticipate the future, and react to changes in the turbulent marketplace. The implementation of comprehensive programs designed to benefit from strategic thinking are based on efforts to maximize lines of expertise and market area planning.

NOTE

1. Machiavelli, *The Prince,* p. 89.

≪ **10**

LINES OF EXPERTISE

The internal organizational structure of the corporate portfolio must change. It is the firm that establishes links among the SBUs within its portfolio that is in a position to create a sustainable competitive advantage over its competitors. In the course of implementing strategic thinking, the portfolio's internal horizontal organizational structure must reflect the new realities of the intensely competitive marketplace. The firm intent on achieving related diversification through related lines of business needs to establish the links from the start that maximize the interrelationships among the SBUs.

The program for adopting a horizontal organizational structure is comprised of three parts: SBU interrelationships, economies of scale, and a new partnership between labor and management. The business environment today requires a renewed effort to establish lines of expertise to give the firm a distinct advantage to meet the targeted needs in which it seeks to specialize. This entails a tangible organizational structure that is sensitive to the potential benefits horizontal links represent and commitment to competitive strategies that complement the firm's culture and strengths of management. In the same manner that the physical structure must reflect the new business environment, so must competitive strategies reflect the strengths of individual corporate officers and the intangible personal culture of the firm, its image to the outside world, its history, and its identity within the company.

The purpose is to secure a set of SBUs exploiting opportunities in related lines of business that can complement each other, thus resulting in a portfolio worth more than the sum of the unrelated business units were they to be stand-alone entities. That intangible synergy, that special essence, is recognition of a distinctive expertise in a capacity that no other competitor can offer. The end result is a firm that offers a particular value to its customers' value chains that cannot be satisfied by any other firm. Thus the internal structure of a portfolio determines whether the full potential of strategic thinking will be realized.

HORIZONTAL STRUCTURE

The overextension of debt throughout the West interferes with normal economic activity. The strains of the structural deficits cross all national boundaries to such an extent that the 1980s have been characterized by slowing growth rates among the Western nations. The lackluster performance of such countries such as Japan, West Germany, and France, for example, contributes to the inability of the United States to increase exports. The saturation of domestic markets in the United States and an uninspired economic growth rate, furthermore, result in more fierce competition for market shares among firms. The slower growth rates and the economic dislocation of the past decade squeeze corporate profit margins even further.

Under these circumstances firms have had to shift their focus away from growth towards profits. Profits, however, are best maximized through a program to establish competitive advantage. The reason for harnessing the economic power of interrelationships is to lower costs, increase differentiation, and enhance marketing. The firm's competitive standing improves through these links among SBUs in related lines of expertise. It is this emphasis on profit enhancement, however, that gives rise to the arguments in favor of related diversification.

The horizontal structure, moreover, is based on a long-term view of the firm's ultimate objectives. Corporate strategies aimed at securing competitive advantage are at the root of strategic thinking. This, in turn, implies the notion that long-term competitive considerations play the central role in establishing interrelationships. The short-term issues concerning financial matters and shareholder views take a back seat to the firm's viability in the marketplace in the long run. This should come as no surprise. The emphasis on the long-term is what accounts for the success of many foreign firms who have paid the price of patience in order to reach the enviable positions they now occupy. The West Germans and the Japanese came to dominate the global economy through a long-term strategy designed to create lines of expertise against which few American firms can compete effectively.

The first step in creating a horizontal structure is for the links among the SBUs to be structured in order to benefit from the economies of scale that are now possible. A natural outgrowth from these reinforced links is economies of scope. The flexibility offered by cutting across traditional divisional barriers between the SBUs gives rise to synergies which, when explored, contribute to superior performance. The economies of scope, moreover, complement the long-term requirements of strategic thinking. In order to reap the benefits of competitive advantages, top management needs to allocate sufficient time for the economies of scope to become apparent. This not only requires a solid relationship with shareholders, but it also alludes to a firm partnership between labor and management. The breach of trust that has occurred during the cost-cutting programs of the past decade must be restored. The damage done to morale among the rank-and-file, SBU managers, and the executive officers must be repaired before an effective strategic thinking program can be implemented throughout the firm.

SBU Interrelationships

An efficient program to establish links among the SBUs that benefits from the potential economies of scale requires the identification and selection of functions which either are standardized by or benefit from volume purchases. The actual functions a firm targets for linking, of course, depends on the nature of its lines of business. Regardless of the functions selected, executive officers need to select functions that cut through SBU divisional barriers in order to maximize cost savings. There are, however, basic business functions that transcend industry and market considerations. The following are areas that should be selected for horizontal interrelationships:

Administrative Services, Graphics—All printed matter, from business cards and stationary to posters and brochures, must be handled by one central department which serves the printing needs of all the SBUs.

Administrative Services, Official Directory—The use of a central directory service for locating employees and updating phone lists, office numbers, mailing addresses, and related issues should be handled by a single office that serves the needs of the portfolio.

Computer and Word Processing Services—A central computer and word processing division should be established for the typing and presentation requirements among the business units. One pool charged with using the Wang and Macintosh systems offers an optimal resource for the compilation of materials other than routine letters and memoranda.

Corporate Communications—All communications to employees on company business, everything from company picnics to the procedures for filing W-2 forms, should be approved and produced by one center responsible for the distribution of all internal communiqués.

Corporate Strategy—The planning, execution, and compliance functions of the firm's strategies must originate from one office. This way the firm can best monitor the progress of each SBU as well as the overall portfolio. This is necessary if problems and weaknesses are to be identified and solutions implemented in a short time span.

Events and Receptions—The planning and hosting of dinners, receptions, and other events is best handled by a single office. For events other than informal functions among the employees within an SBU, the experience of a professional special-events staff, familiar with available caterers and the requirements, is preferred.

Federal/State Regulatory Services—The compliance with all federal and state laws should be monitored by one office. This function could be performed by either the human resource or legal services offices, depending on the lines of business the firm operates.

Government Regulatory Services—One central division should monitor compliance with the trade, tariff, quota, duty, and customs requirements of domestic and foreign governments.

Human Resources—The personnel needs of the entire portfolio must be handled by one office. This streamlines procedures, standardizes the procedures for hiring new employees, ensures that all the required paper work is completed, and identifies the availability of candidates seeking transfers and relocations within the firm. In addition, more specific functions must be consolidated into one central office:

- Benefit Plans Common to All—The negotiations of health, dental, and disability insurances can best be administered by the personnel office, billing costs on a per-employee and a per-participation basis to each SBU.

- Benefit Plans Common to Portfolio—The costs of operating a common human resources office should be distributed among the SBUs.

- Clerical and Secretarial Support—The allocation of clerks, secretaries, and receptionists can be operated according to the size of the firm. The larger company can benefit from a generic pool of support employees and can assign them to different business units on a temporary basis to replace employees who may be out ill, on vacation, or working on special projects requiring help in the short term.

- Executive Services—The special nonpecuniary benefits of top management should be handled by one office. In recent years such services as financial planning and fitness programs, for example, have been afforded top management and these benefits should be the responsibility of one office.

- Hiring—The procedures for hiring employees and monitoring compliance with applicable labor laws and immigration issues should be coordinated by one central office.

- Office Space—The responsibility for securing adequate office space, entering into leases, subletting, and recommending office space projects must be administered by one central office that can monitor changes in the needs of the SBUs and the portfolio.

- Relocations/Transfers—Individuals willing to relocate or seeking transfers can be matched up to opportunities in other business units through one central listing for the company. Such intra-company transfers and relocations save the costs of losing employees or hiring from outside to fill needs as they emerge.

Legal Services—The legal requirements of the firm should be handled by one office in order to protect the firm. All legal matters need to originate from one central office for consistency and to approve of all legal issues affecting the firm.

Marketing and Sales—The marketing and sales functions of a similar nature can be linked. Firms operating in related lines of businesses can be expected to group complementary products into packages that can be sold as units to customers. The degree to which marketing and sales forces can be combined within a portfolio will vary greatly among different firms.

Media and Public Relations—Official communications outside the firm and all inquiries from the public need to be cleared by a single office. The failure to approve of press releases and letters to the public and shareholders, and public statements can cause confusion and embarrassment if each SBU is allowed to operate on its own.

Motor Vehicles—The management of company cars needs to be centralized to reduce the costs of automobile, van, and truck purchases, their maintenance, and the costs of leasing these vehicles to the SBUs.

Planning Research Functions—The analysis of market trends, shifts in customer profiles and competitor moves that affect the industry and the continuous evaluation of what strategic and policy changes are necessary for the SBUs to accomplish their mission are best handled by a single office.

Primary Materials and Inputs—The bulk purchases of basic inputs that several SBUs require plays a pivotal role in reducing production costs and should be the responsibility of a portfolio-wide entity.

Procurement Functions—The procurement functions not related directly to the manufacturing process but necessary for the smooth operation of offices needs to be handled by one office. These function are:

- Contracts—The proper maintenance of an office requires certain maintenance functions the building leasing company may not handle. These range from companies that provide bottled drinking water to vending-machine maintenance, flower arrangements for reception areas, the maintenance of office plants, and carpet steam cleaning.
- Mail and Messenger Services—In order for the SBUs to qualify for volume discounts with overnight and overseas carriers and local messenger services,

their businesses may have to be consolidated into a single account with different pick-up and drop-off points handled by a company-wide office responsible for overseeing these functions.

• Office Supplies and Furniture—The bulk purchases of all office supplies, from copy machine paper and legal pads to pens and binders, must be handled by one office. The same office should keep the inventory of office furniture, from desk lamps and chairs to framed prints and sofas, in order to purchase in large quantities and maintain an accurate inventory of the company's business units.

Technology Development—It is apparent that a firm whose SBUs are diversified in related lines of business market products and services that are complementary in the sense that they fulfill several points on their customers' value chains. Thus as the emphasis on technology and innovation becomes more evident in disturbed economic times, the need to have but one technology development center becomes crucial to the firm's success. In the years ahead technology will take center stage in strategic thinking and the formulation of competitive strategies across all industries.

Travel—In order to keep travel and entertainment expenses within company guidelines, one office should be charged with selecting the services that are approved—whether for air carriers, hotels, car rentals, or restaurants. This does not imply that SBU personnel are not allowed to make plane reservations themselves, but rather that they must use the approved travel agencies, stay at the hotels, rent from the car rental firms, and dine at the restaurants that are mandated by the firm.

The economy of scale made possible by incorporating these functions in the services shared among the SBU and controlled by the portfolio is great. The costs should be billed to the business units in two ways. For services provided by the firm that constitute overhead, such as corporate strategy and technology development functions, funding should come from all the SBUs as determined by a standard formula. The costs involved in administering these functions should be billed on an equitable basis with a proportional share of the expense of services rendered to all the business units. For services that are user dependent, such as office supplies and word processing work, each SBU should be billed to reflect the actual service provided. The costs of providing these services needs to be on a per-use basis in order for SBUs to remain within their budgets.

The object of exploiting SBU interrelationships is to reduce costs through the combined procurement of basic services. The monetary cost savings that are realized through such economies of scale have an added benefit for the firm, however. The role the portfolio officers play in providing these functions to their SBUs allows for a more careful surveillance of developments which can affect the competitive strategies of the firm. It is necessary to keep a constant monitor on the activities of the SBUs, changes in the marketplace and the actions of a company's competitors if threats and opportunities are to be identified in a timely fashion. The rate of technological innovations and the emergence of new products is increasing; competitive strategies must therefore reflect a heightened awareness of the implications of these changes and that strategies based on the preservation of the status quo are futile.

There are, however, opportunity costs of engaging in the interrelated activities discussed above. The firm faces the administrative costs inherent in the process of coordinating these services among the business units. At the same time there are costs arising from the need for consistency. The firm has to establish a pattern of behavior that is consistent in order to establish cycles that can be analyzed. This involves engaging in functions that are suboptimal; for example, it may be necessary to buy a basic input in a given quantity that the SBUs cannot process in a timely fashion, thus incurring the additional costs of coordinating production schedules among the business units or the costs of storing the surplus materials. It is easy to see the need for SBU managers to compromise here and there in order to find a sustainable equilibrium. The inevitable gaps that emerge constitute the opportunity costs of implementing horizontal links throughout the portfolio. Thus the costs of coordination and consistency overall must be lower than the actual benefits derived from the economies of scale on which interrelationships are built.

These costs, fortunately, are very much a factor of the nature of the interrelationships developed by the firm. In the above recommendations these functions by and large transcend timing considerations. While primary input procurement efforts and marketing efforts require considerable timing, negotiation, and compromise among the SBUs, most of the other services do not. Motor vehicle maintenance, the purchase of paper clips, and the majority of the functions identified can occur in a consistent manner that requires little, if any, compromise among the business units. Therefore the costs of coordination and consistency rise according to how complementary the SBU lines of businesses are. Since these lines vary from firm to firm, it is safe to say that the challenge lies in maximizing the benefits of SBU interrelationship to promote efforts to adopt horizontal structures.

Horizontal Economies of Scope

The creation of links based on cultivating the benefits derived from the various interrelationships that exist among the portfolio's business units is appropriate for today's competitiveness. The proper use of economies of scale leads to economies of scope. There has been much debate over the ability to think of economies of scope in a tangible manner; it is important to recognize that while the benefits derived from economies of scope cannot be measured in the same concrete terms as those of economies of scale, they are of significance to the portfolio's overall performance.

The intangible nature of horizontal economies of scope, however, does not reduce its benefits to the corporate entity. The idea contained in this discussion of economies of scope lies in the observation that the single most important asset any firm has in its efforts to establish a competitive advantage is its human resources. It is the abilities of its managers, the vision of its leaders, the lines of command, power, and influence within the organization that shape the kinds of expertise the company cultivates. Unless the top officers recognize the intangible benefits derived from the expertise of its managers, no set of competitive strategies can be expected to accomplish its goals.

The introduction of a horizontal organization structure presents the opportunity to cut across traditional divisional barriers. This gives rise to certain economies of scope based on the intangible benefits that come from expertise, know-how, and experience. These qualities, which cannot be measured, are the decisive elements in determining which firm will succeed in securing and defending a market leadership position. The objections to thinking about the effects of these horizontal economies of scope overlook the importance the expertise and character of a firm's managers play in fostering confidence, motivating the rank-and-file, and presenting an image to the outside world about the nature of a firm's intentions.

These intangibles—expertise, know-how, and experience—which are enhanced through business-unit interrelationships, are the basis for assessing the competence of management. Here again the substance of the subjective appraisal of an intangible quality such as competence presents a series of challenges. Nevertheless, in the same manner that economists are able to make accurate calculations about consumer behavior through revealed preferences, so can various levels of competence be determined through revealed behavior. The ability of managers to overcome obstacles, implement their policies, assess the economic and business environment, and triumph in the marketplace all speak of an individual manager's or management team's traits. The competence level of a firm's management, moreover, can be determined through the evaluation of observed behavior in the marketplace.

An assessment of how developed the horizontal economies of scope are in a firm can be determined through the examination of the men and women in charge as well as the procedures in practice. These are:

Manager Ability—The ability of a manager to respond constitutes his level of competence. A manager who demonstrates resistance to change undermines his ability to function in the context of increased competition and world economic turbulence. It is not sufficient to assess past track records for the ability to function under a given level of turbulence or within the defined parameters of a specific industry as this does not guarantee that the same level of competence can be expected in a higher or lower level of turbulence or in a line of business that is removed from his area of expertise.

Horizontal Problem Solving Process—There are different levels of scope to be realized through the problem-solving procedures in place in any given portfolio organization. The fact, however, remains that problem-solving procedures based on historical performance are less effective in times of turbulence than are procedures that attempt to create innovative alternatives when possible or those that attempt to select an optimal mix chosen from a set of alternatives based on proven business-unit experiences. The firm that moves away from an emphasis on precedents and instead seeks innovations will meet with greater success.

Management Structure—The kind of management structure required to exploit the benefits of economies of scope is dynamic management structure. As discussed in greater detail later on, strategic thinking cannot succeed unless the expertise of a firm's managers is geared to using extrapolative or entrepreneurial management styles. These management structures are forward-looking and thus seek to anticipate future threats, opportunities, and changes which stand to affect the fundamental structure of an industry or market. The specific and unique know-how of individual corporate officers lends itself to the widespread use of management aimed at solving problems through extrapolative techniques that can quantify the effects of a threat, the possibilities of an opportunity or the implications of industry and market changes.

Information Process—It is easy to understand that in implementing a management structure capable of influencing the future and not relegated to responding to events in the marketplace, the role of information is important. The process by which information is collected, analyzed, and managed determines to what degree the firm will be able to control its own destiny. The best approach that can enhance economies of scope throughout the entire portfolio is an information process that relies on the extrapolation of information from the performance of each SBU and each project while keeping a constant vigil over factors that affect the business environment and economic context of the appropriate areas in which a firm operates. To accomplish this requires management with a solid hands-on experience in the processes of using information and incorporating these into competitive strategies. The ability of managers to compete against competitors is enhanced by a shrewd awareness of the developments that foreshadow change.

Organizational Limits—The ability to benefit from these economies of scope is limited only by the degree to which interrelationships are developed. The higher the level of horizontal organization, the greater the capacity for the firm to handle the volume and the complexity of the strategic thinking requirements. A firm needs to be responsive to market realities and to adapt to change if it is to survive. Thus the kind of manager that can deliver valuable economies of scope to the firm demands an environment that rewards creative and innovative approaches to business. Risk taking must be explicitly encouraged and measures to ensure that the organizational structure of the portfolio can handle the effects of creativity and risk must be in place. This, then, alludes once again to the need to replace short-term with long-term considerations. Unless there is a commitment to a solid set of competitive strategies, the managers responsible for the success of an SBU or a project will grow restless with the perceived impatience. To avoid potential turnover the portfolio's organizational structure must reflect the long-term considerations.

Positional Responsibilities—The final component that determines how much a firm can expect to benefit from the know-how and experience of its corporate officers centers on the way positional responsibilities are defined by top management. In dynamic environments encouraging extrapolative and entrepreneurial styles, creativity and innovations are seen as the foundations of market leadership. In no uncertain terms, then, positions are defined in a manner that reflects the importance of risk, innovation, and a broader sense of freedom to develop insights that can enhance competitive strategies. This requires, in part, a commitment to change and offering technological support to managers. In today's business environment, for example, in-house desk-top publishing for presentations and development of strategies is a requisite to a sound program of strategic thinking. The sense of control afforded managers who have access to the proper equipment and official blessing to *think* about the company's lines of business, the firm's long term, the implications of market developments, and how to develop strategies that reflect all these considerations is a bonus no firm can afford to pass up.

The importance of horizontal economies of scope lies in its ability to encourage the process of thinking, which is the foundation of competitive strategies. The lack of foresight and ill-conceived strategies are to blame for the economic dislocation of the past decade. Not unlike other countries in the nineteenth century which committed similar errors, the United States has too long relied on parochial views and myopic strategies. This must be changed. The necessary changes, however, can only come about through a concerted effort to implement the structural changes that can make use of economies of scope and to recruit managers that have a proven track record and show promise.

The reason why economies of scope are of significant value to the firm is that only when the necessary structure is in place and the individuals with the right kind of expertise and know-how are available can two functions be performed: the identification of inputs to protect the firm and the fine tuning of competitive strategies to reduce vulnerability. It is for these purposes that the arguments against the notion of economies of scale are based on the fact that it is difficult to measure their benefits on the firm. They do exist as a decisive element in a manager's abilities and skills. If superior performance is to be achieved, then managers who can address these two issues need to be identified, recruited, and cultivated. The economies of scope discussed are necessary for these two areas.

Identification of Inputs

The integrity of the firm to operate depends on identifying and securing a reliable source of inputs. In times of economic uncertainty characterized by commodity shocks and shifting sources of inputs, the successful firm must be able to anticipate change and guarantee availability of the basic inputs necessary to deliver products and services to customers. These inputs, whether primary raw materials, secondary materials or skilled employees, are vital to a firm's future and access to an uninterrupted supply is the responsibility of the portfolio managers. In current thinking the one input which has not received the attention it merits is the diminishing number of qualified people in the labor market. The long-term impact of a reduced skilled labor pool presents obstacles to future growth that management needs to resolve before it can exercise greater control over its future.

Portfolio Vulnerability

The quest for the identification of related lines of business that can be developed by the firm requires long-term planning. These efforts center on the identification of threats and opportunities in order to reduce the overall vulnerability of the firm's portfolio. The future becomes less uncertain when management can depend on the expertise of individuals who can identify the significant trends that have long-term implications for the firm and the underlying developments that stand to affect the economic and political context of the environment in which the firm has a presence. Thus it is easier to develop an internal organizational structure capable of adapting to the new circumstances and to establish a formidable presence through lines of expertise.

It becomes apparent that, aside from the objections brought against the intangible benefits from the implementation of horizontal economies of scale, the source of other resistance stems from the structural changes implied. A concrete example is in order. The kind of intangible qualities possible through horizontal economies of scale are based in the expertise and background of the managers at the helm of a business unit or an entire firm. Linda Wachner exemplifies the human synergy that emerges when a firm's structure is molded to reflect the strengths of its executive officer and when the manager's own expertise is perfect for addressing the problems confronting the firm.

When Wachner engineered a buyout of Warnaco, a Bridgeport, Connecticut-based apparel giant, in early 1987, she became its president on April 18, 1987. In the short time she has been at the head of this Fortune 500 company, Wachner has embarked on a program to build on the firm's strengths designed to secure market leadership position in the targeted segments. The challenge for Wachner was to develop interrelationships among its business units in order to reduce costs. The SBUs involved in related lines of business, such as the Christian Dior, Chaps by Ralph Lauren, and Geoffrey Beene brands were reorganized into a menswear division that could profit from the economies of scale of combining similar functions. Similar efforts have gone into other business units including new managers at Olga bras and the recruitment of Lily of France's Jack Cassidy to restructure the lingerie lines. This, coupled with the divestiture of unprofitable business units, has reduced operating lines and streamlined operations. Wachner's new managers are building on the cost savings and momentum fostered by the development of lines of expertise through a committed effort to establish horizontal links among the various SBUs constituting a renewed marketing effort. Wachner's insistence on hands-on experience is admirable; it includes Wachner spending her weekends sizing up the specialty boutiques on New York's Madison Avenue and taking her top managers on extensive shopping sprees at Bloomingdale's during the peak of the Christmas shopping season to expose them to the real world of retailing.

The renewed confidence at Warnaco, the bold restructuring, the strengths of the new managers, and the clear definition of the firm's long-term goal—to become a major force in the apparel industry worldwide—speak well of the value that intangible quality of economies of scope has for a firm. Indeed, the underlying lesson in Wachner's success in the short term demonstrates that firms not operating at their potential need to take strategic actions and adopt policies capable of positioning the firm for a major advance. Warnaco's internal structure reflects sound strategic thinking, an emphasis on taking concrete measures to assure that the long-term goals of the firm are realized, the willingness to take risks by replacing managers, instituting restructuring among the business units, divesting the portfolio of unprofitable lines, adopting an aggressive marketing program, and forming a new alliance between top management and the line managers. These are the steps taken by Wachner that will take Warnaco where she wants to take it.

Labor-Management Partnership

The successful implementation of horizontal economies of scope requires a series of reciprocal measures to facilitate the transition to strategic thinking in terms of management-labor relationships. Recent downsizing campaigns throughout corporate America have created tension, friction, and anger at all levels of the organizational structures. The breakdown of trust and confidence between top management and managers undermines the ability of the firm to benefit from economies of scope. While the experience at Warnaco reveals the sense of momentum and enthusiasm that results when carefully thought out reorganizational programs are implemented, this is clearly the exception and not the rule.

The fact remains that in recent years the organizational restructuring that has been implemented in all industries has been crude. As Thomas Murray reports, "In their zeal to streamline management ranks, however, few companies gave any thought to how drastically the relationships between managers and the organization would change as responsibilities were shifted and subordinates were swept out . . . [and this] will haunt industry over the next decade and cause untold long-term damage to many companies."[1] The dilemma, however, is based on the opposing demands of the competitive environment. There is a fragile balance that must be maintained as firms reduce costs through streamlining operations and the trust issues that affect employee morale.

The collapse of trust and a sense of partnership at PTI during S. Ross Brown's cost-cutting campaign is not unique. General Motors provides a vivid example of the consequences damaged morale portend. "The world's largest industrial company," the *Wall Street Journal* reported, "which in the past year has battled soaring costs and sagging sales and which ousted dissident H. Ross Perot from its board of directors, now is fighting terrible morale."[2] The sense of partnership between top management and the ranks has been destroyed. Roger Smith's efforts to increase competitiveness through the elimination of over 40,000 jobs over a period of time has damaged morale among managers. There is a sense of betrayal at GM that is echoed throughout the country as the management blood bath of this decade continues.

The result, as noted in the *Journal*, "[is changes in the] long-held notions of job security and corporate loyalty for tens of thousands of people."[3] This is a significant change that undermines the ability of companies to implement a thorough program to benefit from economies of scale. That careful balance between the opposing needs for a partnership among the business unit managers and the firm's top officers and the need to achieve a cost advantage is a prerequisite before the structural long-term changes required can occur. Not unlike the experiences of GM and PTI, where there is anger and a sense of betrayal, too many firms across the country are caught up in the formidable task of repairing that fragile tapestry of corporate loyalty and sense of commitment to the firm.

Therefore if strategic thinking is to serve as a useful management tool, corporate officers need to realize that essential element brought about by the unquestioned faith and commitment from labor. It is the duty of a firm's top management to wake the interest and inspire the loyalty of the business units' managers. Wachner's skill in inspiring confidence and a new excitement about Warnaco's future is commendable. The forceful actions and clear vision of market realities and that firm's place in the industry are in sharp contrast with the vacillation of GM and PTI where a sense of fear, apprehension, and disorder prevail. The secret of Wachner's success is no secret at all: it is her commitment to her firm, her grasp of industry realities, and her sense of purpose that account for her ability to instill confidence and a strategic sense of partnership between management and labor.

The ability to identify the elements of success and to take steps to ensure that the components that will guarantee success are secured, coupled with the formulation and implementation of strategies aimed at reducing the long-term vulnerability of the firm, instills confidence. Here, then, is a powerful case that demonstrates the strategic edge that is possible when there is a clear communication between the top officers and the line managers about the strategic goals of the firm. These strategies, moreover, are based on similar lines of thought. The long-term success of the firm is based on an internal organizational structure that reflects the individual needs and demands of the firm's industry and markets. In addition, there is an emphasis on allocating resources to a few selected lines of business to achieve a strong portfolio mix within the context of related diversification. The final step in establishing lines of expertise is the recruitment of highly talented professionals with the expertise, know-how, and qualities who will contribute to management-labor bonding and who can foster a strong sense of commitment at all levels of the firm across all divisional business units. Without a strong sense of reciprocal loyalty success is difficult.

NOTES

1. Thomas J. Murray, "Bitter Survivors," *Business Month*, May 1987, p. 29.
2. Amal Kumar Naj, "Gloomy Giant: GM Now is Plagued with Drop in Morale as Payrolls Are Cut," *Wall Street Journal*, May 26, p. 1.
3. Ibid.

≪ **11**

CORPORATE COMMITMENT

Having laid the tangible internal horizontal organizational structure that maximizes corporate resource utility, the firm is in a position to focus its attention on the intangible inner workings of the corporation's psyche. The execution of corporate strategies requires dedication. The ability to foster the commitment level necessary, however, depends on the viability of the strategies adopted by the firm. This requires realistic agendas for prioritizing the objectives of the firm. The creation of a vision for the firm must be followed by comprehensive steps to achieve these goals. The defining of precise goals and the strategies capable of making these goals a reality is the foundation on which commitment is built.

If management is not convinced of the insight of the market analysis, the appropriateness of the corporate vision, the thoroughness of competitive strategies, and the ability of the firm's SBUs to bring the policies to fruition, it is doubtful that management can maintain the necessary enthusiasm throughout the course of the program. Managers are not stupid; it is impossible to sustain enthusiasm for unrealistic expectations when one's gut feelings create an uneasiness. Pep talks cannot substitute for credible strategies. It follows then that commitment will grow from well conceived strategies based on solid analysis of the market realities and the portfolio's requirements.

Therefore it is evident that a firm's success depends to a large degree on the level of commitment. Commitment plays a central role in the proper development of lines of expertise. A diagnostic self-examination of the characteristic traits of both the firm and the men and women who manage it is fundamental to the identification and targeting of specific lines of expertise. If strategic thinking is to make a significant contribution to the management process, it must do so by providing a mechanism for blueprinting the particular characteristics that define a corporate culture. Only then can competitive strategies be developed in keeping with the personality of the firm and its executives. Management must be committed to strategies chosen to make the vision of the firm a reality, and managers must be committed to the abilities and judgment of top management. This commitment, moreover, is built on pursuing realistic agendas, taking purposeful moves to secure and defend market positions, encouraging educated risks, and shifting the focus to the long-term goals of the firm. When line managers see a focused approach to lay the foundation for a sustained period of growth, the long-haul spirit transcends all the levels of the organization.

REALISTIC AGENDAS

The organizational structure of the firm dictates how priorities are determined. An organizational structure that exploits interrelationships affords greater flexibility in establishing the level of commitment needed for the successful implementation of competitive strategies. The horizontal structure of the portfolio defines the power distribution among the SBUs, SBUs and top management, and among the top officers. The stability of the existing power structure defines relationships within the firm. The more stable the internal power centers, their relationships to each other, and the distinct lines of command, the less uncertainty there is among the rank and file.

This makes it possible for managers to assess what the criteria are for the determination of priorities for the firm. The clear definition of power relations within the firm serves two purposes. First it allows for an accurate profile of the executives in office, their personalities, and roles in the firm. The individual manager's temperament and abilities play a major role in shaping the bonds of loyalty from subordinates as well as shaping opinions about the nature of the marketplace and the firm's role in it. Second, the divisional distribution of power and responsibility reveal a lot about the firm's particular culture. A strategy is only as useful as it is appropriate to the firm. A careful understanding of a firm's history, its culture and sense of place shapes the amount of commitment given various competitive strategies. A sound program that conflicts with a corporate culture can produce mediocre results. The goal of management is to ensure that the strategies are appropriate within the framework of the firm. Only in this manner can rank and file commitment to management be enhanced and top management commitment to the portfolio's goals be assured.

The expected levels of commitment to a set of competitive strategies are affected by the corporate culture. In order to develop realistic agendas it is necessary to analyze the effects of corporate culture and individual managers. The incorporation of these considerations in the analysis process allows the firm greater flexibility in determining the impact of non-market forces. The corporate entity is now in a position to identify the strategies that are appropriate and complemented by the distinctive characteristics of the firm's management and culture.

The strategist must weigh the effects of the firm's culture on the ability to interact in the current economic environment. The analysis of the corporate culture must include the portfolio's objectives, the internal/external activity focus, whether the management structure is static or dynamic, whether threats are handled in a reactive/decisive or extrapolative/entrepreneurial manner, what the attitudes towards change are, and how risk is viewed.

PORTFOLIO OBJECTIVES

The objective of the competitive strategies determines how the culture figures as a factor. A firm trying to establish an internal stability in a volatile market has different considerations on which to reflect than a firm trying to develop new markets through innovative products. A firm trying to downsize operations and increase efficiency, likewise, is faced with different considerations. The objectives of the portfolio to gain, increase, or maximize market shares is an important factor as some cultures are more conducive than others to different goals.

ACTIVITY FOCUS

The focus of the majority of the SBUs, moreover, depends on what goals are being actively pursued. A portfolio concentrating on its internal horizontal structure and SBU interrelationships, such as General Motors, faces different problems than a firm focused on the external market. The aim of MCI, for example, is to increase its share of the long-distance market. This is a different goal from that of GM, which is concentrating on surrendering as little ground as possible. The success of each firm's strategy is dependent on how the corporate culture is suited to their respective tasks.

STATIC VERSUS DYNAMIC

The management style in place, historical or forward looking, affects the success factor of the strategies implemented. In static environments, low industry turbulence is presumed, for the propensity to rely on historical experience speaks of a gradual market evolution. Competitive strategies for stable markets by static management techniques are best suited for certain kinds of cultures. A dynamic management style, on the other hand, requires a different set of strategies for dealing with the higher levels of turbulence, which are normal. The rank and file managers will be committed to the firm's strategies only if they feel comfortable with the course of actions undertaken. Competitive strategies incompatible with the management style in place fosters mistrust in top management and a fatalistic morale.

REACTIVE/DECISIVE VERSUS EXTRAPOLATIVE/ ENTREPRENEURIAL

A natural extension of whether a firm has a static or dynamic management structure is how threats are identified and countered. Firms that handle threats only as they occur have a culture focused on short-term planning and management, whereas firms that anticipate threats and seek change on a continuing basis demonstrate a long-term planning and management process. The commitment to competitive strategies depends on how appropriate these strategies are to the kinds of planning styles in use. How corporate culture relates to turbulence indicates which kinds of strategies are best suited for the firm.

CHANGE ATTITUDES

In the same way that cultures evolve to fit into a given environment, so must competitive strategies. It is very difficult to change a corporate culture overnight. Thus the task for management is to adopt policies that guide changes at a pace appropriate for the firm. In order to generate the level of commitment to the strategies chosen, management must ensure that the policies adopted are appropriate to the predisposition to change of the corporate culture. There is always the danger that policies that force change on passive cultures could foster a hostility that undermines the future success of the firm from within. Line managers who resist change on the SBU level can subconsciously sabotage the portfolio as a whole.

RISK ADVERSITY

This leads to the issue of risk. Competitive strategies to be implemented must reflect the level of risk that fits the corporate culture. The adoption of strategies that require levels of risk with which line managers feel uncomfortable are less successful in the long run. The need to take risks increases as does the level of turbulence. For this reason it is necessary to encourage a culture that is open to calculated risktaking. This, however, cannot be accomplished by implementing policies that run counter to the existing corporate culture.

The intrinsic characteristics of corporate culture include the traits of individual executives responsible for the formulation of policies. The strategies adopted need to reflect the individual executives' imprints. In the same way that Frank Lorenzo's personality affects the strategies pursued by Texas Air, so do all firms reflect the temperament and disposition of their leaders. The strategies, then, must reflect the leadership abilities, the personality, the frame of mind, the power position, the political world view, and the knowledge of the executives in charge of guiding the firm.

LEADERSHIP ABILITIES

The ability to motivate people, inspire confidence, reflect self-assuredness, and be charismatic are fundamental leadership traits. The manager who demonstrates the ability to endear himself to his subordinates is in a position to forge strong ties of loyalty to him. Today's manager must strive to have committed workers whose loyalty is born out of respect for his leadership qualities. The executive whose manner is aloof and distant, whether psychologically or physically, creates fragile bonds based on apprehension and fear. The leader who strives to create loyalty based on his qualities as a leader serves the best interests of the firm and himself.

PERSONALITY

Competitive strategies must also reflect the personalities and dispositions of the executive officers. Patience, temperament, and moods must be reflected in the strategies chosen. Impatient executives will not be committed fully to the long-term strategies. Methodological individuals, on the other hand, will exhibit greater willingness to stay a course until the policies come to fruition. Therefore it is imperative to match the individual traits to the strategies implemented. The careful balancing of the different personalities and various strategic options available must be achieved before a sustained level of commitment to the chosen competitive strategies becomes a reality.

FRAME OF MIND

The private philosophy of each individual manager influences how he sees business problems. How the executive articulates his views, what he considers important considerations, and the time parameters of his thinking reveal a great deal of his frame of mind. The introverted executive who quietly reflects is different from an extroverted officer who talks his thoughts aloud. The executive's conceptualization of the internal and external forces affecting a business matter varies greatly. The officer who believes the firm can play a significant role in shaping its destiny is different from the manager convinced the market determines what the future holds for the firm. By the same token, the executive who bases his actions on the firm's historical performance is more conservative than the executive willing to try the unknown. These factors constitute the frame of mind and competitive strategies needed to reflect this. An officer convinced the firm should evaluate its historical performance, for example, is more likely to be dissatisfied with strategies that require a large degree of innovation.

POWER POSITION

The executive's frame of mind is dependent on his or her power position within the management hierarchy. How much power he or she enjoys, coupled with his or her personal ambitions, determines how much risk he or she is willing to tolerate, for himself or herself and for the firm. While the power and influence struggle is an ongoing affair, the prevailing rank of the current executives presents important issues which must be considered in the strategies selected. The ambitions of the men and women in the boardroom, their power strengths, and their inclinations to use their power greatly affect the strategies implemented. This in turn affects the balance of power within the organization. The political factors are at times as important in determining the success of the competitive strategies as market conditions.

POLITICAL WORLD VIEW

The external manifestation of political power takes the form of how the individual sees the world. Each officer's personal values and history shape his or her political world view. This view affects the thoughts and opinions of the executive. In order to evaluate what factors contribute to success in the world, how people interact in the marketplace, what factors about human nature affect their economic decisions, and what will determine the success of the competitive strategies, the manager relies on his or her own philosophy of the realities of the world. These perceptions and judgments about human nature and the world are an intrinsic aspect of personal character that affect the executive's decisions and indecisions. Strategies that conform to the manager's view of human nature and the political world have a greater propensity to demand commitment than strategies at odds with his or her intuitive views.

KNOWLEDGE

The manager's education and knowledge of the firm, the industries, and the marketplace determines how his or her expertise affects the degree and sincerity of commitment to the firm's policies. Competitive strategies that contradict an executive's firsthand knowledge and formal schooling stand poor chances for a sustainable support. This becomes more important during times when the degree of uncertainty impairs the ability to depend on past experiences or on theoretical tools. The need to consider the individual knowledge and experience of each executive is great. The executive's intimate awareness of how the firm functions in the marketplace shapes commitment levels to specific policies which cannot be dismissed.

These are the culture and management factors that determine the commitment level of the rank and file to the firm's agendas. The process by which various activities are prioritized is important in shaping the competitive strategies acted upon. Commitment from the line managers is a crucial factor in determining which set of policies will ultimately meet with success. The first step, however, is an appropriate agenda that reflects the propensities and characteristics of one's corporate cultures and the firm's executives. While it may be desirable to change certain features of that culture, these are best effected through an evolutionary process. Unlike officers, corporate cultures cannot be replaced. While individual manager's traits are an important factor in the success of competitive strategies, in the short term it is important to work within the existing corporate framework and play down personality conflicts. The road to the future is easier this way.

Once a comprehensive diagnostic personality evaluation of the firm's culture and executives is complete, the commitment requirements of successful lines of expertise can be incorporated into the management process. The role of commitment is central to the contention that a sustained competitive advantage can only be achieved through the long-term allocation of resources to the SBUs pursuant to a realistic and sound program of corporate posturing. The distinct characteristics of a firm's profile shape the form competitive strategies take. These strategies, moreover, must closely mirror the core traits of the firm before a long-term commitment is possible.

When the competitive strategies reflect the personality of the firm, the firm is in a position to establish an optimal horizontal structure that exploits the interrelationships among the SBUs. In this fashion linkages are forged that determine the lines of expertise a firm can develop. On a more narrow scale the diagnostic portrayal of the firm allows for the identification of strategies that enhance the level of commitment from each SBU to the portfolio's goal and from the executive officers to the vision of the company. This is an indispensable proposition, for it allows the firm to take concrete steps to realize its goals. Furthermore, once customized strategies are identified, the firm can proceed to implement a program designed to maximize the portfolio's horizontal organizational structure.

The lines of expertise are complete only when the firm takes deliberate moves to secure leadership positions, encourages calculated risktaking among the SBUs, and shifts its strategic focus to a longer-term perspective. The internal structure of the firm must funnel energies into a coherent series of purposeful actions aimed at delivering market leadership positions in the targeted contexts. The details of each strategy differs from firm to firm, although they reflect the profiles of their respective firms. The executive officer is responsible for the ability of the SBUs within the portfolio to work together to achieve the long-term objectives of the firm. Thus it is necessary to take the insights offered by an analysis of a firm's culture and incorporate this new information into corporate policies regarding leadership moves, risks, and long-term priorities.

DELIBERATE LEADERSHIP MOVES

The deterioration of market leadership positions is caused by one of two things: failure to take deliberate moves to secure market leadership positions or the inability to defend an existing market position. Once the agenda that reflects the corporate culture has been compiled, the firm must orchestrate concrete steps designed to implement strategies compatible with a firm's goals. The diagnostic analysis of corporate culture and executives' traits enables the portfolio strategist to customize a program that will complement the firm's particular circumstances. Competitive strategies can deliver concrete results only if they can cultivate loyalty. This is an easier task if the officers charged with carrying out a set of policies believe in them.

Thus commitment from the SBU managers and their subordinates is vital if deliberate moves to secure leadership positions are to be successful. An aggressive stance is an inherent part of any attempt designed to reverse the decline of market shares. Aggressive measures, however, are born out of faith and confidence. It is not difficult to see that effective strategies based on sound analysis and realistic goals create the enthusiasm necessary if these strategies are to be effective. An aggressive campaign designed to secure market shares is more effective when medium- to long-term priorities are pursued. A short-term gain is not indicative of a turnaround or of a sustainable advance.

In the past two decades a disproportionate emphasis has been placed on short-term goals. This leads to the implementation of suboptimal strategies. The need for purposeful moves is great. Corporate energies need to be directed in comprehensive programs designed to benefit from the interrelationships among SBUs. The synergy created by this approach enables the firm to increase market share. An emphasis on the long term, moreover, complements the effort to increase market positions. This is also true for the loss of market shares. In the same manner as complacent attitudes regarding the need for aggressive market leadership moves, complacency about the status quo has contributed to the demise of market shares.

It is no longer acceptable to be satisfied with the prevailing distribution of market shares. As the level of turbulence increases, it is necessary to direct efforts into defending existing market shares. The aggressive moves of Touchstone, a Disney movie SBU, have more than tripled Disney's box-office share from 3 percent in 1983 to 10 percent in 1986. This is a direct result of the planned actions of Jeffrey Katzenberg to establish Disney studios in a leadership position in the movie industry. The success of such films as "Splash," "The Color of Money," and "Down and Out in Beverly Hills" has revitalized the Disney studios to a point where the dynamic atmosphere at Touchstone resembles that of Paramount when its turnaround made it the most profitable studio in Hollywood thanks to movies such as "Flashdance" and "Saturday Night Fever." Katzenberg, who was at Paramount then, perfected his knowledge of what it takes to succeed in Hollywood and is making legendary use of it at Disney.

The strategy of specific plans to establish leadership position in a specific niche has been successful. Although he has earned a reputation as the toughest deal maker in a town infamous for deal makers, Katzenberg's shrewd strategy has paid off. Katzenberg was determined to turn the direction of Disney's movie and television division away from the traditional emphasis on the Magic Kingdom to films and shows based on contemporary markets. This is exactly what the new Disney owners wanted. Katzenberg's efforts to increase market shares are not limited to films. One of the most successful new television shows is Touchstone's "Golden Girls" carried by the NBC television network. The subject matter of this show has raised a few eyebrows among traditional Disney employees. Nevertheless, Katzenberg has been successful in establishing this Disney SBU as a major force in Hollywood, and its increasing market shares demonstrate that his reputation as a wonder boy is well deserved. More important, however, is that the slow decline of Disney studios has been reversed, and the products coming from Touchstone are sensitive to the tastes and morality of contemporary society.

Other Disney SBUs have not ignored Touchstone's lead. While in mature markets the threat of competitors is reduced, a firm cannot take the status quo for granted. The role of innovation and technology, shifts in customer needs, and the volatile marketplace all work to increase threats looming on the horizon. Under these circumstances it becomes important to establish a consensus about the actions required to secure market leadership positions and to defend market shares. The key to this consensus lies in the personal conviction of managers that the policies pursued are the best set of strategies possible for delivering the firm's long-term goals. This is an important proposition, for in times of turbulence, these strategies require risk and short-term sacrifices. Faced with the slowing rates of visitors to the California Magic Kingdom theme park and the introduction of new cartoon characters, from Smurfs to Transformers, Disney realized that an entire generation was growing up more familiar with Big Bird and the Ewoks than with Snow White or Sleeping Beauty. Thus the managers of this SBU decided to embark upon a program to capitalize on the trademark innovation of Disney and incorporate characters already in the consciousness of its target audience in the theme park. The result is Michael Jackson as Captain E/O and the collaboration between Disney and George Lucas on "Star Tours." The addition of these two attractions have helped increase the attendance at the Anaheim theme park. The Magic Kingdom is building on its strengths and employing its proficiency in the creative use of technology and innovations in animation to establish its leadership position. The experiences of Disney demonstrate that if there is to be renewed commitment to the vision of the firm, from both the rank-and-file manager as well as among top officers, the ability of the chosen competitive strategies to deliver must be unquestioned. This is no easy task.

RISKTAKING

The business world today demands higher levels of risk. For this reason corporate guidelines on risktaking must be spelled out. Faced with a formidable onslaught from foreign firms, the downsizing that has occurred throughout corporate America has resulted in the emergence of great apprehension among middle managers. In the wake of massive layoffs, the survivors have grown disillusioned about their role in the company. Once a firm takes short-term actions that frighten their employees, the concept of partnership is damaged. The result is the proliferation of insecurity and inability to make decisions among managers. Eastman Kodak, for example, destroyed its "Father Yellow" image when it initiated a program to layoff over 10,000 employees during the past few years. The historical relationship between top management and line managers was thrown into question by these unprecedented layoffs.

The consequence of Kodak's actions is ironic. Faced with stiff foreign competition, Kodak embarked on a program to cut operating expenses and speed up development of new products. To accomplish these goals it began a series of layoffs while starting up new SBUs charged with specific product development tasks. The success of the SBUs lies in the willingness of Kodak to take calculated risks in order to regain lost market shares. The layoffs, however, created a strong feeling of insecurity among middle managers, which undermines the success of individual SBUs and the entire portfolio.

In an environment where management downsizes operations through layoffs and no efforts are made to articulate the firm's new competitive strategies, a high level of uncertainty is created. The unspoken message sent to middle management is that times are tough and no clear decision on a new direction has been made. This throws into doubt the commitment of top management to any specific set of strategies. Thus a paradox emerges. The inability of the firm to compete necessitates force reductions, while a firm facing stiff competition needs to take risks in order to make headway. These two requirements are mutually exclusive. In the case of Kodak, the short-term goal of reducing operating expenses through layoffs undermines the long-term strategy of introducing new lines of products to build momentum once again.

The actions of Kodak management indicate a revealed preference of high-risk adversity. Thus it comes as no surprise to learn that the SBUs charged with speeding up new products have not met established expectations. "Kodak," Thomas Murray reports, "is already paying the price for middle-management insecurity, according to one insider . . . some of the managers heading up the [SBUs for new product development] have been so apprehensive about making decisions that the businesses are floundering and many key personnel have quit."[1] The SBUs need to know exactly what the acceptable risk parameters for the firm are. Loss of market leadership position stems from the inability to take decisive actions to defend or regain that leadership position. In times of turbulence and competition the need for bold and purposeful actions is greater. Risk is an inherent part of this proposition. But this is a risk that the Kodak managers are afraid to take for fear of losing their jobs.

The ability of Kodak to introduce new products necessary to regain market leadership position is impaired. The absence of an explicit policy on what levels of risk are acceptable in order for Kodak to accomplish the long-term goals expected, coupled with the effective exclusion of the line managers in the formulation and implementation of competitive strategies, undermines the commitment of the SBU managers to top management. The paralysis at Kodak's SBUs indicates that these managers are not privy to the long-term strategies or that they remain unconvinced of the abilities of their superiors. The result, as revealed through the SBUs' inability to perform their assigned tasks, is one in which the line managers are obsessed with the short-term considerations of keeping their jobs over the long-term strategy of the portfolio as a whole.

SHORT- TO LONG-TERM

It becomes clear that as companies work to regain lost market positions, a higher level of risktaking is necessary. The realization that a greater risk propensity is the price that must be paid is not far removed from the notion that the commitment focus of the firm must become long term. The firm implanting long-term strategies fares better in the marketplace. The business environment of today precludes strategies based on the quick buck. A comprehensive set of strategies designed to maximize the individual strengths of the firm must focus on the long-range goals of the firm.

The structure of business in Japan, for example, facilitates long-term commitment to specific goals. The Japanese microchip industry, for one, demonstrates that commitment to long-term goals is a rewarding strategy. The Japanese strategy has been to secure a dominant role in the microchip market. To do this the Japanese have poured millions of dollars into the construction of state-of-the-art facilities in an effort to achieve a cost advantage over American manufacturers. This is possible because the memory chip manufacturers in Japan are divisions of larger firms with the resources to allocate to a capital-intensive and long-term investment. This arrangement allows the Japanese to establish different SBUs, which can contribute monies for other projects requiring time to generate revenues. The long-term view of business in Japan, moreover, facilitates the sustained level of commitment over a period of years. Patience, then, is the cornerstone of long-term competitive strategies. In the the case of Japanese chip makers the patience has paid off. Today the Japanese dominate the memory chip market. With over 85 percent of the world market, the Japanese are in a position to reinvest profits into the manufacturing process to keep their leadership position. Their presence in the market is so formidable, in fact, that the Defense Science Board, an advisory committee to the U.S. secretary of defense, warns of the structural weakness in the domestic chip maker industry. The response from the Semiconductor Industry Association in the United States, moreover, has been a proposed consortium of chip makers, known as Sematech, which will include such firms as IBM and Texas Instruments, designed to regain a competitive edge against their Japanese competitors. The proposed funding for the consortium, $125 million from the participating firms, has yet to be finalized by either the members or the federal government. This, nonetheless, reveals that the potential competitive advantage of committed strategies is a formidable one.

The commitment to developing long-term markets is relevant to every market. Arturo Villar, a Cuban-born businessman, for example, was interested in the idea of a national English-language magazine for the growing Hispanic community in the United States since the 1970s. Attracted to the large community of Hispanics in this country that effortlessly embraced both cultures, Villar worked on the idea of reaching this audience. Villar used the experience he gained from the Spanish-language newswire he and three partners bought to explore his idea further. When a feasibility study confirmed what he suspected all along—that the majority of the Hispanics in the United States prefer to read in English and are functionally illiterate in Spanish—he began the task of marketing his magazine.

The English-language nature of the proposed magazine, *Vista*, had an added appeal: English-language newspapers could now reach the large urban Hispanic populations more readily. When the prototype was prepared in March 1984, the hardsell began. A realistic agenda was prepared in anticipation of the eventual publication of *Vista* magazine and Villar took the necessary risks to make his magazine's debut in September 1985. It has since increased its circulation, readership, and the number of newspapers carried. Mediamark Research reports that its readership is three million. The magazine turned a profit in March 1987.

Villar's *Vista* is now ready for a controlled growth that will allow him to make his monthly into a weekly magazine. The long-term goals of *Vista* are for national distribution that reaches all of the major Hispanic markets in the United States. The most challenging obstacle for *Vista* is to manage its growth without being overwhelmed by it. If it is to secure a leadership position in its market niche, it will need to become a weekly in order to meet the requirements set forth by newspapers. At the same time it must reach the significant Hispanic communities in the New York metropolitan area, south Florida, Chicago, Los Angeles, Texas, and Puerto Rico. The success of Vista thus far, however, suggests that its management is up to the task at hand. Villar has demonstrated that an unwavering commitment to a sound idea, realistic agenda, and concrete actions are required in order to make long-term goals accomplishments.

Thus it becomes more clear to see the importance that commitment plays in the development of lines of expertise. While the internal structure of a firm is important and the degree to which the interrelationships are exploited is crucial to an efficient portfolio, the overlooked notion of the kind of corporate commitment is instrumental to success. Firms must adopt competitive strategies that respect and complement a firm's culture and the personal traits of top management. The foundation of commitment, which is faith, depends on how appropriate and how well tailored strategies are to the individual characteristics of a firm. After all, an executive whose work lacks the essence that comes from conviction cannot expect to succeed.

NOTE

1. Murray, "Bitter Survivors," p. 30.

12

MARKET AREA PLANNING

There are certain characterizations that are appropriate when the strategist assesses the current state of the domestic and global economies affecting the business community. The world's economies are plagued by slow growth rates, an overextension of debt by industrialized and developing nations alike, erratic currency movements, rising real interest rates, and competitive business environments. These factors cannot be ignored for they affect the ability of the firm to attain satisfactory growth rates and targeted market share positions. For this reason a broader analysis of the market areas that affect the firm's related lines of business are called for.

Corporate strategists need to consider the impact of related markets and both vertical and horizontal spillover industries in order to identify major trends that transcend any single market. Therefore, as the firm adopts a series of policies designed to streamline operations and the internal organizational structure to secure the benefits of lines of expertise, it must also see the need for a broader understanding of repercussions in the marketplace. Indeed, it is quite clear that the external aspect of strategic thinking requires a conscious effort on two fronts: understanding the business context and market area planning regarding the firm's related lines of business.

This notion of incorporating context and market area considerations in the company's competitive strategies is a reflection of the economic dislocation of recent years and the inability of American firms to regain lost momentum through traditional marketing methods. While there has been a tendency to blame foreign governments, unfair trading practices and the reluctance of other sovereign states to pursue the monetary and fiscal policies of their own liking and convenience, the real blame lies at our doorstep. As corporate America searches for a catharsis, it must realize that today opportunities are made through preparation. It is the firm with a full grasp of the issues affecting the world, how they interact with its industry, and why markets are changing that is in a position to make that competitive edge a reality. This goal is best served by a conscious effort to analyze the context of a given environment, its effects on markets, and the policy implications for the corporate entity.

CONTEXT

The strategist has to incorporate context into corporate strategies. Lowered expectations regarding growth potentials throughout the industrialized and developing economies worldwide mandates a more careful approach when estimating realistic expectation on SBU performance. Once performance expectations are established, however, careful consideration must be given to the opportunity costs prevailing in the economy. Any variances in actual performance are to be expected during periods of turbulence and increased market volatility. Every estimate of expected business unit return needs to be given a context in terms of what are the returns on alternative investment. Stock market performance when represented in constant terms offers a measurement of the prevailing returns on investments given the existing economic conditions.

The strategist must use the observed returns of the stock market as a barometer that gives a broader context of a firm's forecasts on growth, returns on investment, and overall performance of an individual SBU and the entire portfolio. Economic performance directly impacts the actual, if not expected, growth rates of the business units. No one industry, no matter how independent, is insulated from the effects of the general economic climate. There are vivid examples demonstrating this observation. Economic declines during the Great Depression, for example, left no industry unaffected. Despite efforts to insulate one's firm, the prevailing economic context determines to a great degree whether or not the strategic expectations will be realized. Expectations, then, have validity only so far as the general performance of the economy creates an environment, a foundation which cultivates growth, stability, and the low turbulence required for progress. Conditions in the economic environment that interfere with the ability of a corporate portfolio to perform—such as rising real interest rates, the emergence of structural deficits, absence of international monetary arrangements, and volatility in the currency markets—result in lower actual returns. Knowing the limits the economic context imposes on the ability of the firm to perform is important for it reduces the chances of disappointment if targeted growth rates are not realized.

The importance of context is unquestioned. The issue lies in how to use the stock market performance as a barometer in devising strategic plans. This can be done through a program that takes the performance of the stock market in constant terms and analyzes the economic and political factors that account for the observed behavior. In this way the strategist is afforded a mechanism to interpret the major trends affecting the economy, events that investors believe will impact the economy, and domestic and foreign political events that have a bearing on the economy. Conditions are always changing and events influence the prospects for the economy, an industry, and firms. One only need look back at the volatile reaction caused when Paul Volcker announced he had no intention of staying on as Chairman of the Federal Reserve Board when his second term expired, to see how all the impact of information is processed as it becomes available. Indeed, this increased volatility is now a permanent aspect of the market because of computer trading and the repercussions of the "crash of 1987." The factors that determine stock market performance are the key to a sustainable competitive advantage.

Economic Context

The arguments for using the performance of the constant-dollar Dow have been made. The advantage offered by looking to the stock market lies in its ability to process all information available and reduce all the implications of a development into a rise or drop in the price of the affected stocks. In this way there is a constant assessment of implications of the multitude of business transactions and news developments that occur daily. The utility of the stock market as a barometer of economic health, however, is based on its ability to function as a reference point.

In today's rapidly changing business environment, it is clear that there is a need for a reference point that will allow strategists to establish realistic benchmarks by which to judge an SBU's performance. In a broader sense, however, the stock market as a reference point facilitates the analysis of the economic forces shaping one's industry. Competing firms face similar market conditions. Thus there is a strategic advantage for the firm that is able to see clearly the implications of the economic context of its industry and its markets. In fact, all strategic functions are served by the stock market as a reference point:

Industry—Fluctuations in the stock valuations of one's industry and related industries indicate primary trends that determine the attractiveness of any individual industry. The relative position of the company and the ability of the portfolio benefit or suffer from industry developments. The enhanced strategic position of technology results in greater uncertainty as the status quo of the firms in all industries remains far from guaranteed.

Competitor Analysis—The strengths and weakness of competitors determines the relative standing of one's firm. There are clear indications that the importance of economies of scope will increase in the future. Thus, not only does a firm need to analyze the financial statements of competitors and scrutinize marketing programs, but careful profiles of top officers need to be compiled.

Entry/Exit Barriers—The capital outlays involved in entering and exiting markets imposes mobility constraints on firms competing in an industry. For this reason economic changes that alter existing barriers present the possibility of new entrants into a market or the withdrawal of competitors whose resources are spent.

Competitive Advantage—The formulation of policies in light of economic trends offers new insight into which competitive strategy—cost, focus or differentiation—is the most appropriate one for an individual SBU, a group of SBUs, or the balance of business units in a diversified portfolio. In this manner a sustainable advantage over a firm's competitors can be established for the long term.

Relative Market Strength—The performance of competitors relative to the stock market indicates strengths within the context of alternative opportunity costs. Comparisons of one's firms to the same reference point, furthermore, offers insights into the identification of competitor rankings within the industry. The purpose of relative competitor standing is to point out weaknesses and strengths in terms of cost positions, differentiations success, and growth potential of focused markets.

Strategic Thinking—The information compiled from contextual analyses of competitor and industry positions indicates what actions are in keeping with the long-term strategic goals of the firm. A set of policy actions that complement existing strategies and new, appropriate resource commitments enable the firm to strengthen its lines of expertise and its market area planning process. Since strategic thinking is a continuing effort, the constant input of new facts allows for in-depth analysis of the logic, reasoning, and inferred goals of competitor moves.

Political Context

The stock market reference point reflects political forces. An inescapable part of human interactions, politics influences all aspects of business life. This is why it is better to realize and accept the existence of politics than it is to pretend that politics do not play a role in shaping the business environment. A firm's competitive strategy needs to mirror the potential effects of government regulation, interference, decrees, and turmoil. During the past twenty years the role foreign and domestic government has played in the marketplace has become more erratic, forceful, and discontinuous than at any other time in the post-war era. The collapse of Bretton Woods in the early 1970s left a vacuum that existing international bodies have been unable to fill.

Thus political turmoil among Western nations has increased. This has been intensified by the emergence of a powerful group of nations thrust onto the world scene during the 1973 oil embargo. The massive transfer of economic and political power to the OPEC nations changed the traditional balance of power that existed in the world. This has been compounded by two other developments: the emergence of economic powerhouses all along the Pacific rim and the discomforting decline of Latin American economies. There are more players of significance on the world stage. There are more opposing interests vying for power. All these forces shape the business environment in which firms operate. These factors are then added to the inherent political forces that exist within industry. Thus, the importance of political consideration takes on an unprecedented importance in the wake of a world characterized by greater uncertainty and volatility. Strategic thinking requires an awareness of the role these political considerations have on competitive strategies.

Industry Personalities—Internal industry politics from power struggles to personality clashes among industry leaders have a bearing on the effectiveness of competitive strategies. There are vivid examples of rivalry among firms that went beyond competition in the marketplace. Donald Burr, of the defunct People Express, for example, had worked for Frank Lorenzo of Texas Air and the rivalry between the two men contributed to a great extent to the eventual purchase of People Express by Lorenzo's firm.

Market Forces—The behavior of consumers constitutes a political force. Changes in consumer preference—rational, irrational, and those that are a result of fashionable whims—emerge as unforeseen factors that need to be considered through dynamic management structures. The red food coloring dye scare of the 1970s, for example, presented challenges to the makers of M&M candies. The association of all red dyes with cancer agents resulted in a marked shift in consumer preference that forced the Mars Company to suspend making red candy coating for over a decade.

Role of Government—The ability of government to intervene in the marketplace affects firms. Through legislated incentives, subsidies, and constraints the attractiveness of any line of business can be altered. Issues that affect the national interests of the nation, likewise, can alter the official view of an industry. The potential threat presented by the domination of the memory chips industry by foreign firms, for example, can lead to government steps that alter the structure of the industry. The discovery of side effects of a product can have the same effect. The discovery that asbestos causes cancer is a recent example where the economics of an entire industry are changed.

International Politics—The domestic politics of a competitor's home nation affect American firms. Whether these competitors are protected at home, as is the case with many Japanese firms, or whether they are subsidized and thus have a non-market advantage over American companies, there are strategic implications of these actions. The politics of nations from whom the firm secures primary inputs or to whom the firm exports finished products affects growth and profitability. Brazilian telecommunication markets, for example, are closed to exports from the United States. Thus the international politics affects the ability of AT&T to operate in that country. Many other nations have restrictions on the repatriation of profits. There are many factors regarding international politics that must be considered in the strategic thinking process.

Political Scenario Planning—In addition regional prospects in the broadest terms, such as generalities on the Pacific Rim, Latin America, and the Middle East, must be considered in terms of East-West or North-South viewpoints. Too often regional conflicts and developments are distorted by an East-West conceptualization when these are not appropriate. A forward-looking examination of the issues needs to occur before decisions about the corporate presence in these areas are finalized. The historical parochialism of the United States tends to result in the myopic scenario planning. It is necessary to think about the validity of foreign ways, priorities, and interest in order to establish a mutually beneficial relationship with foreign peoples and in foreign markets.

The systematic incorporation of contextual considerations into strategic planning enhances portfolio management. A well diversified company in a few selected lines of business must be prepared to anticipate changes in the marketplace precipitated by economic and political trends. In our discussion of context thus far, several facts of importance emerge that debunk current myths about the conventional wisdom. Indeed, continued belief in these myths undermines the ability of American firms to implement strategic thinking programs that can deliver a competitive advantage.

The implications of the findings presented here are invaluable to the corporate strategist. Consider the following revelations:

• The Dow Jones Industrial Average is below its 1966 peak in constant dollars;
• Real interest rates in 1987–1988 have not been higher at any other time in the post-war history of this nation;
• The stock market appreciation of the past five years is the result of a deficit-financed aggregate demand and its crash is a result of this debt.

- The emergence of structural deficits discourages capital stock formation;
- The inflow of foreign monies since 1982 have made the United States the world's largest net debtor nation;
- The lackluster economic performance of the industrialized West reduces international cooperation and monetary coordination; and,
- The volatile currency markets will continue, aggravating trade tensions and intensifying the debt problems of many developing nations.

The implication of these facts for the firm is simple. For the remainder of the century the Western economies will reel from the ill effects of the present deficit crisis in the United States. This is manifested in part through lackluster economic performance, which in turn intensifies the competition among firms competing within the same markets. Slower growth rates at home and abroad will continue the present fifteen-year cycle of customary summits by the leaders of the United States, West Germany, Japan, France, the United Kingdon, and Italy to discuss the need for stable currency markets and increased growth rates in the Western economies. Volatility in the international financial markets will continue as the debtor nations—including the United States—fail to get their economic houses in order. The most significant development that is encouraged by the present economic situation is the growing political clout of Japan as a lender of credit to the developing world directly and through its contributions to world organizations such as the World Bank. These are the major forces shaping the economic and political context of the world today. The success of competitive strategies rests on the inclusion of these context issues.

MARKET AREA PLANNING

The strong links between market and context permeate all aspects of portfolio management. These links, moreover, form a dependency between the need for careful market area planning and the impact of current context. The various requirements of this dependency must be balanced in such a way so as to count on a strategic program for specific market areas that is based on accurate assumptions about the forces affecting the business environment. The logic for this is quite simple: if the firm's business units are to behave as relevant actors in their environments, their strategic missions must reflect the current context and the individual characteristics of each market.

The idea behind market area planning is to facilitate the ability of the firm to relate to its environment. A diversified portfolio marketing its related lines of expertise to targeted customers through related lines of business needs to consider the broader issues of spillover effects. This entails a comprehensive mapping of the structural factors of the targeted markets and the advantage of a methodical dissection of the markets in which the firm interacts. Markets, moreover, include not only customers, but also suppliers. In this manner it is possible to compile a thorough portrait of the marketplace from the perspective of the firm. Thus it is in the interest of the portfolio manager to determine the arenas in which the firm operates. In so doing the firm is able to establish strategic arenas which must be protected if the firm is to relate to its environment and achieve superior results.

Strategic Arenas

A fundamental proposition for corporate strategists to consider is the identification of perceived threats to the portfolio's strategic arenas. These areas constitute potential weaknesses that can undermine strategies. The company cannot lose sight of the economy of resource, technology, target, and political arenas which affect its policies. The neglect of analyzing events that may affect these strategic arenas and the failure to anticipate the short- and long-term implications of changes undermines the future success of the firm. As the role of innovation increases and the product life cycles are shortened, it becomes more important to secure uninterrupted and friendly access to the key arenas in which the firm operates.

Strategic Resource Arena

The world is finite. The Club of Rome's studies vividly demonstrate the need for the preservation of natural resources.[1] In the process of assessing the basic inputs that are primary materials in the production chain of goods and services, it is imperative to determine what, if anything, threatens the future supply of and access to these inputs. The basic inputs that the firm can neither make substitute for nor function properly without, constitute the strategic resource arena. The resource requirements of each SBU needs to be determined and analyzed, and policies need to be adopted that seek to guarantee future access to these inputs. The suppliers of inputs, foreign and domestic, must be incorporated into the long-term strategies of the firm as well as the identified supplier substitutes. Supplier substitutes represent alternative sources of the basic inputs. The purpose for this lies in the fact that strategists have to think about not only the theoretical finiteness of global resources but also of the political and natural constraints. These range from political embargoes, as happened during the 1973 oil embargo against the West, to natural disasters, such as droughts, fires, and earthquakes, as well as other conditions which constitute major forces.

The identification of these strategic resources is the first step in understanding how they are threatened and what strategic decisions need to be made if the firm is going to implement resource constraint procedures. The need for resource constraint policies is to anticipate the impact of realized threats against the strategic resources of the firms. In the absence of a national policy it is the firm's responsibility to address the issues of resource constraints. The 1973 oil embargo, for example, raised the national strategic importance of this basic input. The government responded by developing closer ties to oil-producing nations outside the OPEC organization and by creating a strategic oil reserve to protect the national interests should a similar embargo be imposed in the future. The great importance of oil, however, is not the case for other basic inputs affecting selected industries but the integrity of the national economy. For this reason, where there is no national policy to ensure the uninterrupted access to an input, the firm must consider policies that will increase its ability to secure these strategic resources.

Strategic Technological Arena

The importance of technology is greater now than ever before in history. No firm can ignore the fact that today technological advances are weapons. The strategic technological arena is the technological context that affects the related lines of business and threatens to alter the relative standing of the firm. In times of rapid technological changes, the role of innovations and an entrepreneurial approach to the market is required. As the experiences of the memory chips industry suggests, it is now common to invest millions of dollars in a manufacturing process that will become obsolete in a matter of years. The recognition by the Japanese of the strategic importance of this technology has permitted them to use technological innovation as an economic weapon.

The competitive advantage behind such an approach reveals the greater role strategic technologies play in creating opportunities and subverting threats that upset the status quo. The ability to incorporate new technologies as they are developed allows firms to secure long-term competitive advantages. The commitment the Japanese have demonstrated in increasing their global market shares of the memory chips market demonstrates the emerging threat posed by the ability to assimilate state-of-the-art technologies in a timely manner. This is important. The nature of strategic technologies is such that a constant vigil must be maintained if the changes, innovations, and developments that present opportunities and signal threats are to be evaluated and anticipatory measures prepared.

Strategic Target Arena

Markets and customer needs change. There are ongoing structural changes in customers' value chains and the entrance and exit of products affect markets as do changes in customer preferences. This situation is compounded by the fact that product life cycles are now shorter than in the past. This, coupled with the current economic realities, increases the level of uncertainty. The implication for corporate officers is the need to identify strategic target arenas in which to concentrate. Future market growth rates are reduced by competition and market saturation. The key to success lies in profits and quality market shares. Once the strategic targets have been selected, the strategist must identify the areas in the customers' value chains that can be satisfied by the firm. For the corporate officer confronting slower growth rates, the priority is to introduce the necessary economies of scale that constitute the lowest delivered costs. It is the ability to deliver this lowest cost to the customer that will increase profitability.

The overall return is dependent on how thoroughly the firm is able to meet their customers' needs. The evolution of product lines in related lines of business should be coordinated to enhance the complementary nature of the firm's product lines. This requires careful mapping of the markets, needs, and choices the customer faces. The duration of product life cycles takes on a new importance in today's environment. The ability to determine whether the home television shopping phenomenon, for example, is a fad or whether a new market has to be determined. The contentions of Home Shopping Network's Roy Speer, that home shopping is as much a fad as television itself is persuasive given the revealed consumer behavior in this country. Product life cycles, moreover, play a dominant role in determining the long-term prospects for strategic targets. In the final analysis strategists need to determine how the portfolio's lines of businesses can better serve their customers.

Strategic Political Arena

Politics affects business. Whether market, industry, or government related, political considerations play a significant role in affecting the competitive strategies of a firm. Increasing disarray in the world markets serves to increase the pressures to limit the effects of the free market. The parameters of a firm's environment are shaped by political forces. In today's increasingly hostile political context, the threat of protectionism is greater. The pressures to enact tariffs, quotas, and retaliatory measures are on the rise. As corporate America struggles to respond to the difficult challenges posed by foreign competitions, the likelihood of dramatic political responses increases, and so does the political risk exposure of most firms. The possibility of trade wars with the major trading partners, international flaps over American pressures on foreign governments, and the continuing inability to coordinate international monetary policies creates a level of high political turbulence that is unprecedented in the post-war world.

These developments come at a time when firms are concerned with the long-term political considerations within their industries. The volatile nature of the economic environment and the fragility of the political structure—in 1987 there are thirty military conflicts throughout the world—endanger the stability of competitive strategies. The impact of these political and economic conflicts increases the level of uncertainty which undermines competitive strategies. The deterioration in the purchasing power of foreign consumers stemming from the Third World debt crisis, the long-term implications for the development of nations where the working-age population is threatened by disease, the increasing militancy of Western nations, and the increasing level of regional violence are serious issues. The floundering Mexican economy, for one, has serious implications for the American economy as the flood of illegal aliens into this country continues unabated. The spread of disease in African nations brought about because of famine and the spread of acquired immune deficiency syndrome (AIDS) undermines the possibility of development for the next quarter century. The willingness of the United States and France, for example, to use force in Central America and the South Pacific respectively disrupts the ability of regional bodies to plan for development. The continuing conflicts within India and the Iran–Iraq conflicts are vivid reminders of regional conflicts. These are but a few of the continuing disturbances throughout the world that affect long-term planning. The failure of mankind to resolve basic problems imposes growth constraints on firms. Poor people are poor consumers. The problem, however, is that there are more poor people today than ever before, thus limiting the ability of American firms to develop markets abroad. The firm must therefore be able to assess the impact of events and political conditions throughout their strategic political arenas on their lines of business and their ability to achieve their long-term-goals.

The use of strategic arenas is an important tool since it allows corporate officers to analyze the relative merits of control leverage points. The firm is then in a position to include these strategic arenas as control leverage points. Thus the policy implication is clear: invest aggressively in basic industries to exercise greater leverage and influence in focus markets. This practice can be further enhanced through the use of wide distribution: transportation networks, advertising networks, or customer service. The purposeful evaluation of the needs of key strategic arenas is a way to ensure that the level of uncertainty is diminished and corporate officers consider the impact various developments would have on the firm. In this manner strategic arenas take their proper role: assisting the firm in its efforts to achieve optimal profitability in its selected markets.

Market Areas

Once the minimum strategic arena factors are secured, the corporate manager can concentrate on evaluating the needs of the market. No matter how focused corporate efforts are, there is the need to identify the needs of the customer's value chains to identify how the firm can fill other needs. This process requires the identification of customer needs on several levels. The most opportune situation is one in which the firm can satisfy various needs on the value chain in a manner that conforms with the established lines of expertise. There are dire consequences for firms that neglect to map out in minute detail the factors, participants, and developments that alter the nature of the business environment in which the firm operates.

As such the methodical mapping of market areas allows for thorough planning of the best approaches for a presence that can be easily sustained. No other course of action is proper for a nation reeling under the effects brought on by economic dislocation. This economic decline speaks of the mortal blows from within that have struck many in corporate America. These very blows, however, are the result of the inattention paid to the role superior products and service play in the long-term loyalty of customers. In a market economy the bottom line is all that matters, and customers will seek to maximize the value received from firms. The astute businessman realizes that few people buy Japanese cars because they want to contribute to Japan's trade surplus, rather they want to buy the best car for their money.

Products—The firm's goods and services need to be under continuous review in order to determine how closely they match the needs of the customer. Periodic modifications are required as preferences change. Established products may serve as the basis for designing new products when a new customer need is identified. The change in the eating habits of the American public provides an example of old products inspiring new ones. In recent years researchers have documented a growing trend to smaller and more frequent meals growing out of busier schedules for many Americans. The implications of this trend—that many customers would find traditional lunch and dinner meals too large—were reflected by fast food establishments introducing smaller meals. Kentucky Fried Chicken, for example, has introduced "Chicken Littles" which are appropriate snacks and treats to tide people over from one meal to the next.

Services—Over the past few years the cost-cutting programs adopted in virtually all industries have resulted in a sharp decline in the quality of customer service. A dramatic case in point is the airline industry. The fare wars initiated by People Express have become entrenched in the industry as outgrowths of the deregulation that has occurred. Despite the domination of the airline industry by a group of megacarriers, seasonal fare wars continue to characterize the airline industry. As airlines have tried to cut operating costs, the level of customer service has suffered. The decline in customer service has been so severe that consumer complaints have increased during this time by over 50 percent. Airport delays, lost baggage, missed connections, and poor in-flight service account for most of the complaints and indicate a broad decline in all customer service areas. The irritation caused by such delays has been so great, in fact, that one airline is using the draw of excellent service as a differentiation tactic. Alaska Airlines touts its quality service and concern for individual comfort as being well worth the fares charged. The value placed by the customer on service cannot be underestimated and must be included in the corporate market area planning process.

Technologies—The ability to translate a technological advance into a product a customer can use immediately offers a strategic advantage. Many factors determine the rate of technological innovations, but it is the ability to bring these to the marketplace that sets leaders apart from the rest of the competition. In many ways the firm that is in a position to introduce the ready use of technologies to its customers will strengthen a sense of loyalty that ties firms to their customers in relationships. The attempt by American Express to use the most sophisticated computer system available to connect various business travel functions to a single package is a vivid example of the advantages possible through technologies. The American Express effort to connect charge card replacement, travelers' check issuance, medical and legal referrals, insurance coverage, and billing functions into one system that coordinates the financial and planning functions of an entire business trip, through American Express Travel centers and financial services, is a major breakthrough for the traveling public.

Segments—Markets need to be segmented. This allows for an efficient resource allocation program that focuses on the particular needs of specific markets. Market segmentation can occur through one of two methods. A group of customers can be identified and targeted or a group of related products can be marketed together. A firm can, for example, target the entire needs of a group of customers such as cyclists, offering everything from bicycles to clothing and cycling vacations. The opposite is also true. Computerland specializes in the needs of the computer users, business and individual. A difficult, albeit ideal, approach, however, is one in which these two functions merge into one. Sears, Roebuck & Co. is an illustrious example of clear strategic thinking, which accounts for the dramatic reversal of its decline. Faced with stagnant growth rates and a polarization among the U.S. middle class, the nation's largest retailer had to select specific customer groups that were in keeping with the changing demographic profiles of the U.S. population. Thus Sears made a commitment to upgrade its image, products, and services aimed at the secure middle class. The purchase of Dean Witter Reynolds and Caldwell Banker and the creation of the Sears Savings Bank thrust the retailing giant into the financial services market in a formidable manner. The extensive refurbishing of its retail stores and the inclusion of better quality merchandise fit nicely into its strategy of meeting the durable goods, clothing, discretionary household goods, and financial needs of the bulk of the American middle class.

Regions—The strategist can map out the market of a specific region, which can be physical or psychological. The enormous success of the Floridian department store, Burdine's, rests on the retailer's ability to epitomize the ideal Florida lifestyle. The thoughtful cultivation of its image and its innovative marketing programs have made the Burdine's store in the Dadeland mall the most successful store in the nation. This store, moreover, is so entrenched in the essence of south Florida living that its reputation extends to Latin America. It is not uncommon for many wealthy Latin Americans from Venezuela, Colombia, the Caribbean, and Central America to fly to Miami for a weekend shopping trip to Burdine's. Its links to the local community are as strong. There is a firm bond between the store and Floridians which is the envy of other retailers who have been unable to make significant inroads among Burdine's customers. In the Dadeland mall, for example, New York's Lord & Taylor and Saks Fifth Avenue have not detracted from Burdine's appeal among Floridians. In the same vein, psychological regions can be developed to create a loyal following. L. L. Bean, the Maine outfitter, has carved out a psychological image that transcends the geographic region of its identity. Unlike Burdine's, which concentrates on one state and that state's lifestyle, L. L. Bean strives to be the psychological embodiment of an idea, and an image—that of rustic New England. It is so closely linked with the New England image that it can operate the most successful mail order business in the country with little, if any, product differentiation. The fact that the bulk of Bean's merchandise is indistinguishable from Eddie Bauer's or Land's End shows that there is a strong aura about the Freeport, Maine, retailer that goes beyond economics. The careful commitment to the protection of this specific psychological market niche, moreover, assures the New England retailer that it will be as successful as Burdine's in its geographic region.

Dependencies—An alternative strategy is the creation of a product which is so differentiated that no other firm can offer a substitute in its stead. The irreplaceable nature of the product can stem from its tangible or intangible attributes. The customer is then dependent on the firm as the exclusive source of that product. The product does not need to have snob appeal to create that dependent nature. Polaroid, for example, created such a differentiated camera that no other competitor could offer a comparable product. Its exclusive right to use the instant photography gave Polaroid the chance to exploit a specific market to the fullest. Throughout this time the camera maker developed an array of cameras with various options, all derivatives of the appeal of instant photography. This kind of customer dependency is not based exclusively on patented technology. Andy Warhol, for example, created an intangible differentiated product: society portraits. The use of images that were mass produced through mechanical means and the choice of the gaudy colors that made his trademark, this pop artist was able to create a mystique about his portraits that made them highly prized. His portraits of the famous—from Liza Minnelli to Ethel Scull—contained an appeal of glamor that went beyond the pure technique of silkscreening on canvas. Warhol's work, based on the silk screening techniques developed by Stephen Poleskie in the 1960s, had an intangible quality that made them differentiated to those who sought them, just as Polaroid cameras did to mass-market consumers.

The purpose of analyzing market areas is to develop strategies that defend the integrity of the firm's strategic arenas. The above areas allow the firm to concentrate on specific strategies to achieve a differentiated product, a focused market strategy, or to create an image with the customer that forms a bond. This is imperative, for the defense of the strategic arenas is necessary to protect the firm's market position. In addition, the detailed study of the market areas is a requisite that allows the firm to recognize threats. An event that can trigger a threat to any strategic arena poses challenges which the firm must confront. Any threat, no matter how subtle, can contribute to trends that undermine the viability of the firm's presence in any arena. For this reason the firm in a position to anticipate threats has a greater chance of mitigating damages. The same mechanism that identifies threats, however, also identifies opportunities. Considerable efforts must be made to recognize the potential of opportunities that emerge by themselves or which are created through market positions. As growth slows, new markets must be created, opportunities made, and markets developed to secure the future.

RECOGNITION OF THREATS AND OPPORTUNITIES

The advantage of analyzing the economic and political context of the economies and environments in which a firm operates is to gain insights and perspectives. The firm that understands what forces are shaping the world in which it exists is able to identify threats and opportunities on a timely basis. It is no longer enough to sit back and follow the crowd. The successful corporate officer is the one who can identify trends that constitute either a threat or an opportunity. The classification of a development, in fact, reveals a great deal about corporate culture. The two firms discussed below each faced threats and recognized opportunities. Hooker Corporation, under George Herscu, for example, saw the threat of a shopping mall market as an opportunity to use innovation throughout its planned shopping malls. Primerica, under Gerard Tsai, on the other hand, saw the opportunity of the growing financial services sector as a solution to the threats posed by the opportunity costs of remaining in its traditional manufacturing businesses. Each firm took concrete steps to respond to threats or seize opportunities as it saw them. Each firm, moreover, could only have done this through a disciplined and shrewd understanding of the major forces affecting today's economy. In this manner each firm's strategic plans relate to its context, thus they are given new strength.

Threats

The recognized threat is less dangerous than the threat that catches a firm by surprise. A threat, moreover, is a factor that has the potential to interfere with a steady growth in the market shares and profits of an SBU or an entire portfolio. As products mature and markets change, the status quo is upset, creating uncertainty among the affected firms. Hooker Corporation is one such firm. Hooker, Australia's largest developer, is determined to revolutionize the concept of the shopping mall. The United States in recent years has been plagued by a glut of retail space. Most suburban malls are indistinguishable from each other and they have been faced by difficulties in attracting and keeping anchor stores. Mail order selling and discount chains and the emergence of home television shopping services are making inroads to the traditional shopping mall customers.

The result is a saturated industry facing stagnant growth. This threat to mall investors, however, is the very reason why George Herscu, Chairman and CEO of Hooker, believes he can capitalize on the threat faced by the shopping mall industry. With four malls under construction in Denver, Cincinnati, Columbia, South Carolina, and Tampa, Florida, Herscu believes that the smart response to the threat the oversupply of boring malls present is innovation. The threat, Herscu claims, can be overcome by replacing shopping malls with hypermarkets. Hooker is prepared to combine mass marketing with mass entertainment in a series of gigantic shopping centers offering amusement-park entertainment with large department stores, specialty shops, and supermarkets. For a world that welcomes and embraces the gloss of post-modern architecture, there is nothing more appropriate.

The acquisition of Allied Stores Corporation's Bonwit Teller in the spring of 1987 signals that Herscu has found an anchor for all his hypermarket malls. The success of Hooker's ventures remain far from guaranteed. There are, however, certain signs that suggest he will be rewarded for his innovations. The purchase of Bonwit Teller and his plans to increase its stores from thirteen to twenty-eight improves the visibility of the well heeled New York retailer. Bonwit Teller, already an anchor in New York's Trump Tower, could serve as a magnet the way Burdine's makes Dadeland Mall the success it is in south Florida. Thus if Bonwit opens as a major anchor in the malls presently under construction, it will be easier to attract other specialty retailers such as The Gap, The Limited, and Banana Republic to the Hooker malls. The strategic roles for Bonwit Teller are to be a profitable SBU and to attract the upscale consumer to Hooker's malls. Hooker wasted no time in moving; Michael Babcock was named president of Bonwit Teller to enhance the retailer's market position. The turnaround at Bonwit Teller (1985 was the first profitable year in a decade) must continue and its handsome name must enter the consciousness of the American consumer among the ranks of Saks Fifth Avenue, Lord & Taylor, Nordstrom, and Neiman-Marcus. In an effort to build momentum, Hooker also acquired B. Altman and Parisian Department stores in 1987 to function as additional anchors.

The selling of these hypermarkets could be aimed at three segments: teenagers, senior citizens, and working women. A mall with ferris wheels, skating rinks, movie houses, and fast food outlets next to favorite shops has the potential to be a major attraction for many teenagers. If these rides were to offer a season pass for the theme rides during the summer months it would increase the likelihood that teenagers would hang out most of the summer weekends at the malls to go on the rides while being enticed to shop. As the senior population of the nation rises, the patronage of older citizens of the hypermarkets is great. The enormous scale of these projects suggest that more older Americans would visit these malls for several reasons. The most compelling would be the high concentration of stores in one location. The Hooker malls under construction are about four times the size of average suburban malls. In addition the inclusion of amusement rides offers another innovation: day care centers can be established in some malls, thus giving rise to a widespread use of foster grandparent programs. Pre-school children could be dropped off in the morning, be taught, and in the early afternoons they could ride the merry-go-round with a foster grandparent who had just spent the morning shopping. Working mothers, in addition, would welcome the concentration of services. If spas and health clubs were included, the working mother could potentially have a place to buy groceries, leave the pre-school child, shop, and exercise all in one stop.

The marketing of shopping malls as the center of social life is a tremendous innovation. Offering shopping and entertainment services in a higher concentration constitutes a formidable response to the threat faced by the shopping mall industry. The Herscu idea of hypermarkets befits a society centered on the continuous consumption of products and services. Whether or not the Hooker malls prove profitable depends on how the concept is executed. The purchase of Bonwit Teller, however, and the opening of malls in growing markets such as Colorado, South Carolina, and Florida work nicely together, thus enhancing the chances of success. Herscu's attempt to turn shopping malls into miniature shopping vacation resorts stands a fair chance in a market economy such as ours.

Opportunities

The ability to recognize opportunities does not entail rare insight, rather, it implies a sensitive awareness of trends as they emerge. The truth of the matter is that everyday events reveal changes in the direction of the trends that shape the evolution of markets and industries. In a market economy, moreover, trends are identified by profits. Thus when the basic forces affecting the current context are foremost in the executive's mind, it is easier to identify the lines of business in which a firm should concentrate.

The emergence of Primerica as a force in the financial services business is a case in point. Primerica, formerly American Can, found itself caught in a situation in which its traditional bread and butter, can manufacturing, had flat growth, and its profits were squeezed. The manufacturing sector of the economy was in a period of decline as the service sector took center stage. William Woodside realized the significance the emergence of the services sector held for the future. Recognizing that future opportunities lay in the services sector, Woodside welcomed the ideas of Gerard Tsai who had joined the firm in 1981 as an executive vice president.

During this time Primerica recognized the need to shift its focus from its traditional lines of businesses towards the growing financial services sector. To accomplish this goal, the declining and stagnant manufacturing SBUs were sold off and new SBUs in the insurance, mutual fund, and investment sectors were acquired as Tsai envisioned. The gradual refocusing of the portfolio was complete by 1987 with the acquisition of Smith Barney. Tsai, named CEO in 1986 and chairman in 1987, had engineered a dramatic turnaround. In realizing that growth areas signal trends, Primerica saw the clear, long-term opportunities in the financial services sector. The role and purpose for each SBU was radically altered by the explicit decision to enter new lines of business. The portfolio under Tsai reflects the introduction of widespread strategic thinking: new SBUs, new organizational links among the SBUs, and the targeting of different markets. The result is remarkable: in five years a new firm has emerged prepared to exploit business opportunities in growing markets.

Whether the acquisition of Smith Barney in the spring of 1987 will make Primerica a major force in the financial service sector remains to be seen. The early indications, however, are that in the same manner that Primerica has identified opportunities as they emerged, it is prepared to continue taking steps to make its vision a reality. In the summer of 1987 Standard & Poor's Corp. removed Primerica issues from its CreditWatch list, thus signaling growing confidence that the acquisition of Smith Barney will contribute to Primerica's future. The risks taken by Tsai in changing the focus of his firm's activities has thus far been well received. The naming of Kenneth Yarnell, Jr., as President of Primerica in the summer of 1987 signaled a shift to relying on leadership with a proven track record. Yarnell's background complements Primerica's chosen strategy. Having helped Tsai engineer the acquisition of Smith Barney, Yarnell's area of expertise is mergers. His work during his tenure so far indicates that he will help Primerica achieve its long-term goals. In early August 1987, for example, Primerica announced its planned divestiture of its mail order business, Fingerhut Corporation. The proceeds were scheduled to retire debt incurred during the acquisition of Smith Barney. Here, then, is a dual benefit to Primerica: divest an SBU facing stiff competition and shrinking profit margins while at the same time retiring debt to strengthen its financial position to improve the firm's portfolio. By following the money, Primerica has divested itself of the SBUs not profitting from the identified opportunities, thus freeing up resources for the acquisition of strategic business. It is now poised to become a formidable force in its chosen market.

POSITIONAL STRATEGIES

At this point the firm is able to formulate positional strategies. The strategy recommendations emerging from the analysis of context and market area planning are the basis for the definition and refinement of competitive strategies. It is worthy to note a firm's success upon reaching its goals depends on how it positions itself in the marketplace. In many cases position is everything. Strategic thinking requires a comprehensive effort to position the firm's products in the selected market niches aimed at securing market leadership positions. The proper management of the portfolio requires the careful definition of objectives. The role of the corporate strategist is to align goals with realistic expectations as determined by the economic realities of the business environment and the prevailing opportunity cost as reflected in the performance of the constant-dollar Dow.

Theory of Relativity

This task appears formidable. It is not. It does, however, allude to the ability of the firm to draw on experienced and capable managers to use the structure of lines of expertise and market area planning to create a set of unique differentiations among products for specific market segments. The assumption, then, is that the portfolio's strategy must be to build on the principles of thorough market area planning, which is enhanced by the complementary nature of the internal organizational structure. In this manner the corporate officer is able to formulate superior strategies relative to those of the competition.

A story is told of two men who go camping in woods where bears have been spotted on occasion. As the men leave their camp to go on a hike into the dense wilderness, one pauses for a moment, sits on a stump and proceeds to put on his favorite pair of running shoes, which he had in his knapsack. His friend looks at him, caught by surprise by this seeming waste of time, and asks, "Why are you putting on your sneakers?" "Bears," his seated friend responds. "Bears? But no man alive can outrun a bear!" he says, with a perplexed, if not amused, expression on his face. His friend, tying the last of his laces, looks up slowly to his friend and smiles shyly. "I don't have to run faster than a bear," he begins, "I only have to run faster than *you*"

It is the relative strength of strategies that determines winners in a market economy. The West Germans and Japanese are not perfect, but they are relying on superior strategies born from an internal corporate discipline and structure that well serves the superior market planning techniques employed. The creation of superior positional strategies is facilitated by understanding the strategic objectives of the firm, strong leadership with a clear vision of the firm's place in the marketplace, and an aggressive marketing effort capable of securing the targeted market position. These three components are further detailed as follows:

Strategic Objectives—The near- and long-term growth goals of the firm are identified. At the same time the minimum near- and long-term profitability requirements are outlined. Once the growth and profitability benchmarks are determined, corporate management can identify the measures necessary in order to accomplish the growth and profitability projections. The success of the firm to coordinate SBU activities to meet the overall portfolio goals depends on the strategic flexibility. This flexibility, in turn, is a measure of the entry and exit barriers of any market. Thus the level of commitment required at the onset of portfolio management is a function of these barriers. Since an SBU's mobility is limited by entry and exit barriers, the lower the mobility level, the greater resource commitment required. The opposite it true; the higher the mobility level, the greater the strategic flexibility. The officer who fails to realize the importance of strategic flexibility increases the chances that the growth and profitability goals will not be realized.

Leadership with Vision—Success in securing a market leadership position is based on bold leadership moves. The heightened state of competition in the business environment and the uncertainty of the patterns emerging in the macroeconomic policies of the industrialized states pose threats to continued growth. The priority for the firm, then, is to ensure its future. An efficient mechanism for accomplishing this end is for the portfolio to secure strategic market positions for its SBUs. The aim is to maintain an optimal growth and profitability mix within the portfolio. This promotes a sense of continuity and leadership stability.

The prerequisite, however, is management leadership with vision that can incorporate long-term, broad-based, contextual considerations of future political economy of markets and industries into strategies. The leadership with vision required for positional strategies is competent managers who can perform the following functions:

- Identify future goals—A defined vision of the future of the firm should be kept in mind. The steps necessary to make it a reality must be outlined, and corporate strategies need to reflect the parameters in which the firm's business units operate so as to stay on course.

- Establish objectives—The officer needs to establish priorities and to define the role different technologies play in the firm's future. In the future the use of technology as a marketing weapon will be more apparent. Therefore the competitive strategies chosen must be sensitive to technology's enhanced role.

- Assign SBU missions—Each business unit must have precise orders, the human and financial resources necessary to carry out their missions, and a set of links to the other SBUs in the portfolio. These allow the firm to benefit not only from economies of scale, but economies of scope as well.

- Determine risk adversity levels—The acceptable levels of risktaking need to be explicitly conveyed to line managers. In times of higher turbulence, higher risktaking is appropriate. Management with vision understands the need to take more calculated risks and the flexibility that each SBU needs when determining individual risk adversity levels.

- Establish portfolio balance—The portfolio's business units must be well balanced. As each pursues opportunities in the different niches of the related lines of business targeted, the product life cycles, the introduction of new products, and the withdrawal of old ones must be reviewed on a continuing basis. The final portfolio product matrix, however, must conform to the long-term goals of the firm.

- Determine Resource Commitment—The willingness to take risks is revealed through management's commitment of resources to SBUs and individual projects. Conscious efforts to seek resources, provide funding, assign competent personnel, and ensure future access to input reveal the leadership's commitment to an SBU. Recall the lack of commitment of PTG to its international business unit and what it says about the PTG's management's vision of the firm's future.

- Identify Threats/Opportunities—Here is where true leadership manifests itself. Managers who can anticipate threats in the medium and long term and managers who can seize emerging opportunities are rare indeed. The fact that corporate America has failed to be abreast of the market poses formidable obstacles which have not been overcome, as the trade imbalance figures demonstrate.

- Anticipatory Strategies—It follows that the process by which competitive strategies are developed is continuously changing to meet the constant challenges posed by changing markets and customer preferences. As such, what distinguishes superior leadership is the ability to anticipate which emerging trend offers opportunities and foreshadows changes in the marketplace that will affect the firm's fortunes.

- Implementation—The single most important trait that identifies true leadership, however, is action. Strategies must be implemented. The most insightful analysis and the most opportune strategies are of little use if no action is taken. The mark of leadership with vision is the officer whose exercise in strategic thinking ends with policies that are implemented. Thought without action is futile.

Aggressive marketing—The third component is a highly aggressive marketing campaign. In the struggle to implement strategies to gain position, the uninitiated face formidable obstacles. It is no longer sufficient to define a set of strategic objectives. It is no longer enough for leadership with vision. These must work in conjunction with an aggressive marketing effort. The firm must convince the customer that it can meet the needs of its value chains. The firm must be in a position to deliver its products and services in a consistently satisfactory manner. This allows for the high market share that secures a market position that is easily defended.

The ability of the firm to create a portfolio capable of winning customer loyalty hedges on offering a cost competitive, differentiated product. The firm can offer value through a portfolio characterized by a high technology mix. The firm's portfolio must have superior market positions *vis-à-vis* competitor positions. This can only be accomplished through a renewed effort in the marketing functions. The stellar growth of Liz Claiborne rests on the husband and wife team of Liz Claiborne Ortenberg and Arthur Ortenberg. While it is Claiborne who oversees the design, clothing production, and compilation of six seasons, it is Ortenberg who is responsible for their firm's unique marketing program. Through a disciplined program that is unwavering about quality and Claiborne's keen sense of her customer's psyche, their firm is able to develop an unprecedented marketing effort. Their concentration on allocating resources for the high quality of merchandise and into features with strong customer appeal allows Claiborne to introduce an aggressive marketing effort designed to protect the image of the label and increase her control over the retail functions of the firm. In Claiborne's case the absence of a sales force that travels makes it necessary for the retail buyers to visit the firm's New York offices. The same control extends into the firm's say on the nature of in-store promotions and discounts advertised. The result is that the integrity of the label is protected, the high quality of the merchandise is foremost in the consumers' mind, and the label is so in tune with current tastes that per-square-foot sales have tripled the industry average with fewer than average price reductions required to move merchandise.

The success of Claiborne illustrates how an aggressive marketing effort can be successfully launched when a product's differentiation—the highest quality and style plus the market focus of meeting the clothing needs of the modern business woman—enhances the firm's relative standing among its competitors, thus assuring the firm that its efforts will be rewarded. An aggressive marketing campaign that takes risks through innovation is an appropriate mechanism for the success of the firm. As Claiborne suggests, while it may not outrun a bear, it is miles ahead of the competition. Here, then, a coherent program that tries to enhance relative standing through strategic objectives implemented through strong leadership and supported by an aggressive marketing effort has met with superior success. Corporate America can succeed.

An aggressive marketing program can take the form of identifying a market subset and enhancing the targeted audience's value chain. The firm that is able to identify a customer profile and then proceeds to identify the needs of this customer is in a position to understand what products or services are required. The identification of a market niche is fundamental to any successful marketing program. New York's Grand Bay Hotel is a fine example of identifying target markets.

As a new hotel opening in New York during a time when significant hotel space has gone onto the market, the Grand Bay followed a strategy of identifying a given customer profile and catering to the needs of its selected market niche. The Grand Bay's strategy is a simple one: meet the needs of demanding business travelers who are accustomed to comfort and pampering. The new 200–unit New York hotel on 51st Street at 7th Avenue has taken great care to assure that it can give the weary business traveler an oasis of comfort and luxury in the midst of midtown Manhattan. As James Petersen, the hotel's controller said, "Our purpose is to pamper the sophisticated traveler. All our efforts - which began months before the hotel opened its doors - were aimed at ensuring that that small segment of demanding and hurried business travelers find in this hotel the comforts and attention which are too rare in our industry. This is a small segment of upper level management businessmen that is not used to the mass appeal of other mass market hotel chains."

The result is striking; the Grand Bay has a certain personality and level of service that distinguishes it from other hotels catering to business travelers. The understated hotel's success is assured given a sophisticated marketing campaign that identifies its targeted audience. In the course of operation thus far the hotel's objectives have been met. In much the same manner that Liz Claiborne's subtle marketing strategies have paid off handsomely, so will the Grand Bay's pay off also. The success of this hotel in a market that is characterized by an excess supply demonstrates that thoughtful strategies carefully implemented are successful. Liz Claiborne and the Grand Bay demonstrate that aggressive marketing campaigns do not have to be accompanied by much fanfare to be successful.

NOTE

1. Copies of the Club of Rome's publications may be obtained by writing:
Club of Rome
1325 6 Street NW #1003
Washington, DC 20005
(202) 879–3038

13

STRATEGIC THINKING FOR TURBULENT MARKETS

The manner in which positional strategies are implemented, however, must reflect the turbulent and volatile nature of the business environment today. The world economic context in which we operate is one characterized by slower, erratic, and unpredictable growth. As the effects of the continuing structural deficits spill across borders, the effects associated with an overextension of debt become apparent throughout societies and economies. The economies of Japan and West Germany, along with that of the United States, are growing at slower paces. Their ability to absorb U.S. exports diminishes as these economies mature and as birth rates stabilize. The newly industrialized nations, on the other hand, have the potential for growth for two reasons: rising populations representing potential future markets and vast resources which have yet to be harnessed. The illiquidity in the international financial markets and the overextension of debt by such countries as Brazil, Mexico, and the Philippines, however, lead to a cycle of bust and booms as a steady and manageable stream of credits is uncertain.

The result is a world in which economies grow at sharply different rates, business cycles are exaggerated by the turbulence in the international financial markets, and foreign multinationals can exploit the economies of scale possible through off-shore production facilities, sophisticated distribution systems, and aggressive marketing campaigns. The results are tenuous institutional practices and intensified competition at all stages of the value chain. It is more difficult to secure defendable market niches and to offer to customers a service for which there is no substitute.

The corporate officer must realize the underlying principles affecting the observed economic performance which will in all probability remain in place for the remainder of the century. Strategies designed to position the firm in market leadership positions must be sensitive to the circumstances of the economic environment in which we live. The consideration of context refers not only to the national and global economic circumstances but also to the particular obstacles which have come about due to the persistence of structural deficits. The mounting foreign and domestic debt problems and the continuing disjoint movements in economic developments in the industralized West, coupled with the exchange rate advantages of such nations as Taiwan, Korea, and Mexico represent major components in the analysis of the socioeconomic considerations of corporate strategies.

The global village requires managers with a greater breadth of knowledge and experience. The predicted continuance of a turbulent and volatile economy calls for sophisticated and knowledgeable managers who understand the complexities of the economic milieu and can lead corporate America to sustained competitive advantage. Today's turbulence and volatility require nothing less. The same turbulence and volatility reduce the effectiveness of some strategies.

In today's business environment, proper portfolio management must avoid corporate suicide through the implementation of inappropriate strategies. Given the context in which firms must operate, there are certain practices that impair the firm to establish competitive strategies. The dangers of product imitation, buying competitors, overdiversification, and inappropriate political acclimation are pervasive.

PRODUCT IMITATION

A firm that imitates the product differentiation or strategies of its competitors undermines it long-term prospects. The advantage of strategic thinking lies in its ability to change the terms of trade within an industry or specific markets through the introduction of new products and new services or the creation of new markets that can benefit innovative production methods and expanded network linkages. It becomes clear that the very essence of the strategic thinking process centers on innovation. The linking of various services by American Express, for one, is a vivid example of a firm seeking to establish a sustainable competitive advantage through the linking of services and products used by the business traveler, such as travel agents, charge cards, and travelers' checks. Whether or not American Express can continue to succeed by facilitating these functions depends on how these services are packaged and marketed to the customer. Its track record thus far, however, indicates that American Express can count on the ability of its managers and its exemplary use of strategic thinking to develop and implement strategies that can deliver a sustainable advantage.

BUYING COMPETITORS

The free market system is an evolutionary process in which inferior business performance and strategies are discontinued. The problem, however, lies in the tendency to disguise structural flaws as a way of pretending they do not exist, as if denial would render them powerless. This is not the case. In fact, the failure to confront problems head on means the effects of these flaws will emerge as a stronger force later on. The nature of the competitive environment in which we live, however, has resulted in a disturbing practice: buying the competition instead of beating it. For the kind of strategic thinking envisioned in the present discussion, there are dangers to unstructured consolidations within industries that are not the result of market forces. The short-term benefits of acquiring competition quickly evaporates, leaving the firm weaker. The tendency to buy the competition, however, reveals the lack of vision and the absence of remarkable leadership. The dependency on growth through buyouts, however, is self-defeating in the long run. In the final analysis it becomes clear that the competition must be beaten in the marketplace and not acquired.

OVERDIVERSIFICATION

The implementation of lines of expertise reduces the temptation to enter lines of business in which the firm has no competitive strategy. During the past twenty years, American firms have attempted to solve their problems through extensive diversification programs. The result, more often than not, is a far-flung empire of unrelated companies with no central area of common ground to unite them. While the firm's key business unit may be in one industry, the remainder of the business units are in a different one. When this occurs it becomes very difficult to manage the portfolio in an efficient manner. The recent fiasco at Allegis Corporation illustrates the problems of overdiversification. The purpose of Richard Ferris in transforming UAL, Inc., into Allegis was to establish a partnership among the various needs of travelers. After the acquisition of RCA's Hertz unit in June 1985, coupled with the purchase of Pan American World Airways' Pacific routes, Ferris was now in a position to create links among the three business units—United Airlines, Westin Hotels, and Hertz. In this manner, the functions of air travel, car rentals, and hotel accommodations could be linked together, affording the customer new conveniences and user benefits. "Our mission," Ferris declared, "is to use that partnership to care for travelers worldwide.... Allegis is the umbrella for a set of quality and service expectations we want our customers to have when they deal with any one of our companies."[1] This strategy was misguided for a simple reason: Allegis was but a glorified travel agency, and a bad one at that, for it could only book a customer within its system. The Allegis travel services portfolio was overdiversified in relation to management experience, and Ferris was unable to find an adequate management system that could establish the lines of expertise required for his strategy to work. As the level of quality at the units declined and as resistance from both employees and shareholders grew, there were increasing pressures on Ferris to sell off some companies and abandon the partnership strategy. The continuing resistance to Ferris increased as it became apparent that the overall strategy was unworkable. The crisis in confidence was finally resolved with the forced resignation of Ferris in June 1987 and a new management team, headed by Frank Olson. The goal of Allegis under Mr. Olson is to divest the portfolio of Hertz and rename the firm United Airlines, Inc., thus signaling the renewed commitment to the airline industry. Frank Olson wasted no time in disbanding Allegis. One of the hotel units was the first to be sold. On September 4, 1987 Allegis announced the sale of Hilton Hotels to Ladbroke Group PLC. On October 3, 1987 Allegis announced the sale of Hertz Corp. to a group backed by the Ford Motor Co. and later that month the international hotel chain, Westin Hotels and Resorts, was sold to Robert M. Bass Group and to Japan's Aoki Corp. Frank Olson left Allegis and returned to the helm of Hertz Corp. The remaining SBU, United Airlines, is implementing an extensive program to increase its fleet for the purposes of enhancing its ability to service its airline traffic and to incur sufficient debt to discourage hostile bids for control of the firm.

INAPPROPRIATE POLITICAL ACCLIMATION

Strategies that neglect to have the right person for the right job and the right product for the right market will fail. The tendency to approach a business situation from an clinical point of view and to evaluate the circumstances only in dollars and cents paints a one-dimensional portrait of reality. Depth comes to any analysis from realizing the importance of chemistry in business. The value of an individual manager who is the right person for the job creates a dynamism that ensures success. Alan Greenberg, Bears Stearns' CEO, is a case in point. During the course of a decade, Greenberg has made his firm one of the three most profitable Wall Street banks around. His program, centered on focusing on retail brokerage and an expansion financed by a 1985 public offering, has been successful. Greenberg's insistence on working the trading floor daily, coupled with his insistence on hiring people with potential (disregarding Wall Street's love affair with Ivy League MBAs) and his hands-on management style have made Bears Stearns highly profitable. Here is a manager who is perfect for his job, driven by a sense of purpose and a clear vision of his firm's place in its industry. The right political acclimation results in the right kind of chemistry.

The inferior strategies of product imitation, buying out the competition, overdiversification, and poor political acclimation are the roads to corporate suicide. Special care must be taken if the pitfalls are to be avoided, as American Express and Bears Stearns have done. One mechanism that ensures that these troubling strategies are routinely eliminated from the body of the firm's strategic thinking is contingency planning for unforeseen events. This fits nicely into market area planning, for it offers the firm the opportunity to evaluate the likelihood and impact of the new forces shaping the business environment. The fact that many firms fail to avoid these classic pitfalls implies that many corporate strategists have failed to understand the need for a creative approach to the business of conducting business. The world is a turbulent and volatile place. The strategic thinking process of corporate America needs to adapt to these new realities.

THE IMPACT OF SBU SHOCKS

The aim of strategic planning is to reduce the level of uncertainty in the marketplace. It cannot, however, eliminate all the unknowns. The best laid strategies cannot guarantee that an SBU will not suffer a market shock from unexpected events. The impact of sudden customer preference changes, commodity shocks, unseen or underestimated threats, product innovations, or technological changes are the major factors contributing to SBU shocks. These unpredictable events interfere with the SBU's ability to accomplish its strategic mission.

EFFECTS ON SBU

The disruptive effects of a market shock on an SBU's ability to perform as its agenda requires poses a series of complications that at times endanger the very viability of the SBU. The effects of major market and industry shocks result in loss of profits, paralysis of growth, considerable damage control expenses, and opportunity costs. In the face of shocks, the priority of the firm is to confront the potential spillover effects of an SBU shock on the rest of the portfolio. The most challenging task of top management is to redirect activities of the affected SBU, or SBU project, and to protect the ripple effect that can run through the portfolio's interrelated activities.

Loss of Profits

Once a shock has been set in motion, reactive measures are necessary to stem loss of profits. Management analysis must center on the time frame required to minimize loss of profits. The degree of turbulence sets in motion a series of events that wipe out any profits. The magnitude of lost profits depends on three factors: how unexpected the shock is, how long it lasts, and how slow the firm is to respond. The aim of management is to take measures that reduce the loss of profits in the shortest time span possible.

Arrested Growth

An inherent aspect of lost profit containment is the notion of arrested growth. The SBU suffering from a shock is in a position of vulnerability. Competing firms may seize this opportunity to build market shares. The original growth plans, which are closely linked to profitability, are adversely affected by the existence of a shock. How long it takes for the SBU to adjust to the new circumstances will determine the extent to which expected growth rates fail to be realized.

Damage Control Costs

In the response process the SBU, as well as the portfolio as a whole, incurs damage-control costs. The resources required to determine the extent of damage, the needed strategic plan modifications, and the appropriate resource and time commitments necessary to make up for lost time and direct the SBU towards the original plans constitute damage-control costs. Often times entire plans have to be replaced, for an event capable of triggering a shock is of enough significance to affect in fundamental ways the nature of the industry or market in which an SBU operates.

Opportunity Costs

There are, however, instances when plans cannot be modified for they have become obsolete. In such cases the firm is faced with an endgame situation. A shock capable of rendering strategic plans obsolete represents great opportunity costs for the firm. The mere existence of such a condition indicates that the original strategic plans, resources committed, and time spent on the plans was misguided. The implication is that the firm suffered incalculable opportunity costs in a fruitless venture. The SBU or SBU project so affected by the shock should then be abandoned and a new strategy pursued.

EFFECT ON PORTFOLIO

The fate of any single SBU affects the overall returns of the portfolio. It is not enough to isolate an individual SBU or SBU project, for the synergy of a horizontal organizational structure is built on a complex interdependence among the business units within a portfolio. No firm, moreover, can implant lines of expertise unless all the SBUs within the portfolio are prosperous within the strategic areas targeted. To check the progress of each SBU relative to management expectations, the firm should adopt a planned management program. The increased level of turbulence and competition today requires a reduction in the Reactive and Decisive management techniques in use. The corporate officer's dependence on reactive and decisive management techniques reduces his or her effectiveness.

Reactive management is one in which threats are not identified as they become apparent and a firm's response to negative developments is delayed until damage is done. Decisive management, while more forward looking, fares poorly in disturbed economic times. While Decisive management identifies threats as they become evident, countering measures do not prevent the impact of the threat. Although the negative effects of the threats are reduced, there is nonetheless a disruption in the activities of the firm.

The danger lies in random discontinuities in the firm's ability to pursue its competitive strategies. The portfolio that can best sustain SBU shocks is one which uses planned management techniques. A firm that relies on scenario planning is in a position to analyze different opportunity/threat contingency plans. Strategic and operational considerations of potential repercussions must be reflected in the extrapolative or entrepreneurial management in place through planned responses. The goal of management in the wake of SBU shocks is to minimize portfolio losses, arrest opportunity costs, redirect the affected SBU's competitive strategies, modify supporting or complementary SBU activity, and if necessary, decide on an endgame course of action.

Minimize Lost Profits

The proper role of management is to minimize the loss of firm profits due to an SBU shock. The relationship between corporate managers and the SBU is to enact policies that can anticipate threats and contain loss of profits. SBU shocks, moreover, serve to indicate weaknesses in competitive strategies and identify turbulent lines of business. The overall portfolio, then, stands to benefit from corporate management that expects the unexpected. In this manner, planned management must be geared to insulate the remaining SBUs from the shocks. This is more readily accomplished through horizontal linkages and an extrapolative or entrepreneurial approach reaching SBU missions.

Arrest Opportunity Costs

The pursuit of planned management is to identify SBUs whose competitive strategies have the greater likelihood of failure. This is especially important for SBUs charged with entrepreneurial activities or which are penetrating or developing new markets. The deliberate posturing of plans capable of dealing with failed strategies at the onset allow the firm the ability of arresting opportunity costs for the entire portfolio. The objective of diversifying within a specific range of lines of business requires that the selection of market segments and products offered work together to constitute lines of expertise. For this reason opportunity costs represent a significant threat to the integrity of the portfolio.

Redirect Affected SBUs' Competitive Strategies

The impact of a shock on an SBU is a serious matter. It can affect an individual SBU project or the entire role of that SBU in the portfolio. The purpose of the SBU must be reexamined in the wake of a realized threat. To this end, an SBU's competitive strategies, as well as SBU projects, must consider the new circumstances under which the firm operates. Corporate management must redirect its energies into evaluating the long-term implications of a shock on the overall strategy of the firm. If the responsiveness to market realities is to be enhanced, there must be a continuous process by which competitive strategies are redirected in order to channel corporate resources into the optimal activities. This entails the redirection of an individual SBU's competitive strategies or the reassessment of an individual project.

Modify Supporting and Complementary SBU Activities

This must be extended to the entire portfolio. Depending on how sophisticated the horizontal organizational structure is, supporting and complementary SBU activities must be modified in keeping with the new direction of the affected SBU. In order to exploit the interrelationships among the SBUs a certain amount of trouble spillover is inevitable. When shocks occur, the effects are not contained to one SBU or a single project. The extent of the spillover, however, depends on how extensive the horizontal structure is throughout the portfolio. The greater the use of interrelationships, the greater the need to modify the activities of the other SBUs to the new conditions. Moreover, if a portfolio is to work together, it must incorporate supporting and complementary functions that increase the ability of an SBU to accomplish its mission.

Endgame

There are instances, however, when certain SBUs can be sacrificed for the greater good of the long-term goals of the firm. If planned management is to be thorough, it must include endgame strategies. Corporate management must establish criteria that determine when a stock indicates a structural flaw in a firm's competitive strategies thus throwing the *raison d'être* for a project or an entire SBU into question. The experiences of American firms during the past two decades have been characterized by an inability to balance the need for long term commitment to competitive strategies with the advantages of identifying misguided approaches early on. Endgame strategies are intended to suspend misdirected implementations of competitive strategies. While the strategies themselves must be redefined on an ongoing basis, the portfolio's general competitive strategies must be sound from the start. A steady stream of SBU shocks within a portfolio indicates misconceived strategies as well as poor execution of plans. In these cases no endgame strategy can preserve the integrity of the firm's vision.

The benefit of a planned management approach to the administration of corporate portfolios is twofold. The foremost consideration is the nature of planned management. The existence of contingency plans minimizes damage to the portfolio, thus reducing the damaging time lag characterized by reactive and decisive management approaches. The firm able to reduce the disruptions inherent in SBU shocks can better withstand the uncertainties realized threats pose. The second advantage from a planned management approach centers on the effortless incorporation of scenario contingency plans into extrapolative and entrepreneurial management styles within the SBUs. The planned direction from the firm to the SBUs supports their activities and fits well with the expressed goal of developing the use of interrelationships.

NOTE

1. Richard J. Ferris, "From Now On . . . ," *Vis à Vis*, March 1987, p. 13.

14

PORTFOLIO STRATEGIES

The complex issues surrounding the analysis of a firm's business unit pose a series of challenges to corporate officers. If useful evaluations of an SBU's performance are to be made, and if just comparisons among the SBUs within a portfolio are to yield valuable information, analysis tools are needed. In recent years a series of analysis tools for ranking and evaluating the various SBUs within a portfolio have been popularized. The idea behind these various grids and charts is that a well managed firm contains a well balanced combination of business units. SBUs that do not contribute to the overall goals of the firm are shut down or divested, while profitable and promising business units are nurtured. In this manner corporate business units can be managed and sound portfolio strategies can be implemented.

These portfolio grids, or matrices, are two-dimensional graphical representations of the business units within a firm's portfolio. They are used as a method of ranking and comparing a firm's SBUs relative to each other as well as representing the markets in which these business units compete. Their utility as strategic planning tools stem from their ability to suggest in a graphic manner the strategic choices available to an individual SBU. Thus an analysis of the SBU's present position facilitates adopting a plan of action for the SBU in question. These portfolio matrices help determine an SBU's relative competitive position, redistribute strategic resources throughout the portfolio, and identify which SBUs should be divested. The two axes usually measure an SBU's competitive position in relation to its future prospects.

THE BCG GROWTH/SHARE MATRIX

One of the most popular portfolio grid techniques is the growth/share matrix. First introduced by the Boston Consulting Group (BCG), it is frequently referred to as the BCG matrix. The BCG matrix uses volume growth as the criterion for measuring future prospects and market share to evaluate the SBU's competitive position. Growth is represented on the vertical axis, while market share is plotted on the horizontal axis.

For each SBU, estimates are obtained for future growth rate and current market share. Market share is determined by dividing volume sales of the individual SBU by volume sales of the leading competitor in the given market. Relative market share is used as opposed to an absolute market share measurement, since it is a better indicator of the strength of the SBU's market position. Consider an SBU with a 20 percent market share. In a segmented industry with many competitors, this may prove to be a fairly strong market share. In a consolidated market, however, with a dominant market leader, this 20 percent would be relatively weak. A market leader will tend to have a relative market share of greater than one, and a 1.5 cutoff is a standard indicator of market dominance, where the SBU's sales are 1.5 times greater than that of the competition. Past growth rates are typically used for the projected volume growth estimate. To determine whether an SBU is exhibiting high or low growth, historical industry averages are used.

Using these estimates the individual SBUs are plotted on a grid (see Figure 14.1). Each SBU is typically represented by a circle with its diameter being proportional to its expected future demand or sales. The placement of the SBUs on the grid illustrates possible courses of action. There are four quadrants on the grid. Each grid is named to reveal the contribution to the overall portfolio by an SBU located within its parameters. The SBUs are thus classified as either Stars, Cows, Dogs, or Question Marks depending on their location on the BCG matrix (see Figure 14.2). An SBU can overlap the boundaries of the quadrants. This serves to reveal either movement, an SBU leaving one quadrant and entering another, or characteristics, an SBU having characteristics of several quadrants in any given time.

Stars

Star SBUs are those that have the most potential. They have experienced the highest growth and the largest market share of the portfolio. Although they often generate large amounts of cash due to their large market share, they also require large amounts of capital to fund their growth. The net result is an SBU with modest (either positive or negative) cash flow that requires very little resources from the firm. Figure 14.1

Figure 14.1
The Growth/Share Matrix

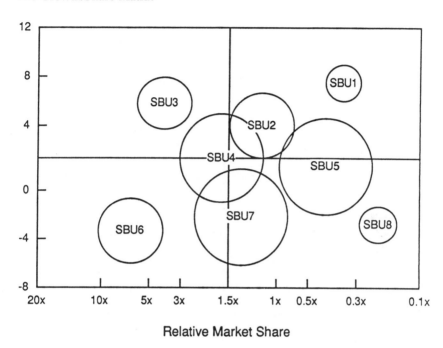

Relative Market Share

Source: International Credit Monitor.

shows that SBU3 exhibits Star characteristics. This SBU is characterized
by its market leadership position and its high growth rate.

Cows

SBUs defined as cash Cows are the work horses of the firm. They are
solidly entrenched in their markets, generating more cash than they
need to fund their low, stable growth. The excess funds are thus available
for use by other SBUs. As the name suggests, these are the SBUs that
the firm "milks" to finance the other activities of the company. In the
graph provided, SBU6 is a Cow, for it generates more cash than it
requires, it is established within its markets, and it has the slow growth
characteristic of maturing markets. For these reasons it is a source of
internal financing for the other SBUs in the portfolio.

Dogs

The Dogs of the portfolio are those slated for divestiture, since they
are the least attractive of the portfolio. They have a small market share

Figure 14.2
SBU Portfolio Analysis Grid: Cash Flow and SBU Implications of the Four
Quadrants

STAR	QUESTION MARK

o Modest cash flow
o Excelent potential
o Optimize SBU
	o Cash drain
	o High growth potential/
	   low market share
	o Either optimize SBU or
	   divest SBU

CASH COW	DOG

o Large positive cash flow
o High market share/ low
   growth
o Control investment & funnel
   cash to SBUs needing it
o Mature SBU
	o Modest cash flow
	o Poor potential for growth
	o Divest SBU

Source: International Credit Monitor

and exhibit little or no growth. These SBUs generate little cash because of their poor market position. In our example, SBU8 is contributing very little to the overall portfolio in terms of sales. Its low growth and low market share status has marked this SBU as a likely target for divestiture for it requires financing without contributing to the overall performance of the portfolio. Dogs should be shut down or sold off.

Question Marks

These SBUs are those that have neither developed into Stars nor deteriorated into Dogs. Their high growth rates indicate that they have good potential, but their low market share means that large amounts of resources must be allocated to develop these Question Marks into Stars. Decisions must be made as to whether these SBUs are attractive enough to continue investing in or whether they are too much of a cash drain. In Figure 14.1, both SBU2 and SBU1 are clear Question Marks. SBU2 has a higher market share than SBU1, while SBU1 has a higher growth rate than SBU2. The decision in this instance may be to divest SBU1 and invest in SBU2 to improve its market share, since SBU1 is contributing relatively little to the overall portfolio in terms of cash generation.

Given the composition of the portfolio as represented on the BCG matrix, the firm is in a position to make decisions on how to best allocate resources among its SBUs. The firm has several courses of action to entertain. It can, for example, transfer cash from highly profitable SBUs (Cows) to developing ones (Question Marks), or to those with the potential for future profitability (Stars). The BCG matrix offers the possibility of four basic strategic moves: to increase an SBU's market share, to hold market share, to harvest, or to withdraw an SBU from a market.

Limitations to the BCG Matrix

The utility of the BCG matrix is limited. The benefits offered by the matrix stem from its role in plotting the market positions of the SBUs and in determining how to optimize the allocation of resources among the portfolio's SBUs. The use of the matrix in conjunction with an objective reference barometer offers more utility. In times of economic turbulence, there is a need for standardized benchmarking tools by which to judge SBU performance. The matrix's relevancy is enhanced when it is used with the stock market barometer to create a context for analytic purposes. Thus the firm can compare the growth and return rates of each SBU with the stock market index to determine how the SBUs are performing given the prevailing economic environment. This becomes more important as turbulence increases. In the microchip industries, for example, the rapid turnover in technologies results in profitless growth. The airlines offer another example of an industry in which merciless, cut-throat competition means profits decline as the number of passengers flown increases. Thus in these two cases, while there is "growth," profit margins erode. Traditional methods of using the matrix give better results when turbulence, technological or market, is low.

In addition to a low degree of turbulence, the utility of the matrix is highest when the market is a stable one with minor shifts in the market share status quo. Factors that contribute to an increasing or decreasing market share undermine the use of the matrix for competitive analysis of the portfolio's SBUs. The matrix, which limits itself to plotting the firm's SBUs, implies that each of the SBU's competitors will remain within reasonable market shares relative to the SBU size. The threat of new entrants or changes in market shares among existing competitors stand to redistribute an SBU's fortunes among competitors. The future must hold the same market share for the firm relative to the existing or possible new entrants.

While the matrix is invaluable in determining the competitive positions of a portfolio's SBUs given certain market share constraints, there are several problems in using the matrix as an analytic tool. The most obvious limitation centers on the inability of the matrix to perform when the presence of turbulence makes future volume growth difficult to tie to profits and when relative market shares are not stable in the short to medium term. The problems of greater concern for the strategic planner, however, go beyond the foregoing observations, for these revolve around structural assumptions of the matrix as used by strategic planners today. These limitations stem from the exclusion of product life cycles and economic context in plotting the SBUs on the matrix.

Reveal Causes—It is not enough to indicate an SBU's position on the matrix without offering an explanation or cause for the position observed. A Star ranking, for example, sheds no light on whether more investment is appropriate. The SBU may be operating at an optimal level. In such a case additional investment will result in two things: the SBU's profitability will decline and there will be opportunity costs associated with denying another SBU those resources. A Cow ranking does not reveal whether it is a mature SBU in a maturing industry and should therefore be milked, or whether there are considerations on the horizon which present opportunities or threats to the continued cow status of the SBU.

Market Shares Role—The relative size of an SBU's market share position within the industry in which it operates is an important consideration when formulating strategy. A Dog could be doing well in relation to its competitors in terms of market share or profitability. An SBU operating in a market facing economic difficulties or intense competition could do well just by holding on to what it has and minimizing long-term losses by emphasizing market share. A Question Mark could be facing similar strategic choices. If it is trying to secure a market niche position in an emerging industry, the long-term strategies could require a program of short-term uncertainty. The relative circumstances must be considered before management concludes that an SBU is positioning itself for future growth that will make it a Star or whether it is drifting aimlessly. The final decision of whether to increase or decrease resource allocation rests on the context in which the SBU operates.

Requires Foresight—The nature of the matrix presupposes that perfect foresight is possible in the sense that the positions of the SBUs can be determined in advance with low probability of variance. This in turn assumes an environment characterized by low turbulence. Thus static conditions reduce uncertainty and allow for more accurate estimates of an SBU's relative strategic positions and growth/profit generations. The problem is that there is high turbulence in the business world. The increased level of turbulence, however, encompasses not only negative volatility in a market, but also underestimates the importance of technological advances, innovations, and entrepreneurial penetration of the marketplace in business.

Assumes Rationality—The matrix assumes that the managers of each

SBU will behave in a rational and detached manner. It is clear that in the process of gathering data and soliciting opinions from each SBU manager there will be a tendency for managers to lose objectivity when evaluating their SBU performance. A logical assessment of the situation based on the facts gives way to gut feelings and individual perceptions. In addition political considerations come into play when defending or recommending increases in resource allocation and time. Managers of Cows, for example, can be expected to be against milking their SBU to finance other SBUs. There is a tendency to resist the withdrawal of investments for they believe that growth has not peaked.

Indeed, the limitations of the matrix as described present a formidable obstacle: power politics among the SBUs as they compete for resource allocation commitments from top management. To pretend that the strategic analysts can ignore the causes behind an SBU's classification as Cow, Star, Dog or Question Mark and dismiss the importance of relative market share while assuming low marketplace turbulence, confident in objective line-manager recommendations is dangerous. The analysis of the performance of the SBUs within a portfolio is a complex issue. For this reason the matrix should play a limited role in the broader context of the other analysis tools described in this discussion. The purpose of reducing the relative importance of the matrix is that a greater emphasis must be placed on making sure the SBUs work together as units of a whole towards a common goal and not against each other.

SHARE/MOMENTUM CHARTS

One of the limitations of the BCG growth/share matrix is that it presents a static representation of the portfolio. It does not indicate the progress the SBUs are making in gaining market share in their relative markets. For this reason, the BCG matrix is more useful when used in conjunction with other analysis tools. Thus the limitations of one tool are compensated for by the strengths of other tools. Along the lines of graphical methods of analysis, the share/momentum chart is useful because it offers a dynamic representation of the relative movements of the SBUs within the portfolio. In addressing these limitations it offers a more complete picture of where the SBUs are headed and indicates their progress towards realizing their strategic missions. The momentum and growth pattern of an SBU enables the corporate officer to determine whether or not an SBU can be expected to contribute to the overall performance of the portfolio.

Not unlike the BCG matrix, the share/momentum grid shows each SBU represented by a circle on a graph (see Figure 14.3). The size of the circle reflects the SBU's sales. The horizontal axis measures the SBU's growth rate within the entire portfolio. The vertical axis plots past rel-

Figure 14.3
The Share/Momentum Chart

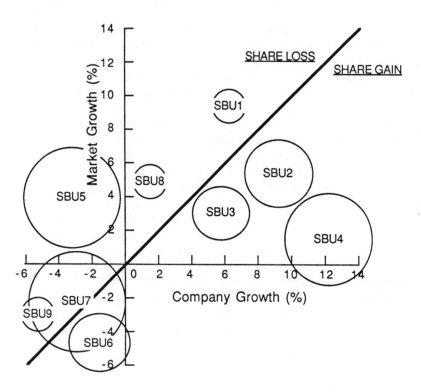

Source: International Credit Monitor.

ative market growth. SBUs below the diagonal line exhibit absolute market share gains, since these SBUs are growing at a rate that is faster than
their respective market rate. In the same manner SBUs that lie above
the diagonal line are losing relative market share. The SBUs on the
diagonal are growing at the same pace as the market. In Figure 14.3,
SBU4 is growing much faster than are its competitors in the overall
market. In the example provided, SBU4 is growing at a rate of 12 percent,
which is remarkable given that the overall market growth is flat. SBU5,
on the other hand, is losing market share in an industry with reasonable
growth potential. Now it is possible to have a more thorough understanding of the forces at work within this hypothetical portfolio. In the
BCG matrix SBU5 was on the borderline between the Question Mark
and Dog quadrants. In the share/momentum matrix, however, a different picture emerges. SBU5 is in trouble. It may be realizing profits in
the short term, but unless its market-share declines can be reversed, it
will soon become a liability and not an asset to the overall portfolio.
SBU5 should be watched carefully and divested if it becomes a Dog.

Moreover, upon careful examination an interesting thing is evident in the lower left quadrant. Both SBU6 and SBU9 are growing at negative rates. In spite of this, however, SBU6 is gaining market share. How can this be? The solution to this seeming contradiction is that the overall market is shrinking. SBU6 is growing at a negative 1 percent annual rate and the market is growing at a negative 4 percent annual rate. The net effect is that SBU6 is actually growing 3 percent relative to the overall market. SBU9 on the other hand, is declining at an annual rate of 6 percent in a market that is contracting at an annual rate of 4 percent. Thus SBU9 is losing market share in a declining market.

In the BCG matrix both SBU1 and SBU2 were Question Marks. The decision whether to invest or divest was a toss-up. Since SBU1 contributed less to the overall portfolio, the decision was to invest in SBU2. On the other hand, the share/momentum chart provides more information that confirms the conclusion reached using the BCG matrix. As Figure 14.3 illustrates, SBU2 is not only contributing more to the portfolio, it is also gaining market share. SBU1, on the other hand, is losing market share. Thus, SBU2 is enhancing its presence in the marketplace and will continue to do so. SBU1, on the other hand, is steadily losing market share, thus it appears likely that its future value to the corporate portfolio will also decline. Thus using the share/momentum matrix in conjunction with the BCG matrix offers more insightful information that is valuable when evaluating the performance of a firm's SBUs within the context of the portfolio and within the markets in which each SBU competes. A more complete appraisal of a firm's business units is now possible.

There are other tools that are of interest when analyzing the firm's portfolio. The learning curve, the profit impact analysis, and the life cycle matrix reveal information necessary in order to make investment and divestment decisions. If an optimal portfolio matrix is to be achieved, each SBU must be judged by standards that are sensitive to the various levels of context in which an SBU operates. These other tools reveal vital information about the various levels of difficulty in the strategic missions the SBUs are assigned. Poor performance may very well indicate a misguided mission rather than shortcomings by an SBU's managers. Unrealistic expectations by the same token, are easily revealed through substandard performance. The proper management of corporate business units, moreover, requires a thorough analysis of a portfolio's performance that reflects all the tools available.

THE LEARNING CURVE

The learning curve is a graphical representation of the fact that as a firm increases its experience in a given manufacturing process production costs decrease. This is illustrated in Figure 14.4. The economies of

Figure 14.4
The Learning Curve

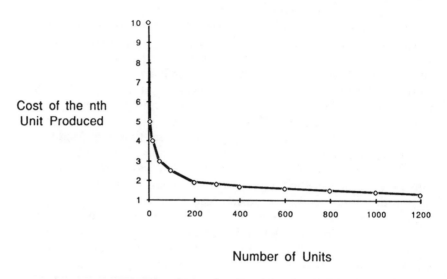

Number of Units

Source: International Credit Monitor.

scale possible through increased production also translates into economies of scope that rise from experienced managers. Initial start-up costs
for the first units are generally high. As the production process improves,
however, workers become proficient in new methods and procedures.
Thus economies of scale, improved technology, automation, bulk discounts for raw materials, standardization, and an experienced and vet-
eran work force all contribute to production cost decreases.

As production continues to increase, the costs level off. Even small
decreases in cost, however, promote the establishment of a strategic
advantage in the marketplace. To see this more precisely, consider a
start-up unit cost of five dollars per unit. By the time production reaches
1000 units, the unit cost may have decreased to one dollar. Although at
this point the slope of the learning curve may have leveled off, the unit
cost when production reaches 500,000 units (500 times as many units)
may decrease to ninety cents. At that point, this relatively minor cost
savings could position the firm as the cost leader for the given product.
Thus a sustainable competitive advantage is now within grasp.

The learning curve is integral to the portfolio analysis process since
it links market growth and competitive position concepts. It is wrong
to think that cost savings can only be achieved through improvements
in worker output. Although the greatest cost savings are obtained during

the manufacturing process, a commitment to cost leadership must be made at every level throughout the firm. The concept of organizational learning, in which the entire organization looks at ways to decrease production costs, either directly or indirectly, must be considered.

The utility of the learning curve as a portfolio analysis tool is in its ability to compare a firm's learning curve to that of the competition. In this way it can introduce context into its analysis. In determining where an SBU is positioned on its learning curve, it can begin to consider what actions are necessary either to maintain or to improve upon a market leadership position. In addition comparing an SBU's learning curve to that of the competition affords the firm information it needs to evaluate critically how its productivity and manufacturing fare relative to that of its competitors.

The market leader in a given industry, for example, will most likely be the cost leader. This is due to larger production economies of scale. Such a firm's major goal is to maintain its cost leadership position. Its relatively advanced position on the learning curve, however, implies that an extensive capital funding program will be required if costs are to be lowered further. The tradeoffs of investing this money have to be weighed carefully. The firm's resources are finite and the opportunity costs of such a financial commitment must be analyzed. There are other factors to consider as well. The construction of an automated production facility, for example, may result in a learning curve that is more steeply sloped than it would be otherwise. This would allow the SBU to decrease its unit costs more rapidly and achieve comparable pricing with a competitor without necessarily being a market leader.

PROFIT IMPACT ANALYSIS

Profit Impact Analysis was developed jointly by General Electric and the Harvard Business School as an analysis technique used to assess the strategic capability of an SBU. The technique uses historical data as the only criteria to determine the expected future performance of the various SBUs within the firm's portfolio. This affords corporate executives the benefit of basing their decisions on a large sampling of data. The benefit of a large data sampling is that it eliminates seasonal or business-cycle fluctuations. It also provides for more accurate statistical analysis. This method, however, assumes a non-turbulent marketplace and future adherance to the status quo. Thus it is more appropriate for firms using a static management structure. While less useful in times of turbulence, it should be used in conjunction with other portfolio analysis tools in order to obtain a more accurate representation of a firm's strategic position.

LIFE CYCLE MATRIX

The life cycle matrix is used to analyze the long-term composition of a firm's portfolio. It also suggests which SBUs to develop or divest to assure a balance between short- and long-term profit potential. The need for a graphical tool to assess a portfolio's short- and long-term balance is best exemplified by the concept of phased cycles. If the business cycles of a firm's SBUs are in phase, then the short-term growth and profit potential are very good. The long-term potential, however, may not be as attractive. While all SBUs for any given portfolio are, for example, Stars in the same time period, they may also become Dogs at about the same time. This could put a firm out of business. The idea is to develop a balanced portfolio over the long term, where at any one time, some SBUs are cash Cows, some are Stars, and other SBUs are being divested and new ones created.

A useful graphical representation of the life cycle balance matrix is provided here (see Figure 14.5). Each SBU is plotted on a table depicting its respective competitive position and growth potential both in the short and the long term. The SBU itself is depicted as a circle. The size of the circle reresents the SBU's relative market share. The life cycle balance matrix provides a simple tool for the corporate strategic planner. Using this approach, the balancing of a firm's portfolio is simplified. First, the SBUs are plotted on the matrix. This represents the short- and long-term profit potentials of the commodities each SBU provides. The information needed is the SBU's growth potential, its future competitive position, market share/market size, as well as expected sales, profit, and investment figures. Second, the firm's strategic objectives in each market area are determined. This is done by an internal assessment of the strategic objectives and resource commitments of the firm. The resources are then distributed among the existing SBUs in such a way that the overall portfolio is balanced. For a portfolio to be well balanced there must be a corporate commitment to both emerging SBUs, growing SBUs, and maturing SBUs. Finally, steps are identified to achieve the portfolio changes needed. This includes plans for the expansion, divestiture, or shutting down of depleted SBUs, as well as developing products and strategic missions for the new and emerging SBUs.

In the example provided here, it is easy to see that this portfolio is well balanced in the short term. There is a good mix of SBUs; some provide capital for current needs and others are poised to be the cash Cows of the future. SBU4, for example, is an emerging business unit with strong growth potential. Other SBUs, such as SBU6, SBU7, and SBU8, are mature SBUs, constituting the cash cows of the firm. These provide funds for the other SBUs of the portfolio. The emerging business units, SBU2 and SBU3, are in the early stages of growth. An examination

Figure 14.5
The Life Cycle Balance Matrix

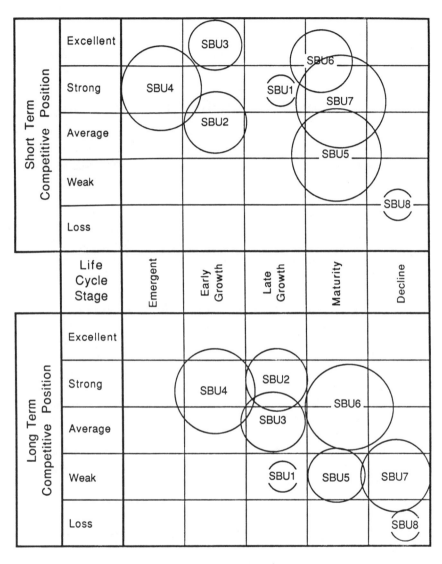

Source: International Credit Monitor.

of the long-term potential of the portfolio indicates that the SBUs reaching maturity will have lost significant market share, thus rendering them divestiture candidates. Of these, SBU5 and SBU7 are weakest and SBU4 is still the strongest, but has reached the last stages of growth. The declining growth rates of SBU2 and SBU3 reveal these will then be mature. From this analysis, it is evident that the future integrity of the portfolio requires a commitment to new and emerging SBUs. The need for viable new products capable of providing future profits is a priority. The prudent manager will take steps to develop new markets and seize opportunities to assure that the continued future growth of the firm is assured. This requires a portfolio that is well balanced in the long term.

COGNITIVE RATIONALITY AND STRATEGIC THINKING

The ideal portfolio is one in which each SBU complements the others while they all benefit from the support and economies of scale provided by top management. This ideal is rare if not impossible. Nevertheless, great emphasis must be placed on activities which attempt to maximize the benefits possible from the interrelated nature of the SBUs. To accomplish this lofty goal, top management has a responsibility to ensure that the most objective method of decisionmaking prevails. The internal cohesion of the portfolio rests on the systematic use of an adequate strategic thinking process. There are three kinds of rationality: cognitive, behavioral, and political.

Cognitive rationality is the conscious effort to evaluate the facts and other data in a logical manner, progressing towards an objective conclusion; behavioral rationality is the unconscious influences on the decisionmaking process by the individual's feelings and emotions; and political rationality is the conscious act of making decisions not based on the logic of the facts, but on individual ambitions, power drives, and alliances.

The requirement for an efficient decisionmaking process is that cognitive rationality be a part of corporate culture as much as possible. The executive officer has to realize and accept the fact that when dealing with human beings, political rationality is inevitable. An open management style of trust that treats employees as an integral part of the company goes a long way in diminishing intrigue and politicking within a company, but there will always be the politics of corporate advancement. While the firm can do only so much to minimize the importance and the proliferation of political rationality among its managers, it can make significant inroads in reducing the effects of behavioral rationality in the decisionmaking process. The most efficient manner of reducing behavioral rationality is by making it explicit that it is not acceptable and by rewarding managers who demonstrate a consistent track record of making cognitive rationality, which may not be politically shrewd, an integral aspect of their management style.

The prudent, if not Machiavellian, executive fosters an atmosphere in which managers are encouraged to be honest and are allowed to make decisions based on the facts, and not on gut reactions. ''The first impression that one gets of a ruler," Machiavelli noted, "and of his brains is from seeing the men that he has about him."[1] The same holds true for a corporate executive today. A firm whose managers are timid and spineless yes-men reveal the sin of pride in their superior officer. Arrogant bullies are the reason why American firms go bankrupt. Executives who rely on intimidating their subordinates get what they deserve: managers whose decisions reflect a disquieting reliance on behavioral and political rationalities. The economic dislocation of the past two decades supports the claim that corporate America has grown too dependent upon behavioral and political rationalities and requires a more widespread use of cognitive rationality.

Therefore it is logical to propose that the firm can achieve a higher degree of internal flexibility and increase its ability to navigate through the turbulent waters of the marketplace by rewarding consistent patterns of cognitive rationalities by line managers. An open environment is instrumental in promoting trust among the SBUs and improving the relationship of the firm to its SBUs. When such conditions exist, the open exchange of information and the evaluation of the competitive strategies pursued becomes a more precise science. The typical firm is plagued by line managers whose evaluations are biased. Managers of Cows are reluctant to admit that their growth has reached a plateau. Managers of Question Marks often foreshadow their own failure by having their lack of a track record interfere with an objective appraisal of their SBU's future prospects. In the political struggles wildcats often have resources withdrawn even though they are the potential Stars of tomorrow. Managers of Stars enjoy political clout and thus overestimate their abilities or their future growth, often receiving more resources than they can efficiently use, while managers of Dogs fear divestiture and carry little clout, ensuring their demise.

Under these circumstances the politics of mismanagement emerge as a dominant preoccupation. This does little to promote the long-term goals of the firm. A disciplined approach has often been lacking. The political infighting at many firms detracts management time and skill from the challenges of competing in the marketplace to competing in the board room. The loser in the long run is the company itself. Thus a program that encourages an efficient proliferation of the use of cognitive rationality across all SBUs within a portfolio enhances the ability of the firm to maximize the benefits derived from economies of scope. The interrelationships that exist among the SBUs must be used to promote a limber and anticipatory management style while minimizing rivalry among the SBUs.

NOTE

1. Machiavelli, *The Prince*, p. 85.

15

COMPETITIVE STRATEGIES AND NON-MARKET FORCES

There are circumstances under which no domestic firm has the resources necessary to compete against a foreign concern. The economies of scale required in many large manufacturing industries are enormous and in so being, they represent prohibitive barriers of entry to many foreign private companies. Nations with smaller natural resources and smaller populations have difficulty achieving the economies of scale necessary to compete on an international level. If these nations were to rely exclusively on market forces to create domestic companies to compete on world markets, they would be at a competitive disadvantage. The result, then, has been that many foreign governments intervene in the marketplace in several industries, from airlines to oil companies and telecommunications firms, to create firms that are often times nationalized or subsidized. Direct government intervention in the marketplace is the only efficient mechanism for many smaller nations to compete in a strategic manner with firms from the larger industrial economies. The existence of firms that respond to political as well as economic influences poses two major challenges for their American competitors.

The first consideration centers on the role governments play when they are the largest single shareholder in a company. The ability of the goverment to increase financing and its willingness to incur losses gives that foreign firm a competitive advantage over firms that do not enjoy access to government support or an understanding shareholder willing to incur losses in exchange for the promise of reaping benefits generations down the road. Many times, then, the question that impacts competitive strategies of American firms is the role of these nationalized or subsidized firms during the penetration of markets or the bidding of projects. The long-term interests of the nation are manifested in the ability of the firm to price goods and services below costs. The role of MITI in Japan, for example, is one in which the partnership between government and industry works to advance the broad goals of the nation and the role each industry plays in the nation's development. The role of government as partner creates a set of priorities that differs from firms which are markedly less political. Through its ability of giving credits and approving plans, MITI exercises an important influence over the ability of Japanese firms to carry out plans. Thus political considerations affect corporate strategies in Japan.

The terms of trade within an industry are changed when a major competitor is concerned not with market forces, but with political ones. The attempts of many U.S. carriers, such as Pan Am, to introduce a more competitive fare structure among the European cities it serves have been thwarted by the adamant refusal of the West European nations to open up their markets, which are dominated by semi-nationalized domestic airlines, to the forces of the free markets. With the exception of British Airways, which was privatized in the winter of 1987, all European airlines are government controlled, and there has been fierce political resistance to the notion of introducing competitive fare structures to flights within the European community. (The only other major private carrier, British Caledonian, was acquired by British Airways in the summer of 1987.) The ability of these airlines to charge relatively high fares on European routes allows them to subsidize overseas routes, competing with many airlines run by developing countries, most of which are former colonies. Air Afrique, for example, links France's former colonies to Paris.

The second consideration is that in many instances the nationalized or subsidized industry is viewed as a strategic industry necessary for the nation's security. In these cases the markets served by the nationalized or subsidized firm is one which the national government is not willing to allow foreign firms to enter. In the case of Aeromexico, for example, the carrier functions not in accordance to the laws of supply and demand, but in accordance to the strategic needs of the nation. The purpose of Aeromexico is to unite all the major urban areas in Mexico with air transportation regardless of the economic utility of the route. Thus many foreign firms are willing to incur losses in order to serve national goals. The goals range from supporting a national firm which is serving the domestic market, such as an airline, to providing a strategic service to the national population, such as supplying the nation's oil requirements, as is the case with British Petroleum.

The implications of these activities on global markets becomes evident when these firms are charged with strategic missions overseas. In many instances foreign firms operate overseas not to make a profit, but rather to create jobs at home. The Japanese semiconductor industry, for example, is more concerned with increasing market share and the domestic political effects of a Japanese dominance in the microchip industry than it is in making a profit in its sales in the United States. Thus foreign firms are willing to earn lower returns in their U.S. operations, or even to incur a loss, in return for higher employment at home. Foreign nationalized or subsidized firms that generate positive revenues from their international operations often times serve national goals other than employment. As the debt problems of many developing nations become critical, the focus of these firms has been to capture hard currencies or to improve the balance of payments. The criteria for continued aid and support from world financial institutions often rests on the ability of a nation to improve its economic picture. The ability to point to an improving balance of payments record helps offset failures, such as ineffective price stabilization efforts.

It becomes more difficult to compete with firms not concerned with short-term market forces. Indeed, American firms have to compete with many companies whose internal structure interferes with the natural outcome of supply and demand. The reason is that the focus of nationalized or subsidized firms is a long-term one. They are managed to operate with the future needs of their national economies in mind and can rely on short-term market intervention to subsidize future growth. In the case of Aeromexico, for example, by incurring losses on unprofitable routes, it is hoped that the communities presently served at a loss to the carrier will develop at a faster pace than they would have otherwise. Thus the future growth of these isolated communities is speeded up, and in the long term the volume of business from the growing community will make the routes profitable. The national priority of these firms determines their behavior in the marketplace. The observed behavior in international markets is one of intervention. When foreign firms compete for markets with these firms, things other than market considerations come into play. The strategies of American firms must reflect the political considerations that affect the markets served, prevailing pricing structures, and commodities offered by their competitors. Airlines competing with Aeromexico on international routes, for example, have to consider that airline's mandate to capture hard currencies. Thus a carrier with a mandate to capture U.S. dollars can be expected to economize on value-chain activities that can be supplied by Mexican companies and offer marginal in-flight service. The competitive strategy for an American competitor such as Pan Am lies in product differentiation—excellent service, in-flight amenities such as movies, and frequent-flier-mileage programs—and in targeting price-inelastic market segments—business travelers as opposed to tourists. Therefore it comes as no surprise that on the New York–Mexico City route, Pan Am targets the business traveler who demands excellent service and is willing to pay a premium for it while Aeromexico caters to tourists who fly coach and are willing to endure some inconveniences in exchange for a good bargain.

The behavior of most nationalized or subsidized firms reflects common patterns: long-term goals prevail over short-term developments, market share is a higher priority than profits. The lesson for American firms is clear. In a world characterized by nations that rely on subsidizing or controlling large firms in order to manifest national policies, the traditional myth of a perfectly competitive marketplace governed by supply and demand rarely exists. The ability of salient firms to enter the U.S. market or to compete against U.S. firms for third party markets means that these firms are willing to accept lower returns. Their priorities may lie in increasing employment at home, earning hard currencies, improving balance of payments schedules, or making a political statement. Under these conditions, the existence of non-market forces must be reflected in the strategic planning process of the firm.

It is too easy to assume that fair competition becomes impossible under these circumstances, but this is not the case. The existence of political risk considerations has always existed and will always exist. The difference is that during times of economic turbulence and technological revolutions that intensify competition, the role of these quasi-nationalized firms becomes more apparent. This is not to say that it is impossible to establish order and detect patterns of behavior whose impact can be quantified and incorporated into strategic planning. On the contrary, several discernable patterns of behavior emerge which result in predictable forces that affect the competitive environment in the global marketplace. The entry of nationalized and subsidized foreign firms into international markets results in increased competition, greater turbulence, higher levels of consolidation within the U.S. economy, and an increase in joint ventures between American firms and foreign companies.

INCREASED COMPETITION

As the effects of the structural deficits and increased turbulence become more apparent, the increased competition in domestic and foreign markets will lead to lower profits. The national economies of the industralized states are increasingly characterized by erratic and slower growth rates. The consequence of slower growth rates and stiffer competition is to put pressures on reducing operating costs and eating away at profit margins. Thus as the focus of competition turns to defending existing market shares, lower profitability can be expected. This will be acerbated by the rise in the inflation rate. There are increasing pressures to monetize portions of the outstanding debt, which cannot be ignored as a politically viable alternative, especially in the wake of slowing economic growth rates. The persistence of structural deficits, increased foreign competition, falling domestic productivity, and lackluster growth will put a squeeze on profit margins.

GREATER TURBULENCE

The interaction of domestic macroeconomic forces and the differing priorities of other nations increase the level of uncertainty in the world arena. The increasing level of uncertainty requires greater flexibility in strategic plans and more widespread use of broad-based analysis tools capable of identifying threats and opportunities early on. In terms of market area planning, greater weight must be given to determining the economic and political context existing in various industries while the utility of tools, such as the BCG matrix, diminishes. The importance of political risk exposure rises, as does the importance of risk taking. The higher levels of turbulence mandate a higher willingness to make bold moves. In the natural intercourse of market forces and competing national interests, the absence of international monetary arrangements and the continuing third world debt crisis necessitates the increased use of scenario planning and focused strategic planning. Increased turbulence puts market leadership positions up for grabs.

INDUSTRY CONSOLIDATIONS

A natural outcome of the increased competition, higher levels of economic and political uncertainty, and the role of non-market factors is an increased tendency towards consolidation within beleaguered industries. The rise in merger and acquisition activities in the United States underscores the subconscious need for achieving greater economies of scale. As if Adam Smith's invisible hand was the moving force, major consolidations in the banking, airline, and semiconductor industries reveal the significant role economies of scale play in competing against formidable companies from abroad. The consolidation within these industries suggests that the need for the elimination of waste, the combining of R&D facilities, the extending of networks and, at times, radical changes in management—labor relationships rather than partnerships—is a requisite to the emergence of firms better able to compete on an international level.

INCREASED JOINT VENTURES

Under these conditions American firms will seek joint ventures with other U.S. firms or foreign firms to bid in and to enter markets. Domestic competitors will enter into agreements to combine their expertise in seeking bid proposals or developing products. The emergence of joint ventures as an alternative to mergers, acquisitions, or hostile takeovers offers the flexibility of combining resources to compete for specific market segments or offer differentiated products to selected customers. The nature of these ventures is to give firms the ability to compete against quasi-nationalized firms with a dominant presence in some strategic markets. The efforts of AT&T competing for a contract with France provide a good case in point. AT&T entered a joint venture bid with N. V. Philips of the Netherlands for a contract awarded in April 1987 by the French government for control of Cie. Generale des Constructions Telephoniques. Three bids were submitted—one each from Siemens AG of West Germany, AT&T and Philips, and Sweden's Telefon AB L. M. Ericsson—and after a hotly contested process, the government of France awarded the contract to the Swedish concern. This led to threats of retaliation against the Paris government by Bonn and Washington, thus revealing the extent to which political considerations are becoming an intricate part of what no longer are economic evaluations. The French denied their decision was influenced by political considerations, citing that the technical merits of the Ericsson proposal were responsible for the decision. Regardless, the efforts of AT&T to submit a bid in conjunction with Philips, moreover, underscore the role joint ventures are playing in enhancing the competitiveness of American firms as they compete in global markets.

The role of non-market forces in determining competitive advantages in global markets is increasing. The impact of quasi-nationalized firms is more apparent as markets face intensifying competition. The result is a world characterized by greater turbulence, slowing growth, reduced profits, increasing consolidations, and the proliferation of joint ventures. The cumulative effect of these forces emphasizes the heightened importance of incorporating context, economic and political, into the development of competitive strategies. The utility of using market area planning in the formulation of corporate policies is more apparent as the degree of uncertainty in the world economy increase. The presence of nationalized and subsidized firms in the international arena undermines the strict adherence to free market principles and alters the terms of trade under which firms compete. It is under these conditions that the role of political and economic context takes on renewed importance. The policy lesson which stands out for the corporate executive is the significant role scenario planning can play in helping firms establish strategies capable of delivering that competitive edge which too often proves to be so elusive.

Thus the lesson of these non-market forces is to reinforce the notion that strategic thinking requires more than mere thought. It demands action. The proper role of the corporate strategist at the end of the twentieth century is not in compiling attractive binders full of information, but in the formulation of strategies which identify one by one the steps, actions and policies required to secure a sustainable competitive advantage. This is accomplished through differentiation, cost advantage, or market focus. The executive officer must be presented with a thorough set of strategies offering the best course of action for each SBU, each good or service the firm markets, and each kind of customer served.

Only then is the firm in a position to evaluate each of the choices presented and to decide upon a course of action. Once competitive strategies are formed, each SBU must endeavor to accomplish its mission. The overall portfolio strategy, moreover, must seek to establish a sustainable competitive advantage. This is only possible if the corporate portfolio reflects strength born out of its lines of expertise and shrewd positional strategies formulated from thorough and thoughtful market area planning. This two-pronged effort—internal cohesion and external relatedness—reinforce each other to achieve superior strategies relative to the competition.

Given the circumstances affecting the world's economies, a sustainable competitive advantage can be achieved through a strategic thinking process that seeks to perfect one of the following areas of concentration.

Product Differentiation

The firm can concentrate its resources on the creation of a portfolio in which the related business units concentrate on a group of highly differentiated products. The differentiation can be founded on various features. The most common mechanism for protecting physical aspects of product differentiation is patents which protect the trade secrets of a feature or group of features the firm's products have. Polaroid, for example, has a patent on the instant photography technology that prohibits competitors, such as Kodak or Fuji, from attempting to duplicate the technology. When a product's differentiation is based on an intangible quality, such as reputation or quality, trade names are used to offer protection. Coca Cola, for one, has a name that epitomizes the soft drink industry. Regardless of actual preferences expressed in taste tests, the consumer chooses a soft drink, not for taste, but for image. This has worked to the advantage for Coca Cola, for the majority of baby boomers associate the soft drink vendor with childhood Americana memories and are loyal to the firm, the product, and the product's aura. Thus the key to successful differentiation lies in buyer identification. The consumer must perceive a certain value that is intrinsic in the product which no other competitor can offer. The successful portfolio builds on one successful product with a high degree of differentiation to create complementary products. Both Polaroid and Coca Cola have used successful products to launch new ones. Polaroid offers several kinds of cameras that use its instant photography technology to reach various price niches in the consumer markets. Coca Cola's Diet Coke, likewise, uses the buyer identification to build a customer base of its own. The signal criteria used are identical: a series of iconic images, a distinct line of packaging or product design, and a solid reputation which create a sense on continuity and reliability. The success of one differentiated product establishes a foundation from which complementary products can be launched, and in so doing, a diversified portfolio is possible.

Cost Advantage

The firm's business units can concentrate on reaching the lowest delivered cost relative to the competitors' cost structures. This can be accomplished through various means. A firm that concentrates on reducing costs through reducing the prices of its inputs can employ four main techniques; its bargaining power, bulk purchases, the use of several suppliers, and transportation. The bargaining power of the firm with its suppliers or its customers offers leverages that can reduce the costs of certain inputs or sales to selected markets. At the same time, the firm can make bulk purchases in order to benefit from volume discounts. This involves the coordination among the portfolio's SBUs in order to establish the horizontal linkages necessary for lines of expertise to be of optimal benefit. The business units can pit one supplier against the other in subtle ways so as to lower the costs of inputs. The last area of external cost cutting efforts centers on transportation efficiencies. The firm that can develop an efficient transportation network can lower its costs enough to achieve a competitive advantage. This, however, is to say that cost reduction is limited to external functions. The greater areas for realizing a cost advantage are internal. Through a careful analysis of the internal value chain functions, whether production, operational, manufacturing, R&D or distribution functions, the firm can sustain market leadership. Anthony O'Reilly, CEO of H. J. Heinz Co., embarked on a cost-cutting program so thorough and successful that today Heinz is the market share leader and the low cost producer in such strategic lines as ketchup, frozen french fries, and vinegar. O'Reilly's success is all the more noteworthy, for it comes at a time when the food industry has been plagued by flat growth and fierce competition that has put pressure on profit margins. The zero-budget developed by Heinz requires managers at the various business units to develop budgets based on the costs of a current start-up. The result is a bare-bones operation which is the business equivalent of minimalism: all the superfluous costs are eliminated. It also calls on the use of the best technology available. O'Reilly is spending over $110 million to automate its plant in the United Kingdom in order to compete with the highest technological standards today. Inherent in the zero-budget concept used by all the SBUs at Heinz are the continuous cost reduction efforts that include all functions from the optimal advertising necessary to market the premium consumer goods to getting the best price on raw materials, and the result is remarkable: profits at Heinz have increased 16 percent a year since 1980. O'Reilly's work at Heinz is not over yet, for he plans to continue reducing costs in the future by concentrating savings in two areas: eliminating a layer of middle managers and reducing marketing budgets even further.

Market Focus

The firm can identify a particular target group and strive to meet the value-chain needs of that market segment. The advantage in concentrating efforts on a few selected markets and customers lies in the specialization that is possible. When each SBU is working towards filling identified market niches which, taken together, constitute a set of products that serve complementary needs of the customer, a certain dependence and buyer identification is fostered that leads to loyalty. Market focus, moreover, is an efficient strategy when each business unit is allowed to develop products that best fit its expertise. The portfolio, then, can develop within the parameters of a series of diversified related lines of business. The result is the emergence of the firm as the authority within the selected market niches. Rolls Royce, for example, epitomizes the ideal of a luxury automobile. It does not strive to be the fastest or give race car performance, but it is the most luxurious automobile made. The marketing strategy is aimed at the customer willing to settle for nothing but the most comfortable vehicle of outstanding workmanship. The use of market focus is not limited to products with snob appeal. Federal Express, for one, has established a formidable reputation as a firm with impeccable customer service. In an age when telephones ring for a minute before a recording puts the customer on hold for another five minutes, Federal Express has an unequalled response time. The market focus, firms who have little patience for waiting and excuses, has contributed to the stellar success of Federal Express. The pattern remains the same, however. Whether it is a car maker specializing in automobiles of uncompromising luxury targeted at a customer willing to pay a premium price, or whether it is an overnight courier service offering unsurpassed customer service to demanding customers willing to pay a premium, the concentration on the needs of a particular customer and on creating a specialized product that is without equal allows for a thorough marketing program capable of achieving a sustained competitive advantage in the selected market niche.

STRATEGIC THINKING FOR STRATEGIC ADVANTAGES

There are times, however, when the existence of non-market forces intrude to such a degree that a firm is not capable of developing a counter strategy alone. The increasing reliance on joint ventures and strategic alliances among large concerns reflects the need to counter the non-market forces at play. The Japanese domination of the memory chip industry, engineered in part by MITI, is a case of a non-market phenomenon. The U.S. semiconductor industry has experienced a continuous decline at the hand of their Japanese competitors. The response thus far has been attempts to create a consortium of American chipmakers who, with government matching funds, would pool the resources of such giants as IBM and Texas Instruments to form a joint effort, known as Sematech, against the Japanese.

These efforts to establish an effort based on large economies of scale is an attempt to secure a strategic advantage. The global macroeconomic policies affecting national economies today are such that the more quasi-nationalized or subsidized enterprises will be competing in the international arena. The need for firms to think about the uses and applicability of strategic advantages is greater. The potential strategic benefits, as Sematech hopes to exploit, through either consortiums or similar efforts may justify the conditional lifting of antitrust restrictions in force. The strategic thinking process requires corporate officers to consider the impact of such cooperation on three strategic arenas: R&D, strategic posturing, and third market penetration.

R&D ECONOMIES

The costs of technological innovations are great. Indeed, the costs of conducting research and development constitute entry barriers into many industries that are dependent on technology. Thus in many smaller countries, it is impossible for private firms to generate enough revenue to fund capital intensive R&D operations. In industries where technology is crucial to success, the option of classifying a group of industries as being of national security is exercised. France, for example, considers aerospace technology a national security matter and actively supports domestic firms operating in that field. Brazil is another case in point. The telecommunications industry is reserved exclusively for domestic concerns. The R&D for the telecommunications and the computer hardware and software industries is supported by appropriate legislation barring the participation of foreign firms. In the United States there are two cases which demonstrate the complex nature of joint R&D efforts. While the semiconductor industry is actively seeking a private business and government alliance in the Sematch venture as a way to pool resources and formulate an adequate response to the foreign threat, the telephone operating companies, which share R&D facilities through Bell Communications Research, or Bellcore, are dismantling through disuse their joint R&D instrument. The goals of the semiconductor industry is to join forces and achieve economies of scale in order to compete against the Japanese microchip makers. The regional telephone operating companies, on the other hand, are competing against each other in ways that are straining the traditional relationships among them. Bellcore, which is owned by the telephone operating companies, is a common research and development facility whose advances assist all the owning partners. There has, however, been a significant shift in focus on the role of Bellcore as the regional holding companies compete with each other in an increasing number of areas. The failure of the operating companies, for example, to reach an agreement on the Open Network Architecture demonstrates that the firms are now concerned more with their individual goals and priorities than with programs that would benefit each other in an equal manner. In this sense as each firm tries to establish a competitive advantage vis-à-vis the other regional firms, they stand to win at home at the expense of overseas opportunities. Indeed, while British Telecom, NEC, and Bell Canada have formidable market shares in the international telecommunications market, none of the regional holding companies, as epitomized by PTG's fiasco, has a remarkable presence in the global economy. The direction of the future, however, lies in seeking a strategic advantage through a mechanism as is sought by the semiconductor industry through Sematech. It is not without irony that what the regional companies have in Bellcore and are not using to its fullest potential, national commitment, the semiconductor industry faces an uphill battling in securing.

STRATEGIC POSTURING

The search for strategic advantages reaches beyond the benefits of economies of scale. With the importance of combining R&D efforts, a second reason for using alliances is their ability to enhance the firm's strategic posture in the marketplace. American Airlines' alliances with Avis, Inc., rental cars, Sheraton Corporation, and Intercontinental Hotels Corporation hotels allow for an extensive bonus-miles reward program using advanced computer systems. This has allowed AMR

Corporation, American's parent company, the ability to position itself in the marketplace in a more successful manner than did Allegis. Here one can see how rational programs of diversification in related lines of expertise can be successful. AMR Corporation demonstrates that a strategic advantage is more feasible when firms enter into agreements that allow each firm to concentrate in its areas of expertise. Robert Crandall, AMR and American president and chairman, has engineered a program with hotel companies and car rental firms that do not interfere with the successful operation of each firm within its industry. Unlike Allegis and Richard Ferris, it is the firm that respects its internal lines of expertise that stands to improve its position in the marketplace. American Airlines' strategy allows for airline, hotel, and car rental companies to be managed by professionals experienced in their respective industries. This is a prerequisite to success, especially for firms, like airline, hotel, and car rental that face different business cycles and are not very complementary. Crandall has been able to concentrate on the airline industry, strengthening American's posture, while expanding the services available to travelers who are less brand loyal today than ever before. The introduction of an advanced computer system that enables customers to link their computers into the Easy Saver network has been successful so far. Through the use of Easy Saver the consumer can check hotel and car rental rates and availability and make reservations independent of the airline. The result, as San Francisco-based Information Systems analyst Roy Nolan said, "is an information and reservation system that offers the customer great flexibility, freedom and superior service that is unequalled within the airline industry."[1] Crandall's efforts underscore Ferris' tragic mistake: in a competitive environment, the successful firm must develop its lines of expertise in related lines of businesses that allow it to strengthen its market position. Crandall understands that hotel people can't run airlines, car rental executives know little about room service, and airline managers don't know how to rent cars. Crandall also understands that the formation of bonus-miles reward programs with hotels and car rental companies do establish links that allow for strategic posturing.

THIRD MARKET PENETRATION

The third and most compelling reason for forming an alliance that delivers a strategic advantage is to use the combined resources to allow for the easy penetration of third markets. There are instances when strategic alliances or joint ventures may not prove adequate for the rigors of global competition. The decision by Moet-Hennessy and Louis Vuitton, two French luxury goods firms, to merge demonstrates this point. The acquisition of 37 percent of Yves Saint Laurent S. A. (YSL) by Cerus

S.A., Carlo de Benedetti's French holding company, in early 1987 began the consolidation of the French luxury goods industry. The increasing competition for international market shares made it necessary for Moet and Louis Vuitton to merge in order to combine resources. The threat presented to these two concerns by the acquisition of YSL by the Italian financier's holding company proved too formidable for either one to confront alone. The proposed merger, which if approved by the French authorities would create France's sixth largest company, will result in a company with a respectable presence in several luxury goods markets. The new firm is to be called LVMH Moet-Hennessy Louis Vuitton and will be headed by Alain Chevalier, Moet-Hennessy's chairman, while Louis Vuitton's chairman, Henry Recamier, will preside over the Strategic Committee. Together the firm will have a dominant presence in the perfume and champagne global markets. The firms hope to establish strong links among the various SBUs, which will continue to market such brand names as Moet & Chandon and Dom Perignon champagnes, Parfums Christian Dior, Hennessy cognac and Louis Vuitton luggage and handbags. Chevalier and Recamier plan to establish a horizontal organizational structure that cuts across divisional boundaries, thus allowing for economies of scale and economies of scope which are necessary for the new firm to increase its presence in third markets. This merger, then, is the formal globalization of the French luxury goods industry, allowing for the penetration of third markets outside France. The challenge posed by Italy's De Benedetti, coupled with the renewed marketing efforts of other American and Japanese luxury goods makers, has increased competition. The strategic advantages this merger represents to Moet and Louis Vuitton are founded in the clear strategic thinking of Chevalier and Recamier as they embark on a program to enhance their presence in the international markets.

NOTE

1. Telephone Interview, May 10, 1987.

16

SUMMARY

The discussion presented illustrates the dire consequences for portfolio management that emerge when there is little substance behind style. The competitive nature of the business world of 1990 requires nothing less than an unwavering commitment to strategic thinking. The dramatic deterioration of the American predominance in the world arena reveals the hollow management that has come to dominate corporate America since the end of Bretton Woods in the 1970s. The inability to manage properly portfolios using objective reference points and reflecting the realities of the structural deficit economy fosters distortions in the strategic planning process. The need for substance—for clear thinking—is the essence of sound strategies capable of securing a lasting competitive advantage.

The need for sound strategic thinking that builds on the past, looks forward to the future, and has a thorough understanding of the present is the basis on which superior performance can be maintained. This requires, above all else, sophisticated managers. The dependence on individuals who are trained in narrow fields of expertise, lacking a comprehensive understanding of the forces that shape the present, is a major contributor to the failure of American business. Whether this takes the form of hiring recent MBAs from Ivy League schools who have no education in the intricate role culture and history play in shaping the economic landscape, or recruiting middle-aged officers who lack a winning track record, this nation can no longer afford either scandals, such as Drexel Burnham Lambert's Dennis Levine, or fiascos, such as PTG's

Pacific Telesis International under S. Ross Brown. The new rigors of the global realities prohibit corporate America from assuming a complacent, business-as-usual attitude to the grave problems it now encounters.

The resolution to the problems arising from the failure of traditional strategic planning and portfolio management, however, is within reach. The answer lies in a portfolio management system that takes into account the various factors that affect how a firm relates to its environment. The use of economic and political context is a requisite to the establishment of realistic goals for the portfolio. The stock market constitutes an unequaled measure of the opportunity cost prevailing at any given moment and must be used to signal changes in the economic current. Armed with this information the corporate officer can then proceed to formulate competitive strategies capable of realizing the firm's long-term goals. The successful firm, moreover, is one that shows the necessary commitment to its strategies. This commitment, however, can only be realized when there is a strong sense of confidence that is born naturally out of the innate strengths and clarity of vision of the firm's leaders. There is no substitute for substance and there are objective reference points which measure the success of any set of strategies. Indeed, it is the innate nature of competitive strategies that result in success. Digital Equipment Corporation was able to identify opportunities in a slumped industry and implement a long-term program to which it was fully committed in order to capitalize on its assets. This strategy has met with astounding success, which has made DEC the envy of its industry. PTI, on the other hand, squandered millions of dollars while disgracing its parent company. The secret of DEC's—or Japan's and West Germany's—success lies not in the size of their bank accounts, but in the quality of their thinking. These are difficult and complex issues, but they are not impossible to tackle. In the course of this discussion we have surveyed some of the firms in corporate America that are taking the lead in establishing and defending their market positions.

The business environment that has emerged as a direct result of the structural deficit economy and the decline in the quality of thought throughout corporate America are the underlying causes for the economic dislocation of the past twenty years. Here, then, are the root causes of the demise of American preeminence in the world economy. Even foreign markets, where the United States has traditionally had a major presence, such as Mexico and Nicaragua, are now being exploited by the Japanese and West Germans with renewed success. Although the emphasis of most current discussions on the state of corporate America has centered on the prevailing exchange rates and trade barriers, the answer to the dilemmas facing corporate America lies within us. No firm can expect to compete effectively unless there are structural changes that create internal lines of expertise within a firm's portfolio in order to exploit the benefits of interrelatedness and an external emphasis on market area planning to secure market leadership positions in the targeted niches. The most efficient mechanism for this is a strong program of strategic thinking that considers objective reference points and pursues related lines of businesses. In the course of the discussions in this book, it has become evident that the absence of context is one of the reasons why corporate America's strategies have been lacking in substance and have been weaker in relation to those of foreign firms. Corporate officers have seen their market shares and profitability decline as foreigners have made substantial inroads. However willing American firms have been on reversing the decline, the fact remains that few firms have been able to implement sound programs to achieve their ends. Results, after all, are all that matter in a market economy. In our discussion, however, we have surveyed many case studies of American success stories—and a few failures—in the hope of identifying that certain intangible quality that is the mark of a leader. Strategic thinking, it must be noted, is that intangible essence that affords the corporate officer the means through which effective competitive strategies can be formulated resulting in a competitive advantage necessary for the proper management of corporate business units. The successful implementation of strategic thinking will assure that the future is ours for the taking.

BIBLIOGRAPHY

Ansoff, H. Igor. "Planned Management of Turbulent Change," *Encyclopedia of Professional Management*, New York: McGraw-Hill, 1979.

———. "The Firm of the Future," *Harvard Business Review*, September/October 1965.

Baumhart, Raymond. *Ethics in Business*. New York: Holt, Rinehart and Winston, 1968.

Beer, Stafford. *The Brain of the Firm*. New York: Wiley, 1981.

Bogue, Marcus C., and Elwood S. Buffa. *Corporate Strategic Analysis*. New York: The Free Press, 1986.

Boston Consulting Group. *Growth and Financial Strategies*. Boston, Mass.: Boston Consulting Group, 1971.

Boyatizis, Richard. *The Competent Manager*. New York: Wiley, 1981.

Burck, Charles. "A Group Profile of the Fortune 500 Chief Executive," *Fortune*, May 1976.

Carter, E. Eugene and K. J. Cohen. "Portfolio Aspects of Strategic Planning," *Journal of Business Policy*, Summer 1972.

Crozier, M. "Less Problemes Humaines que osent les Structures de l'Enterprise dans une Societe en Changement." Paper presented at Cannes Colloquium, March 1973.

Drucker, Peter F., *The Changing World of the Executive*. New York: Time Books, 1982.

———. *Managing in Turbulent Times*. London: Heinemann, 1980.

———. *Technology, Management and Society*. New York: Heinemann, 1970.

Fahey, Liam and William R. King. "Environmental Scanning for Corporate Planning," Business Horizons, August 1977.

Galbraith, John K. *The Affluent Society*. 2nd ed. Boston: Houghton Mifflin, 1969.

———. *The New Industrial State*. Harmondsworth: Penguin Books, 1968.

Hall, William K. "Survival Strategies in a Hostile Environment," *Harvard Business Review*, September 1980.

Hamilton, Ronald H. "Scenarios in Corporate Planning," *Journal of Business Strategy*, no. 2 (Summer 1981), pp. 82–87.

Lorsch, Jay W., and Stephen A. Allen. *Managing Diversity and Interdependence: An Organizational Study of Multidimensional Firms*. Cambridge, Mass.: Harvard Graduate School of Business Administration, Division of Research, 1973.

Machiavelli, Niccolo. *The Prince and The Discourses*. New York: Random House, 1950.

Meadows, Dennis, et al. *The Limits of Growth*. New York: Universe Books, 1972.

Osmond, Neville. "Top Management: Its Tasks, Roles and Skills," *Journal of Business Policy*, Winter 1971.

Pfeffer, Jeffrey and Jerry Salanicik. "Who Gets Power and How They Hold Onto It," *Organizational Dynamics* 5, Winter 1977.

Porter, Michael E. *Competitive Advantage: Creating and Sustaining Superior Performance*, New York: The Free Press, 1985.

———. *Competitive Strategy: Techniques for Analyzing Industries and Competitors*, New York: The Free Press, 1980.

Potts, Mark and Peter Behr. *The Leading Edge*. New York: McGraw-Hill, 1987.

"Putting Excellence into Management," *Business Week*, July 21, 1980, pp. 196–197.

Rubin, J.Z. and B.R. Brown. *The Social Psychology of Bargaining and Negotiation*. New York: Academic Press, 1975.

Sahal, D. *Patterns of Technological Innovation*. Reading, Mass.: Addison-Wesley, 1981.

"Shell's Multiple Scenario Planning," *World Business Weekly*, April 7, 1980.

Steiner, George A. "A New Class of Chief Executive Officer," *Long Range Planning*, August 1981.

Teece, David J. "Economies of Scope and the Scope of the Enterprise," *Journal of Economic Behavior and Organization* 1 (1980), p. 223–47.

Wagle, B. "The Use of Models for Environmental Forecasting and Corporate Planning," *Operational Research Quarterly* 20, 1969.

Warhol, Andy. *The Philosophy of Andy Warhol*. New York: Harvest/HJB, 1975.

Yip, George. *Barriers to Entry: A Corporate Strategy Perspective*. Lexington, Mass: Lexington Books, 1982.

Zaleznik, A. and Manfred F. Kets de Uries. *Power and the Corporate Mind*. Boston, Mass.: Houghton Mifflin, 1975.

INDEX

About the Authors

LOUIS E. V. NEVAER is Director of Political Analysis at International Credit Monitor, a consulting firm specializing in political risk assessments, of which he is the co-founder. He has extensive experience in overseas work, and has worked as a consultant for foreign governments and international firms. He is the author of the POP curve, a macroeconomic tool useful in understanding the national debt capacity of an economy as well as determining the point of diminishing returns of government debt. He and Steven Deck are the coauthors of *Corporate Financial Planning and Management in a Deficit Economy* (Quorum Books, 1987).

STEVEN A. DECK is Executive Director of Data and Statistics at International Credit Monitor, of which he is co-founder. He has worked for, and more recently consulted to multinational companies specializing in information systems, project tracking, and financing. With Mr. Nevaer, he is the coauthor of *Corporate Financial Planning and Management in a Deficit Economy* (Quorum Books, 1987).